FROM A
RECTORY KITCHEN

Italian Food Cooked And Served In The Joy Of The Lord

Buon Gusto

Franca

Franca Bosio Bertoli

and

Fr. Matthew R. Mauriello

Blessings +

Father Matt

From A Rectory Kitchen

Italian Food Cooked And Served In The Joy Of The Lord

by Franca Bosio Bertoli and Fr. Matthew R. Mauriello

Printed in the United States of America

ISBN 9781619046955

Cover design by: Fr. Matthew R. Mauriello and Blake Powers

Cover Photos by: Scott Mullin, Ridgefield, CT

For additional copies of this cookbook, please contact

Franca at: 203-775-6511 or franca.b.bertoli@gmail.com
        or Fr. Matthew at: 203-869-4176 or frmattmaurie@aol.com

An additional book by Fr. Matthew R. Mauriello is:

Mercies Remembered: Reflections and Reminiscences of a Parish Priest which is available through Fr. Matthew at his contact information above.

Both of these books are also available through amazon.com and barnesandnoble.com

DEDICATION

In loving gratitude

to our dear mothers, grandmothers

and other family members who have helped,

by their recipes and love for cooking,

to inspire us.

TABLE OF CONTENTS

INTRODUCTION

FROM MOUNTAIN TO SEA

Dear Readers,

This cookbook is the product of nearly twenty years of friendship between Franca Bosio Bertoli and Fr. Matthew Mauriello. On St. Valentine's Day, February 14, 1992, Fr. Matt began his assignment as a parish priest at St. Joseph Church in Danbury, CT. At that time, Franca was a cook for the priests in the Rectory and her cuisine was well-known and much loved among the clergy who dined there.

Franca and Fr. Matt immediately hit it off, often exchanging cooking tips and recipes. Soon, Fr. Matt was invited to visit Franca, her husband Donald and their beautiful daughter, Donna at their home to enjoy delicious meals there. Fr. Matt always loved to see Franca in action at the stove as she created her "culinary magic," as he calls it. He was fascinated by the unique flavors of Franca's cooking, inspired from a treasury of products typical of the Emilia-Romagna and Lombardia (Lombardy) regions of northern Italy.

Franca was born in the Province of Cremona, in the northern Italian Region of Lombardy. Her husband, Donald, has his roots in the northern Italian Province of Parma, in the Region of Emilia-Romagna, considered by many to reflect the pinnacle of Italian cuisine. It has given the world such treasures as Parmigiano-Reggiano cheese, the world-famous Prosciutto di Parma, and porcini mushrooms, just to name a few of its well known products.

After immigrating to America and marrying Donald in Queens, NY in 1963, Franca continued the wonderful culinary traditions that she learned from her own mother and sisters as well as those handed down from Donald's beloved grandmother, Nonna Terenzia. Ever evolving and adding to her culinary repertoire, whenever she visits family in Italy, Franca always returns with a few new tasty ideas observed from her sisters.

Fr. Matt's own love of Italian cooking came from his dear Grandmother Serafina, who comes from the south of Italy, inland from the Bay of Naples. He thus brings with him the culinary treasures of the sea as well as other specialties typical of southern Italy. Nonna Serafina was born in Italy in 1907 in Tricarico, and along with her husband, Rocco Fiore, came to the USA on the ship "Augustus" shortly after their marriage in December 1928. After arriving in New York's Ellis Island, they settled in Newark, NJ. His mother, Susan (Assunta) was born in the 1930's and Fr. Matt was born in 1956.

His grandmother became a widow in 1952, at an early age. When he was growing up, Fr. Matt's family lived a few houses away from her. After school, he would go to his Grandma's house and there in the basement, she was preparing dinner for herself and her own mother, Assunta. It was always a festival for the eyes to see her in her full glory at the stove and of course, the aromas were delightful!

Fr. Matt's mother is also a great cook, having learned from Serafina, her mother. When younger, Fr. Matt would be in the kitchen, doing his homework from school at the kitchen table, but with one eye on the stove. His mother recalls that no matter how many toys he had as a child, he loved to play with pots and pans and bang them with wooden spoons!

In his travels and studies for the priesthood, Fr. Matt also sampled and learned recipes from other parts of Italy, including Milan, Orvieto and Rome. His sister, Suzanne was a New York model who later went to Milan, Italy, where she met her future husband; they were married in 1990. Whenever he would visit her and the family in Milan, Fr. Matt and Suzanne enjoyed cooking together and he thus learned some recipes from that region of Lombardy. "Finocchio in Padella alla Susanna," on page 272 in the *contorni* /side dishes section of the book, is one example.

In his studies for the priesthood, Fr. Matt was privileged to live in Rome as a student and enjoyed the delightful Roman cuisine. Through his friendship with a brother seminarian, now a priest in Orvieto, he also got to sample and enjoy the cuisine of Umbria and southern Tuscany. Each time that he has had a tasty experience in Italy, when he returned, Fr. Matt tried to incorporate some of those ideas into his own repertory.

After one year of friendship and exchanging recipes, Franca and Fr. Matt decided it was time to write things down and thus began their collaboration on this cookbook, which reflects the two unique and distinct culinary traditions of Northern and Southern Italy. The project included many an afternoon seated at Franca's dining room table, discussing and sampling recipes, with Fr. Matt typing the end results on his computer. We wish to express our sincere gratitude to Franca's daughter, Donna Bertoli Vinci for all her hard work in helping to edit, proofread and format the manuscript

We truly hope that this cookbook, which is a product of love and friendship, will bring you as much joy as Franca and Fr. Matt's friendship and mutual love of cooking has brought to them. Enjoy the recipes and the food and may it be accompanied by much love and joy at your table. Buon Appetito a tutti and may the good Lord bless you and always keep you in His loving care.

The Authors

CHAPTER I: BASICS

Basic Pasta

- Egg Pasta
- Spinach Pasta
- Carrot Pasta
- Tomato Pasta

Sauces and Custards

- Meat Stracotto Filling and Sauce Northern Italian Style
- Ragú Bolognese a la Franca
- Ragú Bolognese in Bianco
- Pesto Sauce
- Salsa Napoletana (Neapolitan Sauce)
- Tomato and Fresh Basil Sauce
- Marinara Sauce
- Vodka Sauce
- Basic Béchamel Sauce
- Hollandaise Sauce
- Lemon Sauce
- Crema Pasticcera (basic custard)

Pastry Crust

- Quiche Crust
- Nonna Terenzia's Famous Crust
- Sweet Pie Crust
- Rich Pastry Crust
- Crostata (pie tart crust)

Bread and Pizza dough

- Basic Pizza Dough
- Basic Focaccia I
    - Focaccia al Rosmarino (Focaccia with Rosemary)
    - Focaccia alle Cipolle (Focaccia with Onion)
    - Focaccia Ripiena (Stuffed Focaccia)

- Basic Focaccia II

EGG PASTA

This recipe can be doubled or reduced proportionally.

Ingredients:

4 cups unbleached, all-purpose flour
6 large eggs
2 Tbs. olive oil
3 Tbs. lukewarm water
Pinch of salt

1. Place the flour in a large bowl or on a clean surface. Form a well in the center of it and add the eggs, oil, water and salt inside.

2. With a fork, beat the eggs and work the flour in from the sides into the liquid. Continue until all flour is mixed with liquid.

3. If this was mixed in a bowl, transfer the dough onto a clean surface. Knead for 15 minutes. Pasta should be pliable, but not sticky. If the pasta feels too soft, gradually add more flour. If it feels hard, add another tablespoon of water.

4. After kneading, the dough should appear very smooth. Sprinkle the top and bottom with flour, cover with an inverted bowl and let rest for 10 minutes.

5. Pasta is now ready to use.

SPINACH PASTA

To the above recipe for Basic Pasta, substitute the water with ½ lb. fresh spinach leaves, cooked, drained and finely chopped.

Continue recipe as above.

CARROT PASTA

To the preceding recipe for Basic Pasta, substitute the water with 1 cup of boiled, fresh carrots that have been mashed. If pasta becomes too soft, add additional flour.

Continue recipe as on preceding page.

TOMATO PASTA

To the preceding recipe for Basic Pasta, substitute the water with 2 Tbs. tomato paste.

Continue recipe as on preceding page.

MEAT STRACOTTO FILLING AND SAUCE

NORTHERN ITALIAN STYLE

Ingredients:

4 Tbs. butter
3 Tbs. olive oil
1 medium onion, finely chopped
1 carrot, chopped
1 small stalk celery, chopped
2 cloves garlic, finely chopped
1 sprig fresh rosemary
2 sage leaves
1 lb. lean beef
½ lb. lean pork
Salt and pepper to taste
1 Tbs. flour
1 cup beef stock
One 28-oz. can tomato puree
Two 28-oz. cans crushed tomatoes
1 cup grated Parmesan cheese
2 eggs, lightly beaten
½ cup breadcrumbs
Pinch nutmeg

1. Heat half of the butter and all of the olive oil in a pan. Add the chopped onions and sauté over moderate heat for several minutes. Do not allow to brown.

2. Add the carrot, celery, garlic, rosemary and sage. Add the meat, season to taste with salt and pepper and brown well on all sides.

3. Sprinkle with flour and add the stock and tomatoes. Cover and simmer for about 2 hours. When the meat is tender, take it from the pan, cut into pieces, place in a food processor and blend until smooth.

4. Place this mixture in a bowl and add one cup grated Parmesan cheese, eggs and the breadcrumbs. Add nutmeg and salt and pepper to taste. Mix all ingredients well and set aside to be used for ravioli filling.

5. Place a strainer over a bowl. Pour the sauce into the strainer and with a spoon, press down the contents, discarding the solids that remain. Return the sauce to the pan and let simmer slowly. Add the remaining butter and let rest.

RAGÚ BOLOGNESE ALLA FRANCA

This is a true treasure from the north of Italy, from the culinary capital of Bologna, but it is made much lighter with Franca's touch.

Ingredients:

¼ cup olive oil
1 large onion, finely chopped
1 stalk celery, finely chopped
2 medium carrots, finely chopped
1 clove garlic, chopped
1 Tbs. chopped basil
1 Tbs. chopped parsley
2 lb. ground beef
½ cup dry white wine
1 can (28 oz) tomato puree
1 can (28 oz.) crushed tomatoes
1 clove
½ bay leaf
1 tsp. sugar
1 beef bouillon cube
Freshly ground pepper and salt to taste
2 Tbs. sweet butter

1. Heat the olive oil in a deep saucepan over moderate heat. Add the chopped onion and sauté until a light golden color. Add celery, carrot, garlic, basil and parsley and sauté in the oil for around 10 minutes over moderate heat. Do not allow to brown too much.

2. Add the chopped meat, stirring occasionally and using a wooden spoon to separate it, and sauté all ingredients for an additional 10 minutes. Add the wine and cook until evaporated. Add the tomatoes, bay leaf and clove, sugar and bouillon cube. Check for seasoning, adding salt and pepper if desired.

3. Reduce heat to low and simmer, stirring occasionally for 45 minutes. Turn off heat and add sweet butter, slowly incorporating into sauce.

Ragú Bolognese in Bianco

This is the "white" version, closer to the traditional recipe from Bologna.

Ingredients:

¼ cup olive oil
1 large onion, finely chopped
2 medium carrots, finely chopped
1 stalk celery, finely chopped
1 Tbs. chopped parsley
2 lbs. ground beef or your choice of meat
1 clove garlic, chopped
1 Tbs. chopped basil
½ cup dry white wine
1 cup heavy cream
1 beef bouillon cube
Salt and freshly ground pepper to taste
¼ cup milk

1. Heat the olive oil in a large saucepan over moderate heat. Add the chopped onion and sauté for about 10 minutes until golden, but not too dark. Add the rest of the vegetables and sauté another 10 minutes.

2. Add the ground meat, stirring with a wooden spoon to separate it. Sauté for an additional 10 minutes. Add the white wine, allowing it to completely evaporate. Add the cream, bouillon cube and salt and pepper to taste.

3. Simmer about 20 minutes. Add milk if the sauce appears too dry.

Pesto Sauce

This is well-loved by many and has its origin in Genoa.

Ingredients:

1 cup firmly packed fresh basil leaves
½ cup extra virgin olive oil
2 tbs. pine nuts
Freshly ground pepper
2 tsp. minced garlic
½ cup grated Parmesan cheese
1/8 tsp salt

Place all ingredients into a food processor and blend until smooth. Makes approximately two cups.

Salsa Napoletana

Neapolitan sauce

A rather quick sauce to make that has the aromatic flavors of the south of Italy. Fr. Matt makes in a hurry, but it is always a real hit.

Ingredients:

¼ cup olive oil
2 cloves garlic, finely chopped
1 large onion, finely chopped
1 and ½ lb. Italian pork sausage (sweet, not hot, with fennel seeds)
One 28-oz. can tomato puree
Two 28-oz. cans crushed tomatoes
6 basil leaves, torn
Salt and pepper to taste

1. In a large saucepan, heat the oil over moderate heat. Add onion and garlic, cooking for about 5 minutes until translucent in color, not allowing to brown.

2. Remove the sausage from the casing and place it in the saucepan, separating with a wooden spoon. Sauté until golden brown.

3. Add the tomatoes and basil and bring to a boil, then reduce the heat to moderate and cook for about 30 minutes, stirring occasionally.

4. Add salt and pepper if desired.

TOMATO AND FRESH BASIL SAUCE

As Franca would say, this is "cucina svelta" or fast cooking!

Ingredients:

¼ cup olive oil
1 small onion, finely chopped
2 cloves garlic, finely chopped
2 cans (28 oz. each) crushed tomatoes
1 and ½ tsp. fresh parsley, finely chopped
2 Tbs. coarsely chopped, fresh basil
1 tsp. sugar
Salt and pepper to taste
2 Tbs. butter

1. Place the oil in a saucepan over medium heat. Add the onion and sauté until golden. Add the garlic and stir for 30 seconds. Add tomatoes, stir well and add the parsley, basil, sugar, salt and pepper.

2. Cook over a lively flame for about 15 minutes, stirring frequently so it does not burn. Remove from heat, add the butter and let rest until ready to use.

Serves 8

MARINARA SAUCE

Ingredients:

1 can crushed tomatoes
¼ cup olive oil
2 garlic cloves, minced
1 tsp. fresh oregano, chopped
½ tsp. red pepper flakes
1 tbs. basil, chopped
1 tbs. parsley, chopped
Salt and pepper to taste

1. Sauté the garlic and oil over medium heat until sizzling. Add the tomatoes, red pepper flakes, oregano, basil, parsley and salt and pepper to taste.

2. Cook under a lively flame for 15 minutes. Remove from heat. Sauce is now ready to use.

VODKA SAUCE

In recent years, this has become one of the new classics throughout the United States and Europe, found on almost every menu. This is our own version.

Ingredients:

1 large onion, finely chopped
2 Tbs. olive oil
3 Tbs. butter
1 cup (8 oz.) heavy cream
Salt and pepper to taste
One 28-oz. can peeled tomatoes with puree
½ cup vodka

1. In a medium saucepan, add the olive oil and two tablespoons of the butter. Melt and sauté the onion until transparent.

2. Take two bowls, break open the tomatoes and remove seeds over one bowl, placing the pulp in the other, until all the tomatoes are done. Put pulp in a blender and chop but do not liquefy. Add strained juice and remaining liquid from the can. Discard all seeds.

3. Add the tomatoes and sauce to the onions, bring to a boil and lower heat to a simmer. Cook for approximately 15 minutes until the mixture begins to thicken.

4. Pour cream into a bowl and add 4 Tbs. of the hot tomato sauce. Stir well to temper the cream. Add all the cream to the tomato sauce, stir well, and add the vodka.

5. Lower heat and simmer, stirring occasionally for another 30 minutes until thickened and creamy.

6. Remove from heat, add the last tablespoon of butter, and let rest, covered, until ready to use.

7. Serve with penne, rigatoni, gnocchi, ravioli or any pasta of your choice.

BASIC BÉCHAMEL SAUCE

Ingredients:

1 stick (1/2 cup) butter
½ cup all-purpose flour
4 cups milk, heated
Pinch of salt and pepper
Pinch of grated nutmeg

1. Melt the butter in a heavy-bottomed saucepan. Add the flour and stir to make a smooth paste. While constantly stirring, gradually add the milk, mixing with a wooden spoon or a whisk until combined.

2. Bring to a boil, stirring. Simmer for 5 to 10 minutes until thickened and smooth. Season to taste.

HOLLANDAISE SAUCE

Ingredients:

3 egg yolks
1 Tbs. cold water
1 Tbs. lemon juice
¾ cup butter, melted and cooled
Salt and ground pepper to taste

1. Put the yolks, water and lemon juice in the top of a double boiler. Beat well until mixture is thick. Add the butter, a little at a time, beating constantly. Mixture should resemble heavy cream.

2. Be sure the pan does not get too hot as the sauce can curdle.

3. Add salt and pepper and additional lemon juice if the sauce is too bland.

LEMON SAUCE

Ingredients:

2 Tbs. butter
2 Tbs. flour
1 cup chicken stock
2 egg yolks
Juice of one lemon
Salt and pepper to taste

1. Melt butter in a saucepan over medium heat. Add flour, stirring well. Stir in stock; bring to a boil for a few minutes, stirring constantly. Turn off heat, season with salt and pepper.

2. Add lemon juice and yolks and stir well with a wire whisk. Serve hot.

CREMA PASTICCERA

Custard filling

The classic filling for cream puffs.

Ingredients:

¼ cup flour
½ cup sugar
2 cups milk
4 egg yolks
1 tsp. vanilla extract
1 Tbs. sweet butter

1. Mix flour and sugar and ½ cup milk. Mix well and add yolks.

2. Heat the remaining milk until it begins to boil. Add into the egg mixture, stirring constantly until well blended.

3. Place the pan over very low heat and cook, stirring constantly, until custard begins to thicken and coat the spoon. Remove from heat, add the butter and vanilla and stir well. Set aside and cool.

PASTRY CRUST

BASIC QUICHE CRUST

Ingredients:

2 cups unbleached, all-purpose flour
½ cup (one stick) unsalted butter, chilled
¼ cup shortening (or an additional ¼ cup butter)
¾ tsp. salt
3 Tbs. ice water

1. In a bowl or on a clean surface, mix the flour and salt.

2. Cut the butter and shortening in pieces and with your hands, rub into the flour to resemble coarse breadcrumbs. You may also use a pastry blender or two knives to cut the butter into the flour.

3. Add the water and mix to combine and form into a ball. Wrap in plastic and chill for 30 minutes. It is now ready to use.

NONNA TERENZIA'S FAMOUS CRUST

This was handed down from Franca's husband's grandmother for the future generations to enjoy... and we have been doing so.

Ingredients:

2 cups unbleached, all-purpose flour
Pinch of salt
¼ cup (1/2 stick) unsalted butter
1 egg yolk
3 Tbs. olive oil
3 Tbs. water

1. Mix all ingredients, just to blend together quickly with your fingertips.

2. Form into a ball, wrap in plastic and chill for 30 minutes before using.

SWEET PIE CRUST

Using quiche crust recipe on preceding page, add one tablespoon of sugar to the dry ingredients.

RICH PASTRY CRUST

Using the Sweet Pie Crust recipe on preceding page, add one egg yolk to the ingredients.

CROSTATA

Pie Tart Crust

Fr. Matt learned this recipe from his sister, Suzanne who lives in Milan, Italy.

Ingredients:

1 and ½ cups unbleached, all-purpose flour
½ cup (or one stick) unsalted butter
Rind of one lemon, finely grated
3 egg yolks
½ cup sugar

1. Mix all ingredients, just to blend together quickly with your fingertips.

2. Form into a ball, wrap in plastic and chill for 30 minutes before using.

BASIC PIZZA DOUGH

Ingredients:

1 envelope dry yeast
1 tsp. salt
1 tsp. granulated sugar
1 cup lukewarm water
¼ cup olive oil
3 cups unbleached, all-purpose flour

1. Mix the yeast, salt, sugar, warm water, oil and one cup of the flour and let rest for 10 minutes until mixture starts to bubble.

2. Add the remaining 2 cups of flour and knead well. If too hard, add an additional splash of water until the dough is smooth and pliable.

3. Place dough in a greased bowl and let rest in a warm place until it doubles in size – approximately 30 to 40 minutes. It is now ready to use.

Variation: Substitute ¼ cup milk plus ¾ cup lukewarm water for the 1 cup of water above.

BASIC FOCACCIA I

Ingredients:

1 package (1/4 oz) active dry yeast
¼ cup olive oil
3 cups flour
1 cup lukewarm water
1 tsp. salt

1. Mix water, yeast, salt, ¼ cup olive oil and 1 cup of the flour and let rest for 10 minutes until it begins to bubble. Add remaining flour and mix well and knead until a soft dough forms.

2. Cover and set aside. When doubled in size (about 40 minutes), place on a lightly floured board and roll dough out to fit a baking sheet.

3. Lightly grease a cookie sheet, place dough in it and brush with the additional olive oil. Make indentations with the tips of your fingers over the top.

4. Let rise a second time for 30 to 40 minutes.

5. Bake in a preheated 375-degree oven for 30 minutes.

Variation I:

Focaccia al Rosmarino (With rosemary): Use focaccia recipe above and add the following:

2 Tbs. Rosemary leaves
2 cloves garlic, peeled and chopped
1 Tbs. coarse sea salt (optional)
¼ cup olive oil

After the dough has risen, brush the top with the olive oil and sprinkle the dough with the above herbs before placing in the oven to bake.

Variation II:

Focaccia alle Cipolle (With onions): Use focaccia recipe above and add the following:

2 medium onions, thinly sliced
½ cup olive oil
2 garlic cloves, chopped
One large sprig of flat-leaf parsley, chopped

Heat oil in a large skillet and add the onions, cook until softened, about 3 minutes, and add garlic. Cook until softened but not brown. Remove from heat, add parsley, mix well and spread onto focaccia before baking.

Variation III:

Focaccia Ripiena (Stuffed Focaccia): Use 2 recipes Basic Focaccia Dough I

For the stuffing:

> *½ lb. salami, thinly sliced*
> *½ lb. provolone cheese, thinly sliced*
> *3 Tbs. olive oil*
> *1 bunch parsley, chopped (about ½ cup)*
> *Black pepper to taste*

1. Divide dough in half. Roll into 2 rectangular pieces ¼-inch thick to fit a cookie sheet.

2. Place the first dough on the lightly greased cookie sheet.

3. Combine the parsley and oil, spread on the dough and layer the provolone and salami on top, leaving ½-inch edge. Sprinkle with pepper and over with the second sheet of dough and seal the edge.

4. Bake in a preheated, 350-degree oven for 45 minutes until golden brown.

BASIC FOCACCIA II

This is an alternate focaccia dough recipe.

Ingredients:

1 package (1/4 oz.) active dry yeast
1 cup lukewarm water
1 tsp. salt
2 Tbs. olive oil
2 cups flour
1 cup Semolina flour
Additional 1/4 cup olive oil

1. Mix the two types of flour together in a bowl. In another bowl, mix water, yeast, salt, ¼ cup olive oil and 1 cup of the flour and let rest for 10 minutes until it begins to foam. Add remaining flour and mix well and knead until a soft dough forms. Let rest, covered, in a warm place until doubled in size – about 40 minutes.

2. Roll out into a rectangle to fit a buttered cookie sheet. Make indentations with your knuckles over the top of the dough. Let rest an additional 15 to 20 minutes.

3. Brush with additional oil and bake in a preheated 350-degree oven for 30 to 40 minutes.

CHAPTER II: ANTIPASTI/APPETIZERS

In a traditional Italian meal, the antipasto or appetizer almost always includes a vegetable such as mushrooms, olives or eggplant that is paired with cheese, meat, seafood or bread. The following recipes are some of the simplest and tastiest antipasti, which can be an impressive introduction to any meal.

- Crostini Portobello
- Bruschetta
- Crostini con Fegatini di Pollo
- Torta di patate / potato pie
- Torta di spinaci / spinach pie
- Marinated eggplant
- Pizzette
- Giardiniera con Tonno e Sardine
- Mussels Arrabbiata
- Caponata Siciliana
- Vongole Ripiene al Forno / Clams oreganate
- Insalata Caprese
- Prosciutto e melone
- Bocconcini di Carne / Meat turnovers
- Bocconcini di Ricotta
- Bocconcini di Gamberi Primavera
- Insalata di Pesce alla Salsa Verde
- Funghi Ripieni alla Parmigiana / Stuffed Mushrooms
- Funghi Marinati
- Peperoni Trifolati alla Fiamma / Roasted Peppers
- Pomodori Farciti Freddi
- Frittura di Verdura
- Insalata di Fagioli e Tonno
- Calamari Fritti
- Ostriche alla Versiliese / Oysters
- Crostini di Polenta al Formaggio
- Carpaccio Classico

CROSTINI PORTOBELLO

Portobello Mushrooms on Toasted Bread

This is tasty and has a trio of flavors and textures: the crunchy bread, the tender and flavorful mushrooms and the delicate melted cheese.

Ingredients:

Three large Portobello Mushrooms
1/4 cup dry white wine
Eight Tbs. olive oil
One loaf of French or Italian bread
Four cloves garlic, whole and peeled
1/4 cup flat-leaf parsley, chopped
Five leaves fresh basil, finely chopped
One half cup shredded Fontina cheese

1. Clean mushrooms, remove stems and slice lengthwise about ¼ inches thick, then cut into 1- to 2-inch sections. Sauté in 6 Tbs. oil for 10 to 12 minutes over moderate heat, stirring occasionally and adding the wine to keep moist.

2. While mushrooms are cooking, slice the bread into ½-inch thickness, making approximately 25 slices. Brush one side of the bread with the remaining oil. Place on cookie sheets and toast in a preheated 350-degree oven for approximately 10 minutes, then remove and rub each slice gently with whole clove of garlic and set aside.

3. To finish mushrooms, add 2 cloves chopped garlic, parsley and basil and heat for an additional five minutes. Remove from heat and place a Tbs. if the mushroom mixture on each toasted bread slice until evenly distributed.

4. Sprinkle the shredded Fontina on top of the mushrooms, then return the cookie sheet with the prepared crostini into the oven for an additional 3 to 4 minutes until the cheese has melted but not browned. Serve immediately.

Serves 6-8

BRUSCHETTA

Tomato Topped Bread Toasts

This has become very well-known in recent years. With the flavors of the tomato, garlic and the tangy basil, it refreshes the mouth in happy anticipation of the meal to come.

Ingredients:

One loaf of French or Italian bread, baguette style

One half cup plus three Tbs. olive oil

Five to six fresh basil leaves

1/2 teaspoon oregano

Two garlic cloves, whole and peeled

Salt and pepper to taste

Six ripe plum tomatoes or any tomato of your choice

To prepare the toasts:

1. Cut loaf of bread into ½-inch thickness, making approximately 25 slices. Brush lightly with the three Tbs. of oil and place on a cookie sheet.

2. Heat in preheated 350-degree oven for 12- to 15-minutes until golden brown. Remove from oven, rub with garlic cloves and set aside.

To make the topping:

1. While the bread is toasting, clean tomatoes and cut off the stem end. Dice tomatoes into small pieces and put into a bowl. Add the remaining oil, salt and pepper, oregano and the basil, which has been torn into small pieces.

2. Stir and let rest for approximately 10 minutes to have the flavors blend. Spoon over the crostini and serve.

Serves 6-8

Variation: Add one Tbs. drained capers in place of the oregano.

CROSTINI CON FEGATINI DI POLLO

Chicken Liver Pate on Toast

The origin of this is from the region of Umbria, just to the north of Rome, and Fr. Matt learned it from his frequent visits to the beautiful hill town of Orvieto.

Ingredients:

Three onions, finely chopped

Three carrots, finely chopped

Three-quarter stick of unsalted butter

One bay leaf

Four Tbs. capers

Two lbs. Chicken Livers

1/2 cup dry white wine

Salt and pepper to taste

One loaf sliced Italian bread, fresh or toasted

1. Place the onion and carrot in a frying pan with two Tbs. of the butter. Add the bay leaf and cook over moderate heat for a minute or two. Add three Tbs. of the capers and the chicken livers, which have been cut into small pieces. Sauté until cooked for 12 to 15 minutes.

2. Add salt and pepper; raise the heat to high, adding the wine and letting it evaporate completely. Turn off the heat, remove the bay leaf and place all the ingredients into a food processor. Blend to smooth consistency.

3. Let cool slightly then add the remaining butter in small pieces and mix well. Put the chicken liver pate into the center of a serving dish and garnish with remaining capers. Place the bread slices around it and serve.

Serves 6-8

Torta di Patate alla Valtarese

Potato Pie Valtarese style

The following traditional "torta" dishes hail from the "Val taro" region of Emilia-Romagna, from among the small villages that surround the Taro River in the foothills of the Apennines.

Ingredients:

One recipe Nonna Terenzia's famous crust (page 12)
Six medium Potatoes
One leek, finely chopped
Five Tbs. olive oil
Salt and fresh pepper to taste
1/2 cup heavy cream
One cup milk
Two cups grated Parmigiana-Reggiano cheese
Three-quarters stick of butter
Three eggs

For the filling:

1. Wash the potatoes and put in a pan, covering them with water. Let boil until cooked, testing with a fork, till soft. Strain, let cool slightly until you are able to handle the potatoes, then peel them and place through a strainer, making a puree.

2. Clean and chop the leek and sauté in three Tbs. olive oil for about 10 minutes. Add the leeks to the potato puree and all the remaining ingredients, except for the egg. Mix well and season to taste. Beat the three eggs lightly, add to the potatoes, reserving two Tbs. of the beaten eggs for later use.

To assemble:

1. Use a baking sheet approximately 18 by 11 inches and ½ inch deep. Grease with 2 remaining Tbs. of olive oil. Roll out the dough until very thin, almost like a filo dough, approximately 24 by 16 inches.

2. Place dough in baking sheet, letting extra dough hang over the edges. Place the potato filling in the center, spreading evenly. Fold the edges over. Brush the top with reserved, beaten egg. Bake at preheated, 375-degree oven until golden. Serve warm. This recipe reheats very well.

Serves 6-8

TORTA DI SPINACI ALLA VALTARESE

Spinach Pie Valtarese style

This is similar to the prior recipe, except that here, spinach is featured in the filling, rather than the potato. The parmesan cheese compliments the spinach perfectly.

Ingredients:

One recipe Nonna Terenzia Crust (page 12)

Four bags (10 oz. each) fresh spinach

Two cups grated Parmigiana-Reggiano cheese

Eight ounces cream cheese

One stick butter

Three eggs, beaten

Two Tbs. olive oil

Salt and pepper to taste

For the filling:

1. Wash the spinach and place it in a large pot with 2 cups water. Bring it to a boil and cook for two minutes, then drain and cool until you can handle the spinach. Picking it up a handful at a time, squeeze out the excess water.

2. Place the spinach on a chopping board and chop coarsely. Place spinach in a bowl; add parmesan, butter, cream cheese and egg, reserving a little to brush on top. Add salt and pepper and mix to incorporate all the ingredients.

For the assembly:

Follow instructions for preceding Potato Torta recipe.

MELANZANE MARINATE

Marinated Eggplant

Fr. Matt learned this when he was a teenager from a friend's Mom in the old neighborhood, and it can even enhance sandwiches, as well as compliment an antipasto platter.

Ingredients:

One large Eggplant

White vinegar

One green bell pepper

1/2 cup olive oil

Two cloves garlic, minced

One Tbs. oregano

Salt and pepper to taste

1. Peel the eggplant and slice crosswise in thin round slices. Stack two to three slices and cut into thin strips. Place all eggplant into a stainless steel pot, add a little salt and cover completely with white vinegar. Place a heavy object, such as a glazed ceramic bowl, on top of the eggplant to put pressure on it. Do not refrigerate.

2. After 24 hours, squeeze all the vinegar out of the eggplant strips, discarding the brown liquid. Cut green pepper into thin strips, mix with olive oil, oregano and garlic. Mix with eggplant and pack tightly into a container. Pour vinegar over all contents. Cover tightly and refrigerate 2 to 3 days before serving.

Serves 6-8

Pizzette

Mini Pizza Appetizers

This is a tasty treat and they are just great when served as passed hors d'oeuvres at a festive gathering.

Ingredients:

One recipe basic Pizza dough (page 14)

For the topping:

One medium eggplant or two medium zucchini, cut into ¼-inch thick slices

½ teaspoon salt

¼ cup olive oil

Three large tomatoes, sliced

One cup shredded mozzarella

One teaspoon dried oregano

1. Prepare dough, cover loosely with a damp cloth and let rise in a warm place until double in size – about one hour.

2. While dough is rising, sprinkle eggplant with salt, layer slices and place a weighted dish on top of it for about 15 minutes. Pat dry with paper towels. If using zucchini, omit this step.

3. In a large skillet, place half the oil over medium heat and add half the eggplant, or zucchini, cooking until golden brown. Place on paper towel to drain. Repeat with remainder of oil and eggplant.

4. Preheat oven to 450 degrees. Punch the dough down and divide it into six pieces. Roll each piece into four-inch circles and place on lightly greased baking sheets. Top each pizza crust evenly with tomato slices, eggplant or zucchini, mozzarella and oregano. Bake until crusts are golden, about 12 to 17 minutes. Serve immediately.

Serves 6-8

GIARDINIERA CON TONNO E SARDINE

Garden Vegetable Medley with Tuna and Sardines

Franca learned this from her days when catering parties for a dear family in Danbury. It is similar to ratatouille, but has additional vegetables and seafood. It is a real crowd pleaser.

Ingredients:

One lb. mushrooms
One red bell pepper
One green bell pepper
One heart celery
Five carrots, peeled
One lb. string beans
Four medium zucchini
One small cauliflower
One eggplant cut in medium pieces
¼ cup capers
Two onions
Two cans (8 oz.) tuna fish
Two small cans sardines
One cup olive oil
Salt and pepper to taste
One bay leaf
One teaspoon thyme
One cup ketchup
1/2 cup Dijon mustard

1. Clean mushrooms, peppers, celery, carrots, zucchini, string beans and cauliflower. Put in a pot and cook in salted boiling water until just tender – about 10 minutes. Drain and let cool slightly. Cut into medium pieces, and put into a large bowl.

2. Chop the onion coarsely, place in a large frying pan along with the eggplant and sauté in the oil for ten to fifteen minutes until translucent, but not browned. Add to bowl and mix.

3. Add the tuna fish, sardines, salt and pepper, bay leaf, thyme, capers, ketchup and mustard. Mix thoroughly and serve cold or room temperature with crackers or crostini.

Serves 6-8

MUSSELS ARRABBIATA

Spicy Hot Mussels

A true taste from the Bay of Naples and seen frequently in many restaurants. Adjust the "heat" of the spiced hot pepper to your liking.

Ingredients:

Two Tbs. olive oil

Two cloves garlic, minced

One Tbs. oregano, fresh or dried

1/2 teaspoon red pepper flakes or ground cayenne pepper

Salt to taste

One 28-oz. can crushed tomatoes with puree

Four-to five-lbs. of Mussels, cleaned and rinsed

1. On a large Dutch oven, sauté the garlic in the oil and add the oregano and pepper to warm. Add salt to taste. Add the tomatoes and simmer for 10 minutes.

2. Add the mussels and cover the pot. Let steam for five minutes until the muscles open and are tender. Do not overcook. This may be served as an appetizer with crusty Italian bread or as an entrée, served over linguini.

Serves 6-8

CAPONATA SICILIANA

Sicilian-style Eggplant Medley

What a treat this is, especially when a little warm. It is tasty spread on crostini, but even when eaten with a fork as part of a larger antipasto platter. It brings a variety of flavors on the palate. From the many invasions of Sicily, sugar was introduced there before the mainland and this dish has a "sweet and sour" taste.

Ingredients:

Two medium eggplants, peeled and cut into ½-inch cubes
1/2 cup olive oil
One clove garlic, finely chopped
Three stalks celery, chopped
One medium carrot, chopped
One medium onion, chopped
One cup canned whole tomatoes, drained and chopped
1/2 cup green olives, chopped
One Tbs. sugar
1/4 cup red wine vinegar
1/4 cup capers
1/2 teaspoon salt
One Tbs. coarsely ground black pepper
One to two fresh basil leaves, finely chopped

1. In a large skillet, heat oil and sauté eggplant and garlic until lightly browned. Remove from pan with a slotted spoon and let drain on paper towel.

2. Add celery, carrot and onions to the skillet, sauté until the onions are translucent but do not begin to brown. Add the tomatoes and simmer for five minutes, stirring frequently.

3. Return the eggplant to the skillet and add all remaining ingredients. Simmer for five minutes. Remove from heat. May be served warm or chilled.

Serves 6-8

VONGOLE RIPIENE AL FORNO

Baked Stuffed Clams

What a great summer dish, especially after spending some of the day clamming and one can enjoy the fruits of their labors.

Ingredients:

18 Clams, cleaned

One half cup olive oil

Two medium onions, finely chopped

Three garlic cloves, finely chopped

1/4 cup chopped flat leaf parsley

Two basil leaves, chopped

Two cups plain breadcrumbs

1/2 teaspoon oregano

Salt and pepper to taste

One lemon cut in wedges

1. Wash the clams, open them and reserve the juice from inside the clam. Place the clam meat in their shells on a baking dish and set aside.

2. Sauté the onion in the oil. Finely chop the garlic, parsley and basil and add to the onion. Sauté for another two minutes, add the bread crumbs, oregano, salt, pepper and one half cup of the reserved clam juice.

3. Remove from stove and, using a tablespoon, cover each clam with the stuffing, distributing evenly.

4. Bake at 375 degrees, uncovered, for approximately 15 to 20 minutes or until the top is golden. Serve hot, with lemon wedges.

Serves 6

INSALATA CAPRESE

Capri-style Mozzarella Salad

A favorite among many, this summer treat originated on the scenic and trendy Isle of Capri, off the coast of southern Italy near to Naples.

Ingredients:

Four large ripe Tomatoes
1/2 cup extra virgin olive oil
Salt and freshly ground pepper to taste
One large package of fresh Mozzarella, approx. 16 oz.

18 small basil leaves
Pinch of dried oregano
One Tbs. of capers

1. Wash the tomatoes and cut into round slices. Arrange on a platter or on individual dishes if preferred. Season the tomatoes with salt, pepper and oregano and drizzle half of the oil over the tomato slices.

2. Place a slice of mozzarella topped with a basil leaf on each tomato slice. Drizzle the remainder of the oil over the dish, sprinkle with capers if desired, and serve. **Serves 6-8**

PROSCIUTTO DI PARMA CON MELONE

Honeydew and Cantaloupe with Parma Ham

It is particularly very refreshing and enjoyable in the summer, when the melons are in season.

Ingredients:

One ripe Cantaloupe melon
One ripe Honeydew melon
One lb. Prosciutto di Parma, sliced very thin
12 fresh strawberries, for garnish

1. Cut the melons in half, remove the seeds and discard. Cut each melon half into four slices and remove the skin. Place them on a serving platter, alternating colors. Place a slice of the prosciutto over each slice of melon.

2. Garnish the dish with the washed and dried strawberries and serve. **Serves 4-6**

Bocconcini di Carne

Bite-sized Beef Turnovers

This is like a mini calzone; just great for hot hors d'oeuvres at a special party has a very savory filling.

Ingredients:

One recipe basic Pizza dough (page 14)
One and 1/2 teaspoons flat-leaf parsley, shopped
One and 1/2 teaspoons basil leaves, chopped
1/4 cup olive oil   One large onion, chopped
Two stalks celery, chopped   Two carrots, peeled and chopped
Two cloves garlic, finely chopped   One lb. chopped Beef
1/2 bay leaf   One whole clove
1/4 cup heavy cream   Salt and pepper to taste

1. Make the basic pizza dough according to instructions, adding ½ teaspoon of basil and ½ teaspoon of parsley, finely chopped. Set aside and let double in   size. Meanwhile, put the oil in a skillet; chop the onion, carrot and celery very fine and sauté in the skillet over moderate heat, until tender.

2. Chop the garlic; add to the vegetables along with the remaining parsley and basil. Sauté for two additional minutes. Add the meat, mix all together and sauté over moderate heat, mixing occasionally.

3. Add the bay leaf, clove and heavy cream and cook for an additional 20 minutes over very low heat, stirring occasionally so it does not burn. Remove from heat and let cool. Remove the bay leaf and clove and discard.

4. When the dough is double in size, pinch off 18 separate pieces and roll them into four-inch circles. Spoon the meat stuffing by Tbs. onto each dough round, distributing equally, leaving about ½ inch around the edge plain. Fold the circles into half moon shape and seal the edges well with your fingers. Place on very lightly greased baking sheets.

5. Pierce each turnover with a fork and place in a 375 degree oven for at least 15- to 20 minutes or until golden. Serve warm or room temperature.

Serves 6-8

BOCCONCINI DI RICOTTA

Ricotta Cheese Turnovers

This is an enjoyable meatless variation of the previous recipe.

Ingredients:

One recipe Pizza dough (page 14)

One lb. Mozzarella

One lb. Ricotta

One and 1/2 teaspoon chopped parsley

1/2 cup grated Parmigiana-Reggiano cheese

Two eggs, beaten

Ground white pepper and salt to taste

1. Make the basic pizza dough according to instructions. Meanwhile, dice the mozzarella, place into a bowl and add the ricotta, chopped parsley and Parmesan cheese.

2. In a small bowl, beat the egg, salt and pepper lightly and add to the cheese mixture and combine. Refrigerate until ready to use.

3. When the dough has doubled in size, pinch off 18 separate pieces and roll them into four-inch circles. Spoon the ricotta mixture into each dough round, distributing equally, leaving about ½ inch around the edge plain.

4. Fold the circles into half moon shapes and seal the edges well with your fingers. Place on very lightly greased baking sheets. Pierce each turnover with a fork and place in a 375-degree oven for at least 15 to 20 minutes or until golden. Serve warm.

Serves 6-8

BOCCONCINI DI GAMBERI PRIMAVERA

Shrimp Bites Spring Style

Here is yet another delicious variation of the stuffed hors d'oeuvre. This time the emphasis is on shellfish. Quickly sautéed scallops or lump crabmeat can also be substituted for the shrimp.

Ingredients:

One recipe Quiche crust (page 12)

For filling:

One lb. Shrimp
1/4 cup virgin olive oil
One medium onion, finely chopped
One stalk celery, shopped
Two cloves garlic, finely chopped
One Tbs. parsley, chopped
One Tbs. basil, chopped
One Tbs. unsalted butter
One Tbs. flour
1/4 cup dry white wine
1/4 cup water
Salt and fresh ground pepper to taste

1. Prepare the quiche crust and refrigerate as directed. Meanwhile, prepare the filling. To cook the shrimp, using a large saucepan, fill half with water and bring to a boil. Place the shrimp in the boiling water and cook for three minutes. Drain under cold water, remove the shell and devein. Cut in small pieces and set aside.

2. In a skillet, heat the olive oil and sauté the onion and celery until softened, about five minutes. Do not brown. Add the garlic, parsley and basil and stir for one minute. Add the flour and mix quickly until fully incorporated. Add the wine and stir quickly, then add the water and stir, bringing to a boil. Add the shrimp and the salt and pepper and stir for one minute. Remove from heat and set aside.

3. Remove dough from refrigerator and place on a lightly floured board. Roll onto thinly and cut into about 18 four-by four-inch squares.

4. Spoon the shrimp filling into each square, distributing equally and leaving about ½ inch around the edge plain. Fold into a triangle shape, seal edges will with your finger and place on lightly greased baking sheets.

5. Pierce each turnover with a fork and place in a 375-degree oven for at least 15-20 minutes or until golden. Serve warm or room temperature. **Serves 6-8**

Insalata di Pesce alla salsa verde

Seafood Salad in Green Sauce

This is a true Italian classic when it comes to the preparation and enjoyment of shellfish. The combination of the various aromatic herbs is accented by bright taste of the vinegar.

Ingredients:

One onion, quartered
One celery stalk cut in chunks
Peel of ½ lemon
Two peppercorns
Two cloves garlic, peeled and chopped
One lb. Bay Scallops
Three Tbs. chopped parsley
Two Tbs. capers
One large bunch of arugula leaves, washed

One carrot cut in chunks
Five Tbs. white wine vinegar
One sprig parsley
12 Tbs. olive oil
One lb. medium Shrimp
Three Tbs. scallions, finely chopped
One cup fresh basil leaves
Salt and freshly ground pepper to taste
Radicchio for garnish

1. In a large saucepan, combine four cups water with the onion, carrot celery, and lemon peel, two Tbs. of the vinegar, the parsley sprig and peppercorns and bring to a boil.

2. Reduce heat and simmer for 20 minutes. Add the shrimp and bring to a boil, about 3 to 4 minutes, and remove from heat. Let the shrimp rest in the water to absorb the flavors for about five minutes and then remove with a slotted spoon.

3. Reheat the water and bring to a boil. Add the scallops and simmer. Cook for one minute and remove from heat. Let the scallops rest in the water for five minutes then remove with a slotted spoon.

4. To make the sauce, in a food processor, combine the basil and four Tbs. of the olive oil. Blend until it becomes a paste. Add the remaining three Tbs. of the vinegar, the remaining olive oil, the capers and the scallions and blend until smooth. Season with salt and pepper and transfer to a bowl.

5. Shell and devein the shrimp and add to the scallops. Combine the seafood with the sauce. Serve immediately over a bed of arugula and radicchio. This may also be refrigerated and served the next day at room temperature.

Serves 6-8

Funghi Ripieni alla Parmigiana

Cheese-stuffed Mushrooms, Parma Style

It seems that there are everyone's favorite, and the addition of the prosciutto it adds a special touch to a classic recipe from the Emilia-Romagna region.

Ingredients:

One lb. medium Mushrooms (about 24)
1/4 cup butter
One Tbs. olive oil
1/2 cup onion, family chopped
One clove garlic finely chopped
1/2 cup breadcrumbs
1/4 cup grated Parmigiana-Reggiano cheese
Two Tbs. chopped parsley
1/2 teaspoon finely chopped basil
One half cup prosciutto, chopped
Two Tbs. milk
1/4 teaspoon freshly ground pepper

1. Rinse and dry mushrooms with a paper towel. Cut ends from mushroom stems and discard. Remove stem from mushroom and chop finely.

2. In a skillet, heat the butter and oil, sauté the onion, garlic and mushroom stems until tender for about five minutes. Add the parsley, basil and bread crumbs. Mix well and remove from heat. Add two Tbs. milk, the Parmesan cheese, prosciutto and pepper to taste and mix well. Stuff each mushroom with mixture until well filled.

3. Pour ¼ cup water in a baking dish. Place each stuffed mushroom, filled side up, in the dish and bake at 350 degrees for 20 minutes or until mushroom is tender and has a golden top. Serve hot or warm.

Serves 6-8

FUNGHI MARINATI

Marinated Mushrooms

These are perfect as part of an antipasto platter and the garlic compliments the dish perfectly. It can also be used as a cold side dish with the main entrée in the summer.

Ingredients:

One lb. button Mushrooms, or of your choice
One half cup olive oil
Two green onions with tops, finely sliced
One quarter cup fresh parsley, coarsely chopped
One quarter cup freshly squeezed lemon juice
One clove garlic, finely chopped
Salt and freshly ground pepper to taste

1. Rinse the mushrooms and pat dry with paper towels. Cut off tips from mushroom stems. Quarter the larger mushrooms and halve the smaller ones.

2. Put ¼ cup water into a medium saucepan and heat until boiling. Add the mushrooms and cook three minutes on high flame, stirring constantly. Remove from stove and let mushrooms cool completely.

3. While mushrooms are cooling, mix the remaining ingredients in a glass bowl. Add the cooled mushrooms and mix well. Serve chilled or room temperature in your favorite serving dish.

Serves 6-8

Peperoni trifolati alla Fiamma

Roasted Peppers in Savory Sauce

The traditional roasted peppers are enhanced by the addition of the chopped garlic and parsley and the flavorful olive oil pulls the flavors together perfectly. There is a smoky flavor as well from the roasting of the peppers.

Ingredients:

Three red bell Peppers
Two green bell Peppers
Two yellow bell Peppers
One cup olive oil
Two Tbs. finely chopped parsley
Two medium garlic cloves, finely chopped
Salt to taste

1. Wash peppers, do not dry. Place them on the open flame of a gas burner. If using an electric stove, place on a cookie sheet and under the broiler. Turn each side until pepper is completely charred and skin looks black.

2. Place the peppers in a paper bag and let rest for 10 minutes. Open bag and peel off the charred skin and remove stems and seeds.

3. Slice peppers lengthwise about 1-inch wide and place in a bowl.

4. Combine parsley, garlic, oil, and salt and pour over peppers, mixing well to coat. Serve with bread crostini over sliced, fresh mozzarella.

Serves 6-8

POMODORI FARCITI FREDDI

Stuffed Cold Tomatoes

This is the perfect summer cold appetizer and a tradition from the Eternal City of Rome.

Ingredients:

Eight cups salted water
One cup white rice or Italian Arborio rice
One half cup shelled baby peas, fresh or frozen
Six large ripe Tomatoes
One half cup green pitted olives, sliced
One half of a red bell pepper, diced
Three leaves fresh basil, chopped
Two sprigs flat leaf parsley, chopped
Two scallions, chopped
Two Tbs. olive oil
One Tbs. mayonnaise
18 capers, rinsed and drained

1. Bring a large pot of eight cups salted water to a boil. Add rice and cook uncovered, over medium heat, stirring occasionally until rice is tender, about 15 to 20 minutes. Drain rice and rinse under cold running water. Drain again. Put rice in a large bowl and let cool.

2. Boil the peas in salted water until tender. If using frozen peas, cook according to package directions. Drain and cool.

3. Wash and dry the tomatoes. Cut off the stem end and remove and discard the seeds and reserve the pulp. Make a small slice on the bottom end of the tomato so it will sit flat.

4. Add all chopped ingredients to the cooled rice. Also add the reserved tomato pulp, the peas and the olives. Mix the olive oil with the mayonnaise, salt and pepper to taste and combine with the rice mixture.

5. Mix well and stuff the tomatoes, garnishing with three capers on each. Serve room temperature or cold.

Serves 6

Frittura di Verdura

Breaded Vegetables

Fr. Matt enjoys these when they are nice and hot and first enjoyed them at a trattoria by Lake Albano not far from Castel Gondolfo, the summer residence of the Pope.

Ingredients:

Two large Portobello mushrooms
Two fresh artichokes or frozen artichoke hearts
Two zucchini
One half cauliflower, parboiled and cut in florets
12 squash flowers
3 eggs, beaten
One half cup milk
Flour for dredging
Three to four cups breadcrumbs
One quarter cup grated Parmigiana-Reggiano cheese
Two Tbs. dried parsley
Salt and pepper to taste
Three cups olive oil or vegetable oil for frying

1. If using a fresh artichoke, remove the stem, strip hard leaves off until you come to the tender center, then cut the prickly spine tops and split the heart of the artichoke. Remove the choke and rub with lemon juice to prevent discoloring. Cut in ¼-inch slices and set aside.

2. Wash the zucchini, cut off and discard the ends and cut into ¼-inch thick slices. Wash the squash flowers, remove the green stem and pat dry with a paper towel and set aside. Remove the stem end from the mushroom and discard. Rinse the mushroom and dry with a paper towel and cut into ¼-inch thick slices.

3. Put the three eggs in a deep bowl and beat lightly with 1/2 –cup milk. Add salt and pepper. Mix breadcrumbs with cheese and parsley.

4. Dredge the vegetables, including cauliflower, lightly in the flour, dip in the egg mixture and then roll in the breadcrumbs, coating each side. When all the vegetables are done, heat oil in a skillet until very hot, but not smoking.

5. Fry the vegetables; turning to be sure they are golden on each side. Remove from the skillet and place on absorbent paper towels. Continue until all vegetables are done. Arrange in a dish and serve with your favorite dressing.

Serves 6-8

INSALATA DI FAGIOLI E TONNO

Bean and Tuna Salad

One of Fr. Matt's favorite appetizers and it is always well received by his guests. Use a fruity olive oil for a flavorful taste.

Ingredients:

Three cups water

One half lb. dried white kidney beans or two cans cannellini or other white beans, drained

One third cup olive oil

Three Tbs. balsamic vinegar

One medium onion, thinly sliced

2 five oz. cans of Tuna, drained

Two sprigs flat leaf parsley, finely chopped

Salt and freshly ground pepper to taste

1. Heat water and beans to boiling, for two minutes. Remove from heat, cover and let stand one hour. Add water to pot to cover beans if necessary.

2. After one hour, heat again to boiling then reduce heat and simmer until tender, for one to one and 1/2 hours. Do not boil or beans will burst. Drain and cool.

3. Mix oil, vinegar, salt and pepper. Pour over beans and onion in a shallow bowl. Cover and refrigerate, stirring occasionally, at least one hour.

4. Transfer bean mixture to a serving platter. Break tuna into chunks, arrange on bean mixture and sprinkle with parsley.

Serves 6-8

CALAMARI FRITTI

Fried Squid

This is an old stand-by in many an Italian pizzeria to nibble on while waiting for the pizza to arrive. Do try soaking the calamari rings in lemon juice or white wine for an hour before preparing, as it tenderizes the meat.

Ingredients:

Two lbs. Squid
One half cup unbleached all-purpose flour
One egg, separated
Two Tbs. olive oil
Four ounces dry white wine
Water as needed
Oil for frying
Salt and pepper to taste

1. Clean and wash the squid and cut into ½-inch rings.

2. Place the flour in a bowl and add the oil, egg yolk, wine and salt and pepper. Mix well and add cold water as needed to make a smooth batter, not too thick, about the consistency of heavy cream. Let it rest for about an hour.

3. Beat the egg white until it forms stiff peaks and fold in the batter.

4. Dip the squid rings into the batter and fry until golden brown. Drain on absorbent paper and serve very hot with spicy Marinara sauce. **Serves 6-8**

For Marinara Sauce:

Garlic
Olive oil
One can crushed tomatoes
¼ tsp red pepper flakes
1 Tbs. each of fresh parsley and oregano
Salt to taste

1. Sauté garlic and olive oil in a large pan.

2. While sizzling, add crushed tomatoes and lower heat to simmer.

3. Add red pepper flakes, fresh parsley and oregano and cook briskly for 10 minutes.

OSTRICHE ALLA VERSILIESE

Oysters Versilia-style

This is a very tasty and elegant dish from the area of Versilia, which is a picturesque coastal town in Tuscany.

Ingredients:

24 Oysters

Two cloves garlic, chopped

1/2 of an onion, chopped

One Tbs. chopped fresh parsley

Two Tbs. breadcrumbs

Two Tbs. olive oil

Juice of one lemon

Salt and freshly ground pepper to taste

Lemon wedges for garnish

1. Wash and open oysters carefully. Discard the top shell, leaving the oyster meat in the bottom.

2. In a bowl, prepare the sauce. Chop the garlic and onion together. Add the parsley, breadcrumbs, oil, salt and pepper and lemon juice. Mix well.

3. Spoon the sauce over the oysters, place them in an ovenproof container and bake in a moderate 350-degree oven for about 10 minutes. Garnish with lemon wedges and serve very hot.

Serves 6

CROSTINI DI POLENTA AL FORMAGGIO

Corn meal Crostini with Cheese Topping

Polenta seems to have made a "comeback" from the old days and is especially enjoyed when cooled, sliced and grilled. The topping is a creamy and luscious perfect compliment. A good glass of Chianti would be great with this dish.

Ingredients:

One cup yellow Cornmeal

Three quarters cup cold water

Three and 1/4 cups boiling water

Two teaspoons salt

One Tbs. butter

Eight ounces Fontina cheese, sliced

Eight ounces Gorgonzola cheese, crumbled

1. Mix cornmeal and cold water in a 2-quart saucepan. Stir in the boiling water and salt. Cook, stirring constantly, until the mixture thickens and boils; reduce heat. Cover and simmer, stirring occasionally, for about 20 minutes. Remove from heat and stir until smooth.

2. Grease a cookie sheet with the butter and spread the polenta until about ½-inch thick. Allow to cool until firm.

3. Using a 2 and ½-inch cookie cutter or an inverted glass, cut the polenta into circles. You may also cut into 2 and ½-inch squares. Place in a greased baking sheet and top with a slice of Fontina cheese and a spoonful of crumbled gorgonzola cheese.

4. Bake at 375 degrees until the cheese melts and starts to bubble. Serve hot.

Serves 6-8

CARPACCIO CLASSICO

Raw Meat Salad

This dish originates in the north of Italy. The Tartars, from the Hungarian region of central Europe, introduced raw meat as a specialty wherever they traveled. This is a contemporary version of a truly classic dish.

Ingredients:

One Tbs. fresh lemon juice

Three Tbs. olive oil

Salt and pepper to taste

Seven ounces very lean Beef filet, sliced paper thin

Six mushrooms, sliced thin

Four ounces Parmigiana-Reggiano cheese, shaved

Lettuce leaves (for garnish)

Note: for easy slicing of the beef, place meat in the freezer 20 minutes before using.

1. In a bowl, combine the lemon juice, oil, salt and pepper to make the dressing.

2. Line six plates with lettuce leaves and drizzle a few drops of dressing on them. Toss the meat and mushrooms in the remaining dressing

3. Arrange the meat and mushrooms on the lettuce leaves and top with the shaved cheese. Serve cold.

Serves 6-8

CHAPTER III: PRIMI/FIRST COURSES

In a traditional Italian meal, the "Primo," or first course, usually involves a starch, such as Pasta, Soup, Polenta, Gnocchi or Risotto.

Pasta:

- Ziti Napoletano al Forno
- Ziti ai Funghi Gratinati
- Rigatoni Quattro Formaggi
- Fettuccine Verdi al Funghetto
- Fettuccine alla Panna
- Fettuccine alla Siciliana
- Tagliatelle alla Ciociara
- Tagliatelle con Verdura
- Tagliatelle Festaiola
- Paglia e Fieno
- Pasta al Pesto
- Pappardelle alla Selvaggina
- Spaghetti alla Carbonara
- Penne Estive
- Orecchiette alle Cime di Rapa
- Pasta e Fagioli
- Farfalle al Salmone
- Cappellini fra Diavolo
- Penne alla Vodka
- Penne agli Asparagi
- Rigatoni alla Boscaiola
- Gemelli alla Gorgonzola
- Spaghetti alle Vongole in Bianco
- Spaghetti alle Vongole in Rosso
- Pasta alle Cozze in Bianco
- Pasta alle Cozze in Rosso
- Spaghetti Aglio e Olio

Lasagne

- Lasagna alla Bolognese
- Lasagne Bianche con Pasta Verde
- Lasagne alla Napoletana
- Lasagne a l'Ortolana
- Lasagne alla Melanzana

- Manicotti
- Crespelle alla Fiorentina
- Cannelloni Ripieni di Carne
- Rotoli di Spinaci
- Conchiglie Ripiene
- Tortelli d'Erbetta
- Ravioli di Ricotta
- Ravioli di Carne
- Tortelli di Zucca
- Tortellini alla Panna
- Tortelloni Classici

Gnocchi

- Gnocchi di Ricotta al Forno
- Gnocchi di Ricotta alla Nonna Serafina
- Gnocchi di Patate alla Gorgonzola
- Gnocchi Verdi in Salsa Rosata

Risotti

- Riso Stile Spagnolo
- Insalata di Riso Freddo
- Riso a Strati al Forno
- Risotto Milanese
- Risotto con Verdura
- Risotto ai Funghi
- Risotto di Zucca
- Risi e Bisi
- Risotto alle Erbe e Prosciutto
- Risotto alla Pescatora
- Risotto con Finocchio e Salsicce
- Risotto ai Formaggi

Polenta

- Polenta base
- Polenta con Cotechino e Fagioli
- Polenta Pasticciata alla Contadina
- Polenta Avellino
- Polenta Boscaiola
- Polenta Gorgonzola

- Polenta al Pesto
- Polenta con Spezzatino di Vitello
- Polenta Rustica
- Polenta Fritta

Soups

- Brodo di Pollo (Chicken Broth)
- Brodo di Manzo (Beef Broth)
- Brodo Base di Pollo e Manzo
- Brodo Vegetale
- Zuppe di Pollo
- Minestra si Scarola e Polpettine
- Tortellini in Brodo
- Brodo con Gnocchetti di Semolina
- Stracciatella alla Romana
- Minestrone al Giardino
- Minestrone Tradizionale
- Minestra di Lenticchie
- Minestra di Piselli Secchi
- Pasta e Fagioli
- Pasta e Fagioli in Rosso
- Passato di Carote
- Passato di Asparagi
- Passato di Broccoli
- Zuppa di Finocchio
- Zuppa di Spinaci
- Crema di Patate e Aglio
- Zuppa di Cipolla alla Contadina
- Zuppa di Vongole al Pomodoro

ZITI NAPOLETANO AL FORNO

Neapolitan-style Baked Ziti

Pasta is a staple in Italy, from the northern to the southern regions. The following section includes recipes for lasagna, baked and stuffed pasta, as well as pasta with traditional northern and southern Italian sauces. This first recipe is a delicious treat from Naples in the sunny region of Campania.

Ingredients:

One recipe Napoletano sauce (page 7)
One lb. Ziti pasta
Two lbs. Ricotta cheese
1/2 lb. Mozzarella cheese, diced
One cup grated Romano or Parmigiana-Reggiano cheese
Two eggs, beaten
Three to four sprigs flat-leaf parsley, chopped
Salt and pepper to taste

1. Prepare the Napoletano sauce. As sauce is simmering, bring a pot of salted water to boil. Add the ziti and cook until "al dente," or six to eight minutes. Drain and return to the empty pot in which they were cooked.

2. Mix the remaining ingredients, reserving ½ cup of the grated cheese. Add about 1 ½ cups of the sauce to the pasta and stir well.

3. Spread ¾ cup sauce on the bottom of a large baking dish. Place 1/3 of the ziti in the dish and spread one half of the ricotta mixture over it. Using a slotted spoon, remove some of the sausage from the sauce and sprinkle it over the top. Repeat the process, ending with the remaining 1/3 ziti as the top layer.

4. Cover generously with the sauce and sprinkle with reserved grated cheese. Cover loosely with aluminum foil and bake in a preheated 350-degree oven for 20 minutes. Remove foil and continue to bake for 15 minutes. Let set a few minutes before cutting and serving in squares.

Serves 6-8

ZITI AI FUNGHI GRATINATI

Baked Ziti with Mushrooms

Very similar to the Baked Ziti in the prior recipe, but the expression "in bianco," means "in white." Here there are no tomatoes featured at all. This is a more typical taste from Franca's region that of Fr. Matt's tradition.

Ingredients:

1/4 cup olive oil
Three Tbs. butter
Two medium onions, finely chopped
2 cloves garlic
Two Portobello mushrooms, cut in half and sliced
Three sprigs flat-leaf parsley, shopped
Two basil leaves, finely chopped
1/2 glass of dry, white wine
1/2 beef bouillon cube
One lb. Ziti
One recipe Béchamel sauce (page 10)
One cup grated Parmigiana-Reggiano cheese

1. Place the oil and butter in a skillet, heat and add the onions and sauté until golden and translucent. Add the garlic, stir quickly then add the mushrooms, parsley, and basil and stir well. Add the wine, bouillon, salt and pepper and sauté for 15 minutes over moderate heat, stirring occasionally.

2. Preheat oven to 350 degrees. Cook the pasta, drain and run under cold water. Place the pasta in a deep baking pan. Pour the mushroom sauce over it and mix well. Add ½ cup Parmesan cheese and mix.

3. Distribute evenly in the baking dish. Pour the béchamel over all and sprinkle with remaining Parmesan cheese. Bake for 20 minutes or until top is golden colored and serve.

Serves 6-8

RIGATONI QUATTRO FORMAGGI

Pasta with Four Cheeses

Typical of the trattorias of Rome, this has been one of Fr. Matt's favorites since he was a student there. It is a true comfort food, like our own American macaroni and cheese.

Ingredients:

1/4 lb. Swiss cheese

1/4 lb. Fontina cheese

1/4 lb. sharp white Cheddar cheese

1/2 recipe Béchamel sauce (page 10)

One and 1/2 lbs. Rigatoni

Three-quarter cups grated Parmigiana-Reggiano cheese

1/2 stick (four Tbs.) butter

1. Cut the three hard cheeses into small cubes and set aside.

2. Prepare the béchamel sauce and set aside.

3. Boil the rigatoni in lightly salted water until al dente. Strain the pasta and return to the pan. Add the butter and béchamel and mix well. Add the cheeses and ¼ cup of the Parmesan. Mix well and pour into baking dish, spreading equally. Sprinkle with reserved Parmesan and bake in a 350 degree oven for 15 minutes or until the cheeses are melted.

Serves 6-8

FETTUCCINE VERDI AL FUNGHETTO

Green Fettuccine in Mushroom Sauce

This is a very tasty dish and the delicate flavors are delightful. We can guarantee that many will be asking for the recipe by the end of the meal.

Ingredients:

One medium onion, finely chopped
Two Tbs. olive oil
Four Tbs. butter
One large Portobello mushroom, cleaned and sliced
One container (14 oz) of white mushrooms, cleaned and sliced
Salt and pepper to taste
½ cup white wine
Two 28-oz. cans crushed tomatoes
One recipe Spinach Pasta (page 2)
1/2 cup grated Parmigiana-Reggiano cheese

1. Put the oil and two Tbs. of the butter in a heavy skillet. Add the onion and sauté lightly over moderate heat for two minutes. Add the mushrooms and the salt and pepper to taste and sauté over moderate heat for 10 additional minutes. Add the wine and let evaporate completely.

2. Add the tomatoes, mix well and let cook over moderate heat for 20 minutes, stirring occasionally. When the sauce is done, add the remainder of the butter, turn off the heat and cover, allowing it to melt. Set aside and stir in the melted butter before using.

3. To make the fettuccine, roll out the dough as thinly as possible with a rolling pin or a pasta machine at the #6 setting. Lightly dust the pasta sheet with flour and loosely roll up the sheets. Take a large, sharp knife and cut the roll of pasta lengthwise into desired width, making ribbons. Unravel the ribbons and place on a lightly floured surface. When ready to cook, boil in lightly salted water for three to four minutes or until al dente. Careful not to overcook.

4. Drain pasta and place in a serving dish. Mix half the sauce into the fettuccine. Spoon about half of the remaining sauce on top and serve the rest on the side, with the cheese.

Serves 6-8

FETTUCCINE ALLA PANNA

Fettuccine in Cream Sauce

This dish was made famous in Rome by Alfred in his restaurant on Via della Scrofa. According to legend, he had invented as a special treat for the American actors, Douglas Fairbanks and Mary Pickford who were on their honeymoon in 1927. This is our own version.

Ingredients:

1/2 stick of butter

One Tbs. flour

Two cups heavy cream

One recipe Egg pasta (page 2) or one lb. dry Fettuccine noodles

One cup freshly grated Parmigiana-Reggiano cheese

Dash of freshly grated nutmeg (optional)

Salt and fresh ground pepper to taste

1. Melt the butter in a saucepan and stir in the flour until well-mixed. Add the cream and keep warm.

2. To prepare the fettuccine noodles, roll out the dough as thinly as possible with a rolling pin or a pasta machine at the #6 setting. Lightly dust the pasta sheet with flour and loosely roll up the sheets. Take a large, sharp knife and cut the roll of pasta lengthwise into desired width, making ribbons. Unravel the ribbons and place on a lightly floured surface. When ready to cook, boil in lightly salted water for three to four minutes or until al dente. Careful not to overcook.

3. If using dry fettuccine, boil according to package instructions.

4. Drain the fettuccine and place in a large bowl. Pour the cream sauce over the pasta and mix well. Sprinkle with Parmesan cheese and mix again. Serve immediately.

Serves 6-8

Fettuccine alla Siciliana

Sicilian-style Fettuccine

The ingredients are typical of the sun-drenched south of Italy and the eggplant adds the unique flavor that is always welcome.

Ingredients:

One recipe Egg pasta (page 2)

Three-quarter cups olive oil

Two cloves garlic, chopped

Two 28-oz. cans peeled plum tomatoes, cut into pieces

One teaspoon hot pepper flakes

One large eggplant, diced

Two Tbs. capers

1/2 cup coarsely chopped black olives

1/2 cup coarsely chopped green olives

One teaspoon oregano

1. Prepare the pasta, roll out the dough as thinly as possible with a rolling pin or a pasta machine at the #6 setting. Lightly dust the pasta sheet with flour and loosely roll up the sheets. Take a large, sharp knife and cut the roll of pasta lengthwise into desired width, making ribbons. Unravel the ribbons and place on a lightly floured surface. When ready to cook, boil in lightly salted water for three to four minutes or until al dente.

2. For the sauce, pour 1/2 cup of the oil into a large saucepan. Add the chopped garlic and lightly cook over moderate heat until slightly golden. Add tomatoes and the remaining ingredients. Season with salt to taste and cook over high heat for 15 minutes, being careful not to burn.

3. Place the fettuccine in a large serving bowl with the reserved ¼ cup olive oil. Mix quickly then pour half the sauce over the pasta. Serve at once with reserved sauce on the side.

Serves 6-8

TAGLIATELLE ALLA CIOCIARA

Tagliatelle in a Creamy Sauce

This recipe is from the area inland from Rome, near to Frosinone. Fr. Matt enjoyed it on his very first visit to Rome at the age of 17 and has served it to many friends throughout the years. When sautéed sliced button mushrooms are added, it is called "alla Papalina," since it has been the favorite of many Popes over the years.

Ingredients:

One recipe Egg Pasta (page 2)

One lb. frozen or fresh baby peas

Four Tbs. butter

1/4 lb. ham, cut into small pieces

One cup grated Parmigiana-Reggiano cheese

Two cups heavy cream

Salt and pepper to taste

1. Prepare the pasta and set aside. Cook the peas until tender, drain and set aside. Melt the butter, add the ham and sauté for two minutes only. Add the peas and cream, salt and pepper to taste and keep warm.

2. To make the tagliatelle, roll out the dough as thinly as possible with a rolling pin or a pasta machine at the #6 setting. Lightly dust the pasta sheet with flour and loosely roll up the sheets. Take a large, sharp knife and cut the roll of pasta crosswise into desired width, making ribbons. Unravel the ribbons and place on a lightly floured surface. When ready to cook, boil in lightly salted water for three to four minutes or until al dente. Careful not to overcook.

3. Drain pasta and place in a serving dish. Pour the sauce over it and gently mix. Sprinkle ½ cup Parmesan cheese and mix again. Sprinkle two Tbs. of the remaining cheese on top and serve with extra cheese at table.

Serves 6-8

Tagliatelle con Verdura Fresca

Tagliatelle with Garden Vegetables

This is our own version of Pasta Primavera, pasta for the "Springtime" that has become very popular in recent years and is heath conscious. Although we use freshly made tagliatelle, dry pasta such as Gemelli can be used as well.

Ingredients:

One recipe Egg Pasta (page 2)

Three fresh artichokes

Two Tbs. butter

One medium onion, finely chopped

Two medium zucchini, diced

1/2 cup finely diced red bell pepper

Six ounces asparagus, cleaned and cut into ¾-inch diagonal pieces

Salt and pepper to taste

One cup heavy cream

Three sprigs flat-leaf parsley, finely chopped

1/2 cup Parmigiana-Reggiano cheese

1. Prepare the pasta as in step 2 on preceding page and set aside.

2. If using fresh artichoke, peel the outer hard leaves (Refer to Frittura di Verdura, page 38).

3. Melt the butter in a large skillet over medium heat. Add the onion and sauté to a golden color. Add the zucchini, red bell pepper, artichoke and asparagus to the skillet. Continue to sauté over medium-high heat until all the vegetables are tender but not overcooked — about 10 to 15 minutes.

4. Add salt and black pepper to taste. Add the cream and cook, stirring occasionally, over a lively fire until it reduces and the consistency thickens.

5. Boil the pasta in lightly salted water until al dente. Drain and place in a large serving dish. Pour over the sauce and mix well. Sprinkle with grated cheese and parsley and serve immediately.

Serves 6-8

TAGLIATELLE FESTAIOLA

Festive Tagliatelle

This is purely Franca's masterpiece and the first time that Fr. Matt was impressed with her cooking was with this very same dish. We hope that it is just as pleasing to you as well.

Ingredients:

One recipe Egg Pasta (page 2)
Two recipes Pesto (page 7)
One lb. shrimp
One lb. sea scallops
Two Tbs. butter
Two Tbs. olive oil
Two cloves garlic, minced

1. Prepare the pasta as on preceding page. Prepare pesto sauce and set aside.

2. Bring a medium pot of water to boil. Add the shrimp and boil for two minutes only. Drain and run under cold water, then peel, clean, devein and set aside.

3. Clean the scallops, pat dry and set aside.

4. Put the butter and oil in a large skillet and add the garlic and cook to a light golden color. Add the scallops and cook over a lively flame, stirring occasionally for five minutes. Add the shrimp, stir, cook and additional minute, add salt and pepper to taste, cover and remove from heat.

5. Cook the pasta until al dente, drain and place in a large serving bowl. Pour in half the pesto and half of the fish, mixing well.

6. Place the remaining fish on top, cover with pesto and serve, garnished with fresh basil leaves.

Serves 6-8

PAGLIA E FIENO

"Straw and Hay" Pasta

The two colors of the green and white fettuccine are reminiscent of straw and hay, hence the name. This is a favorite throughout Italy, from north to south.

Ingredients:

For the green pasta:

Two cups unbleached all-purpose flour
Two large eggs
One Tbs. olive oil
1/2 lb. fresh spinach

For the white pasta:

Two cups unbleached, all-purpose flour
Two large eggs
One Tbs. olive oil
Two Tbs. lukewarm water

1. For the sauce, refer to the Ragu Bolognese a la Franca sauce on page 5. Also needed is one cup freshly grated Parmigiana-Reggiano cheese.

2. To make the paglia e fieno noodles, follow the procedure found under basic pasta. Roll out the dough as thinly as possible with a rolling pin or a pasta machine at the #6 setting.

3. Lightly dust each pasta sheet with flour and loosely roll it up. Take a large sharp knife and cut the roll of pasta crosswise into the desired width, making ribbons. Unravel the ribbons and place on a lightly floured surface. Boil in lightly salted water 3 to 4 minutes or until al dente.

4. Drain and place in a serving dish. Pour sauce over and gently mix. Add ½ cup grated cheese and mix again. Sprinkle two Tbs. cheese on top and serve the rest of the cheese at the table with the Paglia e Fieno.

Serves 6-8

SPAGHETTI AL PESTO

Pasta with Pesto Sauce

Well-known and enjoyed worldwide, this sauce is originally from Genoa in the northern Italy Region of Liguria.

Ingredients:

One recipe Pesto (page 7)

1. Boil one pound of fresh spaghetti or pasta of your choice, such as ziti, in lightly salted water for three to four minutes. If using dried pasta, prepare according to package directions.
2. Drain pasta and place in a deep serving dish. Add half the pesto and mix well. Top with the remaining pesto sauce and serve immediately. Serve with grated cheese. **Serves 4-6**

PAPPARDELLE ALLA SELVAGGINA

Pappardelle Pasta with Wild Game Sauce

Many people enjoy hunting season throughout Italy and this is a recipe similar to cacciatore, which means hunter style.

Ingredients:

One recipe Egg Pasta (page 2)
¼ cup olive oil
Flour for dredging
½ cup grated Parmigiana-Reggiano cheese

One large onion, chopped
1 lb. Portobello mushrooms
1 and ½ cups chicken stock
1 rabbit or pheasant, cut in pieces

Marinade (to be done the night before):

1 sprig rosemary, finely chopped
½ cup olive oil
Salt & pepper to taste

2 garlic cloves, finely chopped
1 cup dry white wine

1. Mix marinade ingredients together, place the rabbit or pheasant in a ceramic bowl, coat with marinade, cover and refrigerate overnight.

The next day:

2. Prepare the pasta and cut into strips 1" thick and 12" long and set aside.

3. Heat ¼ cup olive oil in a large skillet. Clean and slice the mushrooms.

4. Remove meat from marinade and reserve liquid. Dredge the meat in the flour, add to the skillet and brown the pieces until golden. Add the chopped onions, mushrooms, garlic and sauté until the onions are tender – about 10 minutes.

5. Add the chicken broth and reserved marinade and continue to cook over low heat for 1 and ½ hours until very tender and the meat comes off the bone. Remove the meat pieces from pan, then remove and discard the bones and cut meat into large pieces. Return to pan to keep warm.

6. Boil the Pappardelle in lightly salted water until al dente. Drain, place in a large deep platter and add meat sauce, mixing well. Top with grated Parmesan cheese and serve hot.

Serves 6-8

Spaghetti alla Carbonara

Coal-miner Style Spaghetti

A favorite of so many throughout the years! It is considered a classic Roman dish and according to tradition, was originally cooked over charcoal.

Ingredients:

½ lb. smoked bacon
¼ stick butter
3 egg yolks
1 and ½ lbs. Spaghetti
½ cup heavy cream, room temperature
1 cup freshly grated Parmigiana-Reggiano or Pecorino Romano cheese.
Salt & freshly ground pepper to taste

1. Cut the bacon into small pieces. Sauté lightly and drain the grease. Add the butter and keep warm.

2. In a large bowl, beat the egg yolks, the cream and the salt and pepper and set aside.

3. Cook the pasta in a pot of lightly salted water until al dente.

4. Drain pasta and add into the bowl with the egg and cream mixture. Mix well. Add the bacon, butter and grated cheese, stirring. Serve at once.

Serves 6-8

PENNE ESTIVE

Summertime Pasta

Fr. Matt learned this recipe from his sister Suzanne when he was visiting Milan in the hot summer. It has also been called "alla Checca." It is a raw sauce that is said to have originated in Naples, but now is enjoyed throughout all of Italy and we are happy to share it with you!

Ingredients:

8 ripe plum tomatoes
½ cup extra virgin olive oil
1 large clove garlic, minced
8 to 10 basil leaves, torn
Salt and fresh ground pepper to taste
1 lb. fresh mozzarella
1 and ½ lbs. dried Penne pasta
Several basil leaves for garnish

1. Plunge tomatoes into a pot of boiling water for 30 seconds to one minute. Remove and place in a bowl of cold water to loosen the skins. Drain, peel, remove the seeds and cut into small dice.

2. Place the tomatoes into a large bowl and add the olive oil, garlic and basil leaves torn into pieces, and the salt and freshly ground pepper. Let rest, covered, for 1 to 2 hours to allow the garlic to mellow.

3. Cut the mozzarella into small chunks and set aside.

4. Place the penne into a large pot of salted boiling water and cook according to package instructions, or until al dente. Drain pasta and add to the tomato mixture, blending well. Add ¾ of the mozzarella, mix quickly and serve, garnishing with the reserved mozzarella and fresh basil leaves.

Serves 6-8

ORECCHIETTE ALLE CIME DI RAPA

Pasta with Broccoli Rape'

This is a recipe from the area near Bari, in the region of Puglia, near to the Adriatic side of the Italian peninsula. Fr. Matt's maternal grandparents are from a town not too far from there and he was brought up on it. It is still one of his all time favorites to this day. Although he usually prefers it meatless so he can enjoy it on Fridays in the season of Lent.

Ingredients:

1 large head of Broccoli rape

1 lb. Pork sausage (optional)

1 and ½ lbs. dried Orecchiette or Cavatelli pasta

6 to 8 garlic cloves, chopped

½ teaspoon red pepper flakes

½ cup extra virgin olive oil

1. Remove the thick stems from the broccoli rape. Cook in lightly salted boiling water, about 10 to 15 minutes over moderate heat, stirring occasionally.

2. If using sausage, remove from the casing, crumble and brown in a frying pan until all the pink is gone. Remove with a slotted spoon, discarding the drippings. Reserve the sausage meat.

3. Meanwhile, lightly fry the garlic in the olive oil until browned, but do not allow it to burn. Add the broccoli, sausage and red pepper flakes and keep warm.

4. Boil the pasta until "al dente," drain and return to the pot in which it was cooked. Add the broccoli rape, oil, garlic and sausage mixture. Stir well and cover. Let rest a few minutes before serving.

5. May be served with grated Romano cheese at the table.

Serves 6-8

PASTA E FAGIOLI

Macaroni-style Pasta with Beans

We have heard this pronounced every which-way, such as "Pasta Fazool" arising from Italian-American slang. Call it what you wish, but we call simply delicious! It actually is originally from the region of Veneto, in the northeast of Italy, and is the ultimate in comfort food.

Ingredients:

1 and ½ lbs. short pasta, such as Ditalini
3 to 4 cloves garlic, finely chopped
¼ cup olive oil
Pinch of oregano
2 cans (18 oz. each) of white cannellini beans
One 28-oz. can crushed tomatoes
2 to 3 sprigs flat-leaf parsley, chopped
2 basil leaves, torn into small pieces
Salt & pepper to taste

1. Brown the garlic in the oil and add the oregano, beans and tomatoes, parsley and basil. Cook 15 to 20 minutes over moderate heat, stirring occasionally.

2. Meanwhile, boil the pasta in salted water until al dente. Drain and return to pot. Add the tomato sauce and stir well. Add salt and pepper to taste. Cover and let rest for a few minutes before serving.

3. If desired, serve with grated Parmesan or Romano cheese.

Serves 6-8

Variation: You can substitute Chickpeas, also known as Garbanzos, for the Cannellini beans and have the well known dish, Pasta e Ceci.

FARFALLE AL SALMONE

Butterfly Pasta in a Creamy Salmon Sauce

This dish is very elegant and served at many weddings in Italy over the years as the first course.

Ingredients:

1 and ½ lbs. of Farfalle pasta

1 and ½ cups heavy cream

¾ lbs. smoked salmon

2 Tbs. tomato paste

½ stick (4 oz) unsalted butter

Salt & Pepper to taste

1. In a saucepan, heat the cream over moderate heat. Add the tomato paste and mix well. Flake the salmon and add to the pan. Cook the pasta according to package directions in lightly salted water until al dente.

2. When the pasta is done, drain and return to pot. Add the butter and mix well, coating the pasta. Add the salmon and cream sauce and mix well. Pour into a large serving bowl and garnish with chopped parsley, if desired. **Serves 6-8**

CAPPELLINI FRA DIAVOLO

Spicy Pasta with Shrimp

Spicy, enjoyable and always well received.

Ingredients:

3 Tbs. olive oil

2 cloves garlic, minced very fine

1 can (28 oz.) crushed tomatoes

2 to 3 sprigs flat leaf parsley, finely chopped

3 basil leaves, finely chopped

1 lb. large Shrimp, cleaned and deveined

½ teaspoon red pepper flakes

2 Tbs. butter

Salt to taste

1 lb. Angel hair pasta

1. In a saucepan, heat the oil and add the garlic. Fry until a light golden color. Add the tomatoes, basil and parsley, stir and bring to a boil. Cook over a lively flame, stirring frequently to avoid burning for about 10 minutes to reduce the liquid.

2. Add the shrimp and cook for an additional five minutes. Add salt and red pepper flakes to taste and the two Tbs. butter. Turn off flame and cover, allowing to rest.

3. Boil the pasta in a pot of lightly salted water until al dente. Drain well and place in a large serving dish. Add half of the shrimp sauce and mix well. Pour the other half over the top and serve immediately. **Serves 6-8**

PENNE ALLA VODKA

Penne Pasta with Vodka Sauce

This has become one of the new classics, and can be found on almost every menu worldwide. Here is our own version.

Ingredients:

1 lb. dried Penne Rigate pasta
1 cup grated Parmigiana-Reggiano cheese
1 recipe Vodka sauce (page 9)
¼ cup chopped fresh chives

1. Prepare the sauce according to directions under basics and keep warm.

2. Boil the pasta until al dente. Drain and place in a large serving dish or bowl. Add approximately half of the sauce and mix well. Add ½ cup of the grated cheese and mix.

3. Place pasta portions in individual pasta bowls. Top with sauce and sprinkle with chives and additional grated cheese.

Serves 4-6

PENNE AGLI ASPARAGI

Penne Pasta with Asparagus

We invented this recipe together and we sure hope that you will enjoy the variety of flavors that we have incorporated to make this a very tasty combination. It brings together many of our "favorite things."

Ingredients:

2 lbs. fresh asparagus
6 Tbs. extra virgin olive oil
2 garlic cloves, peeled and sliced
¼ lb. ham or prosciutto, sliced
½ cup Gaeta cured olives, pitted

1 cup grated Parmesan cheese
1 cup chicken broth, warm
1 lb. dried Penne Rigate pasta
Salt & pepper to taste

1. Wash asparagus, trim off tough stems and discard. Cut them into diagonal pieces 1" long and set aside.

2. In a large saucepan, heat the oil, adding the sliced garlic, and sauté until a light golden color. Add the warm broth and asparagus and cook over moderate heat until asparagus are just tender.

3. Cut prosciutto into small julienne strips and add to the pan with the asparagus. Add the olives and simmer for an additional minute. Remove from flame, add the butter and let rest.

4. Cook the pasta until al dente in salted boiling water for 8 to 10 minutes. Drain the pasta, place in a serving dish, mix with the sauce, sprinkle with the cheese and garnish with parsley.

Serves 6-8

RIGATONI ALLA BOSCAIOLA

Forest-style Pasta

This recipe is reminiscent of a variety of earthy flavors, hence the name "Forest-style." It is great for the autumn or winter and was first tasted by Fr. Matt while in Tuscany. Meat from Wild Boar can be substituted for the bacon and sautéed zucchini has also been used instead of the mushrooms in some restaurants.

Ingredients:

½ cup dry porcini mushrooms
8 oz. Portobello or button mushrooms.
6 Tbs. extra virgin olive oil
2 Tbs. butter
½ cup dry white wine
1 lb. Rigatoni
¼ lb. smoked bacon or pancetta, cut in strips
1 medium onion, finely chopped
1 clove garlic, finely chopped
Salt and pepper to taste
½ cup grated Parmigiana-Reggiano cheese

1. Soak the dry mushrooms in 1 cup warm water for 10 minutes. Meanwhile, add 4 Tbs. of the oil to the skillet and place over moderate heat. Sauté the onion and garlic until light golden in color.

2. Wash, dry and slice the Portobello or button mushrooms, add to the onion mixture and sauté.

3. Remove the dried mushrooms from the water, finely chop and add to skillet. Strain the mushroom water through a cheesecloth and reserve. Add the white wine and strained porcini mushroom liquid and cook over moderate heat for 20 minutes, stirring occasionally.

4. Meanwhile, in another small skillet, heat the remaining oil, add the bacon or pancetta and sauté for 5 minutes. Remove with a slotted spoon and set aside.

5. Cook the pasta until al dente, drain and place in a mixing bowl, reserving ½ cup of the water.

6. Add the bacon to the pasta with the reserved water and butter and mix well. Pour the mushroom sauce and half of the grated cheese and mix again. Serve with additional cheese at the table. **Serves 6-8**

GEMELLI ALLA GORGONZOLA

Gemelli Pasta in Gorgonzola Sauce

This is our own variation of Pasta with three cheeses. It is very soothing and comforting on a winter's night. It can be followed by a tossed green salad and accompanied by a glass of your favorite wine.

Ingredients:

1 cup whole milk
4 oz. gorgonzola
1 lb. dried Gemelli pasta
4 oz. Fontina cheese, cut in cubes
2 oz. grated Parmigiana-Reggiano cheese
Salt and pepper to taste

1. Warm milk in a saucepan over low heat. Add the gorgonzola cheese. Stir with a wooden spoon until mixture is smooth and creamy.

2. Cook pasta in salted water until al dente. Drain and place in a serving dish. Add the gorgonzola cream and Fontina cubes. Mix well, sprinkle with Parmesan cheese and serve at once.

Serves 4-6

SPAGHETTI ALLE VONGOLE IN BIANCO

Spaghetti with Clams in White Wine Sauce

This pasta is well-known and one can almost taste and smell the sea while enjoying this meal. Typically, Italians discourage the use of grated cheese with shellfish dishes.

Ingredients:

4 dozen small Clams
1 cup dry white wine
3 Tbs. olive oil
1 small onion, finely chopped
4 cloves garlic, peeled and finely chopped
¼ cup chopped flat leaf parsley
Salt to taste
1 Tbs. red pepper flakes
1 lb. dried Spaghetti

1. Wash clams and place in a large heavy-bottomed pan with wine. Cover and heat until they open.

2. Remove all clams from the shell and discard shells. Chop half and leave the rest whole. Strain clam broth through a cheesecloth, add to clams and set aside.

3. In a large saucepan, heat the oil and sauté the onion until translucent. Add the clams with liquid. Add the parsley, hot pepper and salt to taste to the pan and cook through for one minute. Turn off flame, cover and let rest.

4. Cook the spaghetti until al dente, drain, add sauce and mix well. Serve hot.

Serves 6-8

SPAGHETTI ALLE VONGOLE IN ROSSO

Linguini with Clams in Tomato Sauce

This is very similar to the prior pasta, but with the added dimension of the flavor of tomato to help enhance the dish, if that is your preference.

Ingredients:

3 dozen small Clams

3 Tbs. olive oil

4 garlic cloves, finely chopped

1 small onion, finely chopped

2 Tbs. tomato paste

One 28-oz can of crushed tomatoes

Pinch of oregano

Salt and pepper to taste

Red pepper flakes, if desired

1 cup water

1 lb. dried Spaghetti or Linguini

2 sprigs chopped parsley

1. Wash and clean clams. Add water to a large, heavy-bottomed pan, steaming clams until opened. Remove and discard shells. Chop half the clams and leave the other half whole. Strain the liquid through a cheese cloth, add to clams and set aside.

2. In a large saucepan, heat oil, add garlic and onion together and sauté until light golden in color. Add tomato paste, stir and cook, adding crushed tomatoes, oregano, salt and pepper to taste. Simmer over moderate heat for 20 minutes.

3. Add the clams with liquid, stir, cover and remove from heat.

4. Cook pasta until al dente. Drain. Mix with sauce and serve hot. Garnish with parsley.

Serves 6-8

PASTA ALLE COZZE IN BIANCO

Pasta with White Mussel Sauce

Follow the recipe for white Clam sauce, but substitute cleaned Mussels for the clams. After steaming the mussels, remove and discard the shells and the steaming liquid. Substitute 1 cup bottled clam juice.

PASTA ALLE COZZE IN ROSSO

Pasta with Red Mussel Sauce

Follow the recipe for tomato Clam sauce, substitute cleaned Mussels for the clams. After steaming the mussels, remove and discard the shells and the steaming liquid. Substitute 1 cup bottled clam juice.

SPAGHETTI AGLIO E OLIO

Spaghetti with Garlic and Oil

This classic spaghetti dish is famous throughout Italy as a midnight snack. In Sicily, breadcrumbs are added and it is called "Pasta con la Mollica."

1 lb. dried Spaghetti or Linguini	½ cup extra virgin olive oil
4 garlic cloves, chopped	2 sprigs parsley, chopped
½ teaspoon dried red hot pepper flakes (optional)	salt

1. Cook the pasta in a large pot of salted water until al dente.

2. While the pasta is cooking, sauté the garlic in the oil in a large frying pan until a light golden color, for about 2-3 minutes, do not allow to burn.

3. Drain the pasta and add to the frying pan. Toss over medium heat for about one minute. Add the chopped parsley and the crushed red pepper, if desired. Add salt to taste.

   Serves 4-6

L<small>ASAGNA ALLA</small> B<small>OLOGNESE</small>

Lasagna in the Style of Bologna

This is the classic lasagna that has been a tradition in Franca's family for generations. It was always well received whenever it was served to the priests of the Rectory. It was especially requested whenever the bishop was invited for dinner.

Ingredients:

One recipe Bolognese sauce (page 5)
One recipe Egg Pasta (page 2)
One recipe Béchamel sauce (page 10)
One lb. whole milk mozzarella cheese
Two and 1/2 cups grated Parmigiana-Reggiano cheese
Two Tbs. olive oil

1. Prepare the Bolognese sauce. While the sauce is cooking, prepare the Basic Pasta recipe. While the pasta is resting, prepare the Béchamel sauce and set aside. Shred the mozzarella cheese and set aside with the grated Parmesan. Bring a large pot of salted water to boil. Add two Tbs. of olive oil.

2. Roll out past dough thinly. If using a machine, use the # 6 setting for the last rolling. Cut the pasta in rectangles, approximately 4 and ½-inches wide and the same length as the baking dish. This will make the lasagna easier to assemble.

3. Prepare a large baking dish by spreading a thin layer of the Bolognese sauce and a thin layer of the Béchamel sauce with a spoon.

4. Place three to four sections of the fresh pasta into the boiling water. Cook for about 30 seconds to one minute, then remove with a slotted spoon and place into a bowl of cold water. Taking one piece of cooked pasta at a time, let the water drain off it and layer it in the baking pan over the sauce and béchamel, until completely covered.

5. Place another thin layer of the meat sauce and the béchamel over the pasta and with your hand, sprinkle with the mozzarella and Parmesan cheeses. Continue the same procedure for the rest of the ingredients, ending the top layer with meat sauce, béchamel and Parmesan cheese.

6. Bake uncovered for 20 to 30 minutes at 375 degrees. Remove from oven and let rest for about five minutes to settle before cutting into squares to serve.

Serves 6-8

LASAGNE BIANCHE CON PASTA VERDE

White Lasagna with Spinach Pasta

Ingredients:

One recipe Spinach Pasta (page 2)

One recipe Béchamel sauce (page 10)

One recipe Bolognese Bianco (page 6)

One lb. whole milk Mozzarella, grated

Two and 1/2 cups grated Parmigiana-Reggiano cheese

Referring to the recipe for Lasagna Bolognese, follow the same instructions for assembly and baking.

LASAGNA ALLA NAPOLETANA

Neapolitan-style Lasagna

This lasagna is prepared the way that Fr. Matt was accustomed to enjoy at the family table, especially for the holidays. He learned this recipe from his grandmother and his Mom.

Ingredients:

One recipe Egg Pasta (page 2) or two boxes lasagna noodles
One recipe Neapolitan sauce (page 7)
Three lbs. whole milk Ricotta, or part-skim if desired
One lb. Mozzarella cheese, shredded
Two cups grated Parmigiana-Reggiano or Pecorino cheese
Three eggs, beaten
Two Tbs. chopped parsley

Prepare the Napoletana tomato sauce.

1. If using the fresh Basic Pasta recipe, roll dough out thinly. If using machine, use the #6 setting for the last rolling. Cut the pasta into eight-inch strips and cook a few sheets at

72

a time in salted, boiling water for about 30 seconds to one minute. Remove with slotted spoon and place in a large bowl of cold water to cool, then dry on towels. If using dried noodles, cook three to five minutes and cool as well.

2. Mix the ricotta, mozzarella, one cup of the grated cheese and the eggs and parsley in a large bowl.

3. To assemble the lasagna, prepare a large baking dish by placing a thin layer of sauce in the bottom of the dish. Layer the pasta and cover with a layer of ricotta and a layer of sauce. Sprinkle with Parmesan cheese. Continue the same procedure until completed, ending with a layer of pasta covered by sauce and sprinkle with more Parmesan.

4. Cover with aluminum foil and bake in preheated 375-degree oven for 30 minutes. Uncover and continue to bake for an additional 15 minutes. Remove from oven, cover and let sit for about 5 minutes before cutting and serving.

Serves 6-8

LASAGNA A L'ORTOLANA

Garden-style Lasagna

This has the same idea as Pasta Primavera, where fresh vegetables are featured. This recipe was developed as a mutual collaboration between Franca and Fr. Matt.

Ingredients:

One recipe Egg Pasta (pg. 2)
One recipe Béchamel sauce (pg. 10)
One lb. carrots, peeled and sliced
One lb. string beans, cut into 1-inch pieces
One lb. zucchini, sliced
Three Tbs. butter
Two Tbs. olive oil
One lb. fresh spinach, rinsed

One lb. fresh ripe tomatoes
Four Tbs. chopped fresh parsley
Three cloves garlic, chopped
One lb. shredded mozzarella
Two cups grated Parmigiana cheese
Six fresh basil leaves
Salt and ground pepper to taste

1. Prepare the Béchamel sauce and set aside. Make the pasta according to instructions and let rest under an inverted bowl.

2. Chop the parsley and garlic together until very fine and set aside.

3. In a frying pan, heat the olive oil and sauté the zucchini until just tender. Add salt and pepper to taste and a teaspoon of the parsley and garlic mixture. Mix to coat and set aside.

4. Parboil or steam the string beans and carrots in lightly salted water. Drain and place in separate bowls. Add a Tbs. of butter and a teaspoon of the parsley and garlic mixture to each and set aside. Parboil or steam the spinach and wait until it is cool enough to handle. Squeeze out the excess water from the spinach and place in a bowl. Add a Tbs. of butter and a teaspoon of the parsley and garlic mixture.

5. Bring a pot of water to boil. Add the fresh tomatoes and boil for one minute to loosen the skin. Strain the tomatoes, remove the skin, slice and discard the seeds. Place in a bowl with two Tbs. olive oil, salt and pepper to taste and a teaspoon of the parsley and garlic mixture.

6. Wash the six fresh basil leaves, tear them into small pieces and set aside.

To assemble the lasagna:

1. Roll out the pasta dough until very thin, or use the #6 setting on the pasta machine. Cut into pieces approximately four and ½-inch wide and the same length as the baking dish.

2. Bring a large pot of salted water to boil. Add two Tbs. olive oil to prevent pasta from sticking. Place three to four sections of the pasta in the water, cooking for 30 seconds to a minute. Remove with slotted spoon and place in a bowl of cold water.

3. Prepare a large baking pan by placing a thin layer of béchamel sauce in the bottom. Layer the pasta, draining the water as you remove it from the bowl. Place the zucchini on the first layer of pasta and spread evenly. Spread a thin layer of the béchamel with a spoon, sprinkle with the basil, mozzarella and Parmesan cheese.

4. Continue to layer in the same manner, next using the carrots, followed by the string beans, spinach and finishing with fresh tomatoes. The last layer should be pasta topped by Béchamel and grated Parmesan cheese.

5. Place in a 375-degree oven and bake uncovered for 20 to 30 minutes.

Serves 6-8

LASAGNA ALLA MELANZANA

Lasagna with Eggplant

This recipe incorporates eggplant, which has been lightly battered and fried, between the layers. On occasion, the addition of eggplant with a pasta dish has been called "alla Sorrentino" meaning in the style of Sorrento, which is on the Amalfi coast.

Ingredients:

One recipe Béchamel Sauce (pg. 10)
One recipe Tomato Basil Sauce (pg. 8)
One recipe Egg pasta (pg. 2)
One large eggplant
One lb. Mozzarella cheese, shredded

Flour for dredging
Two eggs, beaten
Two teaspoons water
Two cups olive oil
1 and 1/2 cups grated Parmesan cheese
Salt and pepper to taste

1. Prepare Béchamel sauce and Tomato Basil sauce and set aside. Prepare pasta and let rest under inverted bowl.

2. Wash eggplant, cutting off and discarding the ends. Cut lengthwise into thin slices. Discard both the end slices as they will be all skin.

3. Mix the egg and water together in a bowl. Heat the oil in a large skillet over moderate heat. Dip eggplant slices into the egg mixture and then in the flour. Fry in batches and drain excess oil on paper towels.

4. Roll out the pasta very thinly, on the #6 setting, and cut into four and ½-inch squares. Cook two to three pieces at a time for one minute in boiling water. Remove with slotted spoon and plunge into cold water. Drain.

5. Take a large, deep baking dish, cover the bottom with a thin layer of sauce, add a little béchamel and spread evenly together. Place a layer of pasta over the sauce, spread a thin layer of béchamel sauce, sprinkle with mozzarella and grated Parmesan cheese. Place eggplant over the pasta layer, spread a thin layer of tomato sauce, sprinkle mozzarella and grated cheese.

6. Continue layers until all pasta and eggplant are used. If your top layer is eggplant, top it with tomato sauce. If the top layer is pasta, top it with béchamel.

7. Bake at 375 degrees uncovered for 20 to 30 minutes. Take out of oven and let rest for five minutes before cutting and serving.

Serves 6-8

PASTA RIPIENA AL FORNO *(Stuffed and Baked Pasta)*

MANICOTTI

Pasta Crepes

These have been called "feather-light" and are very delicate.

For the crepes:

Two cups unbleached all-purpose flour

Pinch of salt

Three eggs, beaten

Two and 1/2 cups milk

Two teaspoons olive oil

For the filling:

Two lbs. Ricotta cheese

Three eggs, beaten

Five to six sprigs parsley, chopped

One cup grated Parmesan cheese

1/2 lb. Mozzarella, diced

Salt and pepper to taste

One recipe Tomato Basil Sauce (page 8)

1. For the crepes: Sift the flour and salt into a mixing bowl. Beat in the eggs and milk until the mixture is smooth, then stir in the oil.

2. Lightly grease an eight-inch skillet or crepe pan with butter. Heat the pan and pour ¼ cup of the thin batter into the pan. Quickly tilt and rotate the pan so the batter covers the bottom in a thin layer. Cook for about one minute or until the underside of the crepe is golden brown. Turn the crepe and cook the other side for about 30 seconds. Slide the crepe out of the pan into a dish and continue to cook the remaining batter this way.

3. For the filling: In a large bowl, mix the eggs with the ricotta and then stir in the remaining ingredients.

4. Fill each crepe with two Tbs. of the ricotta mixture. Fold one half of the crepe over the middle of the filling and then overlap the other half of the crepe.

5. Cover the bottom of a large baking dish generously with the tomato and fresh basil sauce. Place the manicotti with the seam side down in the baking pan and cover with additional sauce. Sprinkle with more Parmesan cheese if desired and bake at 350 degrees for 20 minutes. Reserve additional sauce to add when you serve the baked manicotti. **Serves 6-8**

CRESPELLE ALLA FIORENTINA

Florentine-style Crepe Manicotti

The addition of spinach in the filling adds another dimension and the combination of both the béchamel and tomato sauces was the brainstorm of Franca! It works every time.

Ingredients:

One lb. fresh spinach

One and ½ lbs. Ricotta

1/2 cup Parmigiana-Reggiano cheese

Two eggs, beaten

One-eighth teaspoon or pinch of ground nutmeg

One crepe recipe (page 76 Manicotti recipe)

1/2 recipe Béchamel sauce (page 10)

One recipe Tomato and fresh Basil Sauce (page 8)

Salt and pepper to taste

1. Clean and cook the spinach, drain well, squeezing out excess water, and chop. Mix with the ricotta, eggs, Parmesan cheese, nutmeg and salt and pepper. Set aside.

2. Make the crepes as directed in the previous recipe. Place two Tbs. of the filling on the center of the crepe. Fold in half, then in half once again.

3. Layer the bottom of a baking pan with béchamel sauce and spot it with tomato sauce. Place the folded crepes in the pan. Cover with additional béchamel and spot once again with the tomato sauce. Sprinkle Parmesan cheese over it and bake in a 375-degree oven uncovered for 20 minutes. Allow to rest before serving. Serve with additional tomato sauce.

Serves 6-8

CANNELLONI RIPIENI DI CARNE

Cannelloni Stuffed with Meat

This is a classic recipe and, in fact, it can be considered as a one dish meal, since the meat is incorporated within the pasta shells.

Ingredients:

1/4 cup olive oil
2 medium onions, finely chopped
1 Tbs. fresh basil, chopped
One Tbs. fresh parsley, chopped
2 carrots, finely chopped
1 clove garlic, finely chopped
1 stalk celery, finely chopped
1 1/2 lbs. lean ground Beef (Veal or Poultry may be substituted)
One Tbs. tomato paste
1 bay leaf (optional)
1 clove (optional)
1 cup grated Parmigiana-Reggiano cheese
1 recipe Egg pasta (page 2)
1 recipe basic Béchamel (page 10)

1. In a heavy saucepan, heat the oil and sauté the onion until translucent. Stir in the rest of the vegetables as well as the parsley, basil and garlic and sauté for another 10 minutes. Add the meat, crumbling with a wooden spoon, stirring constantly until browned.

2. Add tomato paste and the bay leaf and clove if desired. Lower the heat and simmer for 20 to 30 minutes. When slightly cooled, remove and discard the bay leaf and clove. Stir in the Parmesan cheese and One and ½ cups of the béchamel sauce and salt and pepper to taste. Set aside.

3. Make the pasta and roll thin or if using the machine, set at the #6 setting. Cut into 5-inch by 5-inch squares.

4. Bring a large pot of lightly salted water to boil. Cook four to 5 pasta squares at a time for about 30 seconds to one minute. Remove with slotted spoon and drop into a bowl of cold water.

5. Preheat oven to 375 degrees. Prepare a large, shallow baking dish large enough to hold all the cannelloni in one layer. Lightly butter the dish and cover the bottom with a thin layer of the béchamel sauce.

6. Take one cooked square of the pasta at a time out of the bowl, shaking off the excess water. Place two to three Tbs. of the meat filling in the center of each square and fold both sides of pasta over the meat, sealing it. Place in platter, seam side down, and continue procedure until platter is filled. Spread the remaining béchamel over the cannelloni and sprinkle with remaining Parmesan. Bake uncovered for 20 to 30 minutes. Allow to rest for five minutes before serving. **Serves 8-10**

Rotolo di Spinaci

Pasta and Spinach Roll

This recipe is not seen too often, but Franca pulled it out of her archives from the days of cooking with her family in Italy.

Ingredients:

Three bags (12 oz. each) fresh spinach
One stick butter
One lb. Ricotta cheese
Pinch freshly grated nutmeg
Two eggs, beaten
Four to five fresh sage leaves
One and ½ cups grated Parmigiana-Reggiano cheese
One recipe Egg pasta (page 2)

For the filling:

1. Wash the spinach leaves thoroughly and place in a saucepan with ½ cup water. Add a pinch of salt and cook until tender. Drain and let cool. Squeeze excess water out, chop very fine and set aside in a medium-sized bowl.

2. In a skillet, melt ½ a stick of butter and add to the spinach, then add the ricotta, eggs and ½ cup of the Parmesan cheese and a pinch of the nutmeg, salt and pepper to taste.

Assembly:

1. Cut the ball of dough in half and roll each into a single rectangular-shaped sheet as thin as possible. Spread the filling equally on each rectangular sheet of pasta, leaving about an inch around the border plain.

2. Roll the sheet and seal the edges and at each end. Place in a cheesecloth or a linen cloth and tie with cooking thread. Place both rolls in a pot of boiling salted water and cook slowly for 15 to 20 minutes.

3. Remove from water, let drain and remove the pasta from the cloth covering. Cut in slices about an inch thick and place in a lightly buttered baking pan.

4. For the sauce, place the sage leaves and butter in a saucepan over low heat until melted. Pour over the pasta slices and sprinkle ½ cup of the Parmesan cheese. Place uncovered into a 350-degree preheated oven for 15 minutes. Serve hot with reserved cheese. **Serves 6-8**

CONCHIGLIE RIPIENE

Baked Stuffed Shells

This is another festive treat and is especially good when the company gets delayed, since each individual stuffed shell retains the heat. It is the favorite of many over the years and is easy to prepare as well.

Ingredients:

One recipe Tomato and fresh Basil Sauce (page 8)
Two I lb. boxes large pasta Shells
Two lbs. Ricotta cheese
Two eggs, beaten
1/2 lb. Mozzarella cheese, diced
One cup grated Parmigiana-Reggiano cheese
Five to six sprigs flat-leaf parsley, chopped
Salt and pepper to taste

1. Parboil the shells in lightly salted water for about five minutes. Drain and run under cold water. Drain and reserve.

2. In a large bowl, mix the eggs with the ricotta and then stir in the remaining ingredients.

3. To assemble:

4. Cover the bottom of a large baking dish generously with the sauce. With a spoon, fill each of the shells with the ricotta mixture. Arrange them in the dish with the ricotta filling facing up.

5. Cover with sauce and sprinkle with additional Parmesan cheese, if desired. Bake at 375-degree oven for 20 to 30 minutes.

Serves 8-10

STUFFED PASTA

TORTELLI D'ERBETTA

Cheese and Swiss chard Ravioli

This is a classic from Franca's region that she is an expert in preparing. They are the best!

Ingredients:

One recipe Egg Pasta (page 2)
One and 1/2 lbs. Swiss chard or spinach leaves with stalks removed
One lb. Ricotta cheese   *Two eggs, beaten*
Two cups freshly grated Parmesan cheese   *Four Tbs. plus 2/3 cups butter*
Pinch of nutmeg   *Pinch of salt*
5-6 fresh Sage leaves

1. Wash and cook the Swiss chard, drain and squeeze out excess water. Chop very fine and set aside.

2. Melt the 4 Tbs. of butter in a saucepan. Add the chopped chard or spinach and mix over low heat for 10 minutes. Season with nutmeg and salt. Remove from heat and, with a wooden spoon, stir in ricotta and eggs. Add Parmesan cheese and mix until well blended. Set aside.

3. Roll out the dough with a rolling pin or pasta machine into thin sheets. Trim to 5-inches wide sheets. Place walnut-sized spoonfuls three inches from edge and one and 1/2 inches apart. Fold the top edge over the spoonful of stuffing and cut with a pastry wheel along the bottom edge to join.

4. Place your finger between the stuffed pockets and then cut with pastry wheel to form into individual ravioli. Make sure the edges are well sealed. Melt the 2/3 cup of butter in a small saucepan over very low heat. Add 3 sage leaves for flavor. Do not allow to brown.

5. Bring a large pot of salted water to boil. Cook the tortelli for two to three minutes, making sure not to overcook. Drain and arrange them on a serving dish. Drizzle the melted butter over them and sprinkle the Parmesan cheese evenly. Garnish with remaining fresh sage leaves and serve immediately.

6. You may also serve the tortelli with the Bolognese Meat sauce (page 5).

Serves 4-6

RAVIOLI DI RICOTTA

Ricotta Cheese-filled Ravioli

This is more typical in the south Italian tradition, particularly from the region of Campania, the area surrounding Naples. Fr. Matt recalls those Christmas mornings in his youth, when his paternal grandmother, Francesca and his aunts would make hundreds of them fresh that day, to be served to the extended family for Christmas Day dinner.

Ingredients:

One recipe Egg Pasta (page 2)
One recipe Tomato and fresh Basil Sauce (page 8)

For the filling:

Two lbs. Ricotta cheese
One cup freshly grated Parmigiana-Reggiano cheese
1/2 lb. Mozzarella cheese, grated
Two eggs, beaten
3 sprigs flat-leaf parsley
Salt & pepper to taste

1. In a bowl, mix ingredients for the filling, reserving ½ cup of the Parmesan cheese.

2. Roll out the dough until very thin or at the #6 setting if using machine. Make paste sheets 5-inches wide. Place Tbs. of the filling 2 ½ inches from the edge and 2 inches apart. Fold the pasta sheet and with your fingers, press between the little mounds of the filling.

3. With a cookie cutter of fluted pastry wheel, cut around the mound, forming a half circle. Make sure the edges are well-sealed. Continue until all the dough and cheese are used.

4. Bring a pot of salted water to a boil and cook the ravioli gently for two to three minutes. Drain by lifting out of the pan with a slotted spoon and place in a serving dish. Cover with the tomato and basil sauce and sprinkle with reserved Parmesan cheese. Serve immediately.

Serves 6-8

RAVIOLI DI CARNE

Meat-filled Ravioli

This recipe is more typical of the Parma area and this recipe was handed down to Franca from her own grandmother and mother. It is Fr. Matt's favorite treat whenever he would visit Franca and Donald for a Sunday afternoon meal.

Ingredients:

One recipe Meat Stracotto filling with Sauce (page 4)
One recipe Egg Pasta (page 2)

1. Make the stracotto filling and sauce and set aside. Make the pasta and roll out the dough thinly or use the #6 setting on the pasta machine.

2. Make the pasta sheets 5-inches wide. Place Tbs. of the filling 2 and ½ inches from the edge and 2 inches apart. Fold the pasta sheets and with your finger press between the little mounds of filling. With a fluted pastry wheel, cut around the mound, forming a square. Make sure the edges are all sealed. Continue until all the dough and stuffing are finished.

3. Bring a pot of salted water to a boil and cook the ravioli gently for two to three minutes. Drain by lifting the ravioli out of the pan with a slotted spoon and place in a serving dish. Cover with the warm sauce, reserved from the stracotto, and sprinkle with Parmesan cheese. Serve immediately.

Serves 6-8

TORTELLI DI ZUCCA

Pumpkin-stuffed Ravioli

A lovely autumnal dish the can actually be enjoyed all year round.

Ingredients:

One recipe Egg Pasta (page 2)

For the filling:

One 2.5 to 3-lb. Pumpkin
One and ¼ cups freshly grated Parmigiana-Reggiano cheese
1/2 cup breadcrumbs
Two eggs, beaten
Pinch of nutmeg
Salt & pepper to taste
Three to four fresh sage leaves
1/2 cup melted butter

1. Preheat oven to 375 degrees. Slice off the top of the pumpkin, cut in half and scoop out all the seeds. Place both halves face down in a shallow baking dish with a little water and bake for one and one/half to two hours.

2. Remove from oven and allow pumpkin to cool. Scoop out the pulp, place in a large bowl and mash with a fork. Add ¾ cups of the Parmesan cheese, the eggs, breadcrumbs, nutmeg and salt and pepper. Meanwhile, place the sage in the butter and keep warm over low heat.

3. Roll out the dough thinly or use the #6 setting of the machine. Cut two 2.5-inch disks from the dough with a cookie cutter or inverted glass. Place a teaspoon of the pumpkin filling in the center of each disk and fold over, sealing the edges with your fingers.

4. Boil in lightly salted water for two to three minutes. Remove with slotted spoon and place on a serving dish. Drizzle the butter and sage over it and the remaining half cup of the Parmesan cheese and serve immediately.

Serves 6-8

Tortellini alla Panna

Tortellini in Cream Sauce

It is a legend that tortellini originated in the town of Castelfranco Emilia, in the province of Modena, in honor of the visit of Lucrezia Borgia there in the Middle Ages.

Ingredients:

One recipe Egg pasta (page 2)

For the filling:

One whole skinless Chicken breast
½ lb. Beef
1/2 lb. lean Pork
One carrot, diced
One stick celery, diced
Two Tbs. olive oil
Two whole cloves garlic, peeled
¾ cup breadcrumbs
Two eggs, beaten

For the sauce:

Four Tbs. butter
1/2 cup freshly grated Parmigiana-Reggiano cheese
One cup heavy cream
¼ lb. ham or prosciutto, diced (optional)
salt and pepper to taste
Three Tbs. butter
One cup freshly grated Parmesan cheese
Salt, pepper and dash of nutmeg

1. Make the pasta, cover with an inverted bowl and set aside to rest. Put the oil and butter with the peeled garlic cloves, carrot and celery in a large skillet and heat it. Add the pork, chicken and beef and season with salt and pepper. Cook over moderate heat for 45 minutes, stirring occasionally.

2. With a slotted spoon remove the meat, place in a bowl and let cool slightly. Using a food processor or knife, chop very fine but do not make a paste. Put chopped meat mixture back into the bowl and add the parmesan cheese, breadcrumbs and nutmeg, salt and pepper to taste and the beaten eggs. Mix well.

3. To make the tortellini, roll out the pasta thinly or on the # 6 setting if using the pasta machine. Cut into 2-inch by 2-inch squares, placing about ½ teaspoon of filling in the center of each. Fold each square in half to form a triangle and pinch the edges together to seal. Lift the center point upwards with your finger and bring the two opposite side points together. Pinch the corners of the two side points where they join. Let the tortellini rest on a floured board.

4. Bring a large pot of salted water to boil. Meanwhile, prepare the sauce by melting the butter. Add the ham if desired and sauté for two minutes. Add the cream, salt and pepper and heat well without allowing it to boil. Keep warm.

5. When the water comes to a boil, add one Tbs. of olive oil and stir. Put the tortellini into the boiling water and cook two to three minutes. Drain by lifting out of pan with a slotted spoon and place in a deep serving dish. Pour the cream sauce over and toss gently. Sprinkle with the cheese and serve. **Serves 6-8**

TORTELLONI CLASSICI

Classic Tortelloni

These are considerably larger than the prior recipe of tortellini, thus the suffix, "oni" which usually designates something on the larger size in the Italian language.

Ingredients:

One recipe Egg Pasta (page 2)
One recipe Bolognese Sauce (page 5)

For the filling:

One bag (10 oz.) fresh Spinach
Two lbs. Ricotta cheese
1/2 cup freshly grated Parmigiana-Reggiano cheese
Two eggs, beaten
4-5 sprigs flat-leaf parsley, finely chopped
Salt and pepper to taste

1. Wash the spinach and place it in a pot with two cups water. Bring to a boil and let cook for three minutes. Drain and let cool enough to handle.

2. Pick up a handful at a time and squeeze out the excess water. Chop the spinach finely. Place in a bowl and add the ricotta, parsley, Parmesan cheese, eggs, and salt and pepper to taste.

3. Roll the dough out thinly and cut into 3-inch by 3-inch squares. Use one teaspoon of the stuffing and refer to the prior recipe for folding the tortellini.

4. Boil the tortelloni, drain and mix with half of the Bolognese sauce. Sprinkle with additional grated Parmesan cheese and serve the remaining sauce at the table.

Serves 6-8

GNOCCHI DI RICOTTA AL FORNO

Baked Ricotta Gnocchi with Cheese

These gnocchi are more delicate than one would expect and are finished in the light and tasty butter and sage sauce.

Ingredients:

1 lb. Ricotta cheese
5 egg yolks
2 and ¼ cups grated Parmigiana-Reggiano cheese
1 and ½ cups all purpose flour
½ stick of butter
5 to 6 sage leaves

1. Mix the ricotta and yolks in a bowl. Fold in the 2 cups of the cheese and all the flour. Drop rounded teaspoonfuls into salted boiling water. As they rise, remove with a slotted spoon and place in a baking dish. Continue until all the gnocchi are cooked.

2. Place sage leaves in a small pan with the butter over low heat until melted, but not browned.

3. Pour butter and sage mixture over gnocchi, sprinkle with remaining Parmesan cheese and bake in 350-degree oven for 10 to 15 minutes. Serve hot.

Serves 6

Gnocchi di Ricotta alla Nonna Serafina

Grandma Serafina's Ricotta Gnocchi

Fr. Matt would watch his maternal grandmother Serafina make these gnocchi and wants to share this tradition with all of you.

Ingredients:

1 lb. Ricotta cheese
1 egg, beaten
1 and ¾ cups all-purpose flour
Dash of salt

1. In a bowl, mix the ricotta and egg. Sift in the flour and salt and blend well. Form into a ball, then cut into six sections.

2. On a well-floured board, roll out each section into cylinders about ½-inch in diameter – about the thickness of a finger. Cut cylinders into one-inch pieces.

3. Curl each piece against the tines of a lightly floured fork and make an indentation with your finger as you curl. Continue, using all the dough, and place gnocchi on a floured board.

4. Bring a large pot of salted water to boil. Gradually add the gnocchi in batches. Cook until they rise to the surface. Cover and let boil for 30 seconds.

5. Remove with a slotted spoon and continue until all the gnocchi are cooked.

6. Serve with your favorite sauce. Suggestions: Pesto, Tomato and basil, Bolognese, Gorgonzola or Veal stew with mushrooms.

Serves 6-8

GNOCCHI DI PATATE ALLA GORGONZOLA

Potato Gnocchi with Cheese Sauce

When one thinks of gnocchi, it is the potato type that usually comes to mind. Here is our own version that we have developed together.

Ingredients:

6 medium all-purpose Potatoes
2 eggs, beaten
2 cups flour

For the sauce:

16 oz. heavy cream
8 oz. gorgonzola or mascarpone cheese
3 oz. or ¾ stick of butter
1 teaspoon coarsely chopped parsley
Salt and freshly ground pepper to taste

1. Boil the potatoes with skins until fully cooked, approximately 30 minutes. Pierce with fork to check for tenderness.

2. Drain the potatoes and let cool slightly. Peel and mash well, using a ricer if possible. Place on a lightly floured board and make a well in the center. Add the flour and mix lightly. Make a well again and add the beaten eggs. Mix and shape into a ball.

3. On a well-floured board, roll out each section into cylinders about ½ inch in diameter – about the thickness of a finger. Cut cylinders into one-inch pieces.

4. Curl each piece against the tines of a lightly floured fork and make an indentation with your finger as you curl. Continue, using all the dough, and place gnocchi on a floured board.

5. Bring a large pot of salted water to boil. Gradually add the gnocchi in batches. Cook until they rise to the surface. Cover and let boil for 30 seconds.

6. Remove with a slotted spoon and continue until all the gnocchi are cooked.

7. To make the sauce, combine the cream, cheese, butter and salt and pepper in the top of a double boiler or in a saucepan over very low heat, until all ingredients melt into a smooth consistency. Pour over cooked gnocchi and garnish with parsley.

Serves 6-8

GNOCCHI VERDI IN SALSA ROSATA

Green Gnocchi in Pink Sauce

This green gnocchi is also very popular and tasty. Our rose tinted sauce compliments it well.

Ingredients:

1 and ½ lbs. Potatoes
3 cups all-purpose flour
½ lb. spinach
2 eggs, beaten
Pinch of salt

For the sauce:

¼ lb. butter
1 Tbs. tomato paste
½ cup heavy cream
½ cup grated Parmigiana-Reggiano cheese

1. Boil, peel and mash the potatoes. Wash the spinach and cook without added water. Cool slightly and chop very fine by hand or in a blender.

2. Combine all ingredients and work into a smooth dough and dust well with extra flour. Roll into cylinders about ½ in diameter and slice into one-inch sections.

3. Curl each piece against the tines of a lightly floured fork and make an indentation with your finger as you curl. Continue, using all the dough, and place gnocchi on a floured board.

4. Bring salted water to a boil and drop the gnocchi in batches into the water. When they rise to the surface, let boil a few seconds more before removing with a slotted spoon.

5. For the sauce: Melt the butter in a saucepan and stir in the tomato paste. Add the cream and stir until the sauce is smooth and pink. Pour over the gnocchi and serve with Parmesan cheese.

Serves 6-8

Risotti *(Assorted Rice Dishes)*

RISO STILE SPAGNOLO

Spanish-style Rice

Risotto is a staple in northern Italy, often substituted for pasta or used as a main dish. However, it is also popular throughout the peninsula. Here are our favorite recipes. Fr. Matt learned this recipe from his mother many years ago.

Ingredients:

1 and ½ lbs. Arborio (short-grain) Rice
2 Tbs. olive oil
2 cloves garlic, minced
1 green bell pepper, chopped
1 small onion, chopped
10 oz. tomato sauce
¼ cup grated Parmigiana-Reggiano cheese
Salt and pepper to taste

1. Boil the rice in lightly salted water for 15 to 20 minutes until tender but firm. Meanwhile, lightly sauté the onion in the oil for a few minutes. Add the garlic and bell pepper and continue to cook until pepper is softened. Add the tomato sauce and simmer about 10 minutes. Add salt and pepper to taste.

2. Drain the rice and place back into the pot. Add the sauce, and Parmesan cheese.

3. Lightly butter an ovenproof baking dish. Pour in the rice mixture and spread evenly. Cover with foil and bake in a moderate 350-degree oven for 30 minutes. Serve hot.

Serves 6-8

INSALATA DI RISO FREDDO

Cold Rice Salad

Many of the trattorias of Rome and even throughout Italy serve this dish during the hot summer, when everyone is looking to stay cool, even in the culinary area!

Ingredients:

2 cups Arborio Rice
1 cup shelled peas, fresh or frozen
½ cup artichoke hearts, frozen or marinated
2 Tbs. capers, rinsed and drained
1 cup black and green pitted olives, sliced
1 red roasted pepper (page 36), cut lengthwise into thin strips
½ lb. pre-cooked Shrimp
½ cup olive oil
Juice of one large lemon (about ¼ cup)
Salt and pepper to taste
16 steamed and chilled mussels (optional)
2 to 3 sprigs flat leaf parsley for garnish

1. Bring a large pot of salted water to boil. Add rice and cook uncovered about 15 to 20 minutes. Drain and rinse under cold running water. Drain well.

2. Place rice in a large mixing bowl that has been brushed with oil. Cool at room temperature.

3. Boil the peas in lightly salted water until tender. If using frozen peas, boil according to package directions. Drain well, add to the rice and mix.

4. Add the capers, olives, pepper slices and shrimp.

5. In a small bowl, combine the olive oil, lemon juice and the salt and pepper. Mix well and taste for seasoning. Pour the dressing over the rice mixture and toss well.

6. If using the mussels for garnish, steam them in a large saucepan with a cup of water and ¼ cup dry white wine until they open. Remove, chill and place on the perimeter of the bowl of rice for a garnish. Place parsley in the center. Serve slightly chilled or at room temperature.

Serves 6-8

RISO A STRATI AL FORNO

Layered Baked Rice

This is a very warm and inviting dish and so easy to prepare since it is finished in the oven. It is similar to a dish in Naples, which has a baked rice dish called the Sartu' that is layered with mozzarella and peas before baking.

Ingredients:

1 and ½ cups short-grain Rice

3 eggs, beaten

2 to 3 sprigs parsley, finely chopped

1 cup grated Parmigiana-Reggiano or Pecorino cheese

½ recipe Tomato and Fresh Basil Sauce (page 8)

Salt and pepper to taste

¾ lbs. Italian sausage, removed from casing, cooked and crumbled

¾ lbs. shredded mozzarella cheese

1. Boil the rice in lightly salted water until tender, about 15-20 minutes. Drain and let cool. Add eggs, parsley, ¼ cup Parmesan cheese and ½ cup tomato sauce to give the red color and add the salt and pepper to taste.

2. Put 3 Tbs. of sauce on the bottom of a rectangular baking dish. Make one layer using half the rice. Top with a layer of sauce, half the crumbled sausage meat and half the mozzarella cheese.

3. Make another layer with the remaining rice mixture. Top with sauce, grated cheese, sausage meat and remaining mozzarella. Bake in 375-degree oven for 30 minutes or until sauce bubbles. Serve hot.

Serves 6-8

RISOTTO MILANESE

Milan-style Rice

Risotto is typical of Milan, where the typography allows for the best Arborio rice to be grown. There are many variations on the theme of risotto but this is the mother of them all!

Ingredients:

2 cups Arborio Rice

¼ cup plus two Tbs. butter

1 medium onion, finely chopped

1 cup dry white wine

4 cups boiling hot chicken broth

½ teaspoon ground saffron

Pepper to taste

½ cup grated Parmigiana-Reggiano cheese

1. In a large pot, melt ¼ cup of the butter and sauté the onion until lightly brown. Add the rice and stir until coated and lightly browned. Add the wine and stir well and let reduce by half. Add pepper to taste and the saffron. Stir well.

2. Add one ladle of chicken broth at a time and stir until it is absorbed by the rice. Continue the procedure one ladle at a time until rice is cooked. This should take about 20 minutes.

3. Remove from heat and add in the remaining butter and Parmesan cheese and stir well. Serve immediately.

Serves 6-8

RISOTTO CON VERDURA

Rice with Vegetables

This is one of the many variations of the Milanese risotto, this one featuring a variety of fresh vegetables, almost like "Primavera" style.

Ingredients:

1 and 1/2 cups Arborio Italian Rice
1 medium onion, finely chopped
2 cloves garlic, finely chopped
6 Tbs. butter
2 Tbs. olive oil
1/2 cup dry white wine
½ cup grated Parmigiana-Reggiano cheese
2 medium zucchini, diced
1 bunch fresh asparagus, tips only, cleaned and washed
1 package (10 oz.) fresh spinach, cleaned
2 to 3 sprigs flat leaf parsley, chopped
3 basil leaves, chopped
4 cups boiling hot chicken broth
Salt & pepper to taste

1. Place the oil and 3 Tbs. butter in a large pot. Add the onion and cook until lightly golden. Add the garlic and stir well. Add the wine and let it reduce by half.

2. Add all the vegetables and one cup of the broth and cook until just tender, being careful not to overcook. Remove vegetables with a slotted spoon and set aside.

3. Add the rice and stir to coat. Add one ladle at a time of the broth and cook until the rice has absorbed all the broth, or until rice is tender, approximately 20 minutes.

4. Remove from heat, add the vegetables, the remaining butter and parmesan cheese. Mix well and serve.

Serves 6-8

RISOTTO AI FUNGHI

Rice with Mushrooms

As Franca and her husband Donald would often remind Fr. Matt, some of the very best porcini mushrooms grow in the Borgotaro area, very close to Donald's family home.

Ingredients:

1 envelope, approx. one ounce of dried Porcini Mushrooms
1 and 1/2 cups Arborio Italian Rice
1 medium onion, finely chopped
4 Tbs. butter
2 Tbs. olive oil
2 cloves garlic, finely chopped
1/2 cup dry white wine
4 cups boiling hot chicken broth
½ cup Parmigiana-Reggiano cheese
Salt and pepper to taste

1. Soak the dry mushrooms in a cup of warm water for at least 10 minutes and set aside.

2. In a large pot, sauté the onion in the oil and 2 Tbs. of the butter. Add the garlic and stir well.

3. Remove the mushrooms from the water with a slotted spoon and add them to the pot. Add the wine and let it reduce by half.

4. Add the rice and sauté until lightly golden. Add the hot broth one ladle at a time, stirring well after each addition, until it is absorbed. Continue this process until all broth is used, about 20 minutes in total. Add salt and pepper to taste.

5. Remove from heat and add in the butter and Parmesan cheese. Stir well and serve hot.

Serves 6-8

RISOTTO DI ZUCCA

Rice with Yellow Squash

Risotto combined with pumpkin or squash is a recent arrival this side of the Atlantic Ocean, but has been a favorite in Italy for many years. We hope that you see why.

Ingredients:

1 large Acorn Squash
6 Tbs. butter
1 medium onion, finely chopped
2 cloves garlic, finely chopped
1 and 1/2 cups Arborio Italian Rice
4 cups boiling hot chicken broth
Pinch of nutmeg
½ cup grated Parmigiana-Reggiano cheese
Salt and pepper to taste

1. Cut squash in half. Remove the skin and seeds and cut one half into small dice and reserve. Cut the other half into thin slices and from these, cut small triangles and reserve.

2. In a large pot, add 2 Tbs. of the butter, onion and garlic and sauté until transparent. Add the diced squash and pinch of nutmeg, and cook over a low flame for about 10 minutes. Add the rice and sauté till coated. Add the broth, one ladle at a time, until it is absorbed. Continue this process, using the rest of the broth, about 20 minutes.

3. Meanwhile, in a frying pan, add two Tbs. of the butter and the squash cut in triangles and lightly fry, turning occasionally, careful not to break them. Cook until tender when pierced by a fork.

4. Add salt and pepper to taste to the rice. Remove from heat, add the last two Tbs. of the butter and the Parmesan cheese and stir well. Pour the risotto into a large serving dish and garnish around the perimeter with the squash triangles. Serve at once.

Serves 6-8

Risi e Bisi

Rice and Peas

This dish is typical of Venice and a true delight that can be found in virtually every restaurant or trattoria in that beautiful and unique World Heritage city.

Ingredients:

3 Tbs. butter
2 Tbs. olive oil
¾ cup diced lean bacon
1 large onion, finely chopped
3 cups shelled fresh or frozen peas
1 and ½ cups Arborio Rice
6 cups boiling hot chicken broth
Salt and pepper to taste
¾ cup grated Parmigiana-Reggiano cheese
2-3 sprigs flat leaf parsley, chopped

1. Heat the butter and oil together in a large pot. Sauté the bacon and onion until browned. Add the peas and some of the broth to moisten.

2. Cook the peas for only 2 minutes and then add the remainder of the hot broth. Allow to boil.

3. Stir in the rice, lower the heat and cook for 20 minutes or until the rice is tender. Stir occasionally. Add salt and pepper to taste and sprinkle with parsley and Parmesan cheese. Serve hot.

Serves 6-8

RISOTTO ALLE ERBE E PROSCIUTTO

Rice with Herbs and Prosciutto

This is our very own variation on the theme of risotto, where we pulled together some of our most fragrant and enjoyable flavors and added them to the base of risotto. You can vary the spices if you wish, but just add a pinch, so that the subtle flavors can come through.

Ingredients:

1 and 1/2 cups Arborio Italian Rice
1 small onion, finely chopped
2 Tbs. unsalted butter
2 Tbs. olive oil
1 teaspoon grated lemon peel
¼ lb. of Prosciutto ham, cut into thin strips
¼ cup heavy cream
4 cups boiling hot beef broth
Salt and pepper to taste
½ cup grated Parmigiana-Reggiano cheese
Pinch of marjoram
Pinch of thyme

1. In a large pot, melt the butter with the oil over medium heat. Add the onion and sauté until transparent. Add the rice and stir to coat. Add the thyme and marjoram.

2. Slowly add the hot broth one ladle at a time and stir continually until absorbed. Continue until all broth is used and rice is cooked – about 20 minutes.

3. Remove from heat. Add the prosciutto, heavy cream, lemon peel and Parmesan cheese. Mix well and serve hot.

Serves 6-8

RISOTTO ALLA PESCATORA

Fisherman's Rice

Our variations on the theme of risotto continue and this time, we feature shellfish to enhance the basic risotto. Of course, lobster or other fish of your choice can be substituted and the preparation here varies from the classic way that Risotto Milanese is prepared.

Ingredients:

1 and 1/2 cups Arborio Rice
1 medium onion, finely chopped
3 cloves garlic, finely chopped
2-3 sprigs flat leaf parsley, finely chopped
3-4 basil leaves, finely chopped
½ fish bouillon cube
6 Tbs. butter
1 Tbs. olive oil
1 lb. Sea Scallops
1 lb. large Shrimp, shelled and deveined

1. In a medium saucepan, melt 3 Tbs. butter and the olive oil. Sauté the garlic, being careful not to burn it. Add the fish, parsley and basil and the bouillon. Cook over a lively flame for 6 to 8 minutes. Remove from heat and set aside.

2. In a pot of lightly salted water, cook the rice for 20 minutes. Drain and put in a serving dish. Add the remaining butter and mix well.

3. Make a well in the middle of the rice and pour the warmed fish mixture in the center, drizzling some of the juice over the rice. Serve hot.   **Serves 6-8**

RISOTTO CON FINOCCHIO E SALSICCE

Rice with Fennel and Sausage

This risotto combines several unique flavors and makes a delicious and hearty first course.

Ingredients:

1 lb. Italian sweet fennel Pork sausage
1 fennel bulb, finely sliced
1 medium onion, finely chopped
3-4 sprigs flat leaf parsley, finely chopped

½ cup dry white wine
1 and ½ cups Arborio rice
4 cups boiling hot beef stock
½ cup grated Parmigiana-Reggiano cheese
Salt and freshly ground pepper to taste

1. Remove sausage meat from the casing, crumble and add to a large pot. Sauté over moderate heat for 10 minutes. Add onion and fennel and continue to sauté.

2. Add the wine and let it reduce by half. Add the rice and stir well. Add the hot beef stock one ladle at a time and stir well until it is absorbed by the rice. Continue until all the stock is used and the rice is tender – about 20 minutes. Add salt and pepper to taste.

3. Remove from heat and add the Parmesan cheese and stir well. Place in a serving dish and garnish the parsley. Serve very hot.

Serves 6-8

RISOTTO AI FORMAGGI

Rice with Cheeses

This risotto is typical of the northern area close to the border with Switzerland and France. We have incorporated our own version and selected several cheeses, but you can use gruyere if desired in place of one of them.

Ingredients:

1 and 1/2 cups Arborio Italian Rice
1 cup light cream
¼ lb. Fontina cheese, cut in small cubes
¼ lb. Gorgonzola cheese, crumbled
½ cup Parmigiana-Reggiano cheese

1. In a medium saucepan, add the butter, cream and gorgonzola and let warm, mixing occasionally.

2. Meanwhile, cook the rice in a lightly salted pot of boiling water for 20 minutes. Drain and place in a serving dish. Add the cubes of Fontina and mix well.

   Pour the hot cream sauce over the rice, add the Parmesan cheese, mix well and serve hot.

Serves 6-8

POLENTA BASE

Basic Polenta

Polenta is a staple in the countryside of northern Italy, used as a substitute for pasta or even as a main dish. It is easy to make, versatile, and makes for a satisfying meal.

Ingredients:

6 cups water
3 Tbs. unsalted butter (optional)
Salt to taste (approximately 1 and ½ Tbs.)
2 cups yellow Cornmeal
2 cups cold water

1. Bring the 6 cups of salted water to boil. Add butter, if desired.

2. In a bowl, gradually mix the 2 cups cornmeal into the cold water, making a paste. Stir the polenta paste into the pot of boiling water. Keep stirring with a wooden spoon until the mixture comes to a boil again. Be sure to always stir in the same direction to avoid separation. Occasionally, scrape the polenta from the sides of the pot and mix well.

3. Cook, stirring frequently until the mixture begins to pull away from the sides of the pan. This will take approximately 30 to 40 minutes.

4. Pour onto a board or serving dish and serve.

Serves 6

POLENTA CON COTECHINO E FAGIOLI

Polenta with Cotechino Sausage and Beans

This is Donald's very favorite and a typical dish to enjoy on New Year's Day. It is said that this recipe brings prosperity for the year that just arrived. Fr. Matt has enjoyed his sampling of this tasty treat more than once at the Bertoli's home.

Ingredients:

1 recipe basic Polenta (see prior recipe)
1 Cotechino salami (approximately 2 lbs.)
1 bag (8 oz) dried red kidney beans, washed and soaked overnight
3 Tbs. olive oil
2 Tbs. butter
1 large onion, finely chopped
1 stalk celery, finely chopped
3 carrots, finely chopped
2 cloves garlic, finely chopped
2 Tbs. tomato paste
Salt and ground pepper to taste
½ lb. Fontina cheese, thinly sliced
½ cup freshly grated Parmigiana-Reggiano cheese

1. In a large pot of water, boil the cotechino whole until tender: approximately 40 minutes. Be sure to prick with a fork to avoid bursting. While it is cooking, put the washed beans in a pot with 8 cups cold water and bring to a boil. Lower the flame and let cook.

2. Meanwhile, put the oil and butter in a saucepan and heat. Add the onion and sauté until transparent. Add the rest of the vegetables and sauté for approximately 10 minutes.

3. Add the 2 Tbs. tomato paste and stir rapidly for 1 minute. Add the vegetable mixture to the pot of the cooking beans. Add the salt and pepper to taste and stir well. Cook until the beans are tender and sauce is reduced and thickened, approximately one hour.

4. When cooked, take the cotechino out of the water and place in the bean sauce for the last 20 minutes of the cooking. Add the salt and pepper to taste as needed.

5. At this point, make the polenta as directed in the basic polenta recipe. When done, spread half of the polenta evenly in a large, deep serving dish. Lay the Fontina cheese on the polenta and spoon over some of the bean sauce, spreading evenly. Cover with the remaining polenta. Spoon over additional bean sauce, reserving some for serving at the table. Sprinkle with the Parmesan cheese.

6. Slice the cotechino in one inch to one and ½-inch slices. Serve hot with the polenta.
   Serves 6-8

POLENTA PASTICCIATA ALLA CONTADINA

Polenta Peasant-style

The word "pasticciata" means "all mixed up" and here the polenta is cooled, cut and randomly placed in the baking dish before it is baked. Although it may look like a real mess, it tastes so really very good.

Ingredients:

1 recipe basic Polenta (page 102)

¾ stick butter

1 cup Parmigiana-Reggiano cheese

5 Tbs. tomato paste

1 large onion, finely chopped

2 cloves garlic, finely chopped

Salt and pepper to taste

1. Melt ½ stick of the butter, add onion and cook until translucent. Add the garlic and stir well. Add the tomato paste and incorporate all ingredients well. Add salt and pepper to taste. Remove from heat.

2. Make the polenta according to the basic instructions. Pour on a serving platter or a board. Let cool and cut into 2-inch by 2-inch squares.

3. Place polenta chunks randomly in a buttered baking dish. Pour the sauce over them until well-coated. Sprinkle with Parmesan cheese, dot with reserved butter and bake uncovered in a 350-degree oven for 15 to 20 minutes. Serve hot.

Serves 6-8

POLENTA AVELLINO

Avellino-style Polenta

Here we have the rustic flavors of the south and reminiscent of the Province of Avellino where Fr. Matt's paternal grandparents were born and raised before their arrival in America.

Ingredients:

2 Tbs. olive oil
1 large onion, chopped
2 cloves garlic, finely chopped
1 28-oz can crushed tomatoes
3 sprigs parsley, chopped
4 to 5 basil leaves, torn
1 and ½ lbs. Italian Pork sausage
1 recipe basic Polenta (page 102)
Salt and freshly ground pepper to taste
¾ cups grated Parmigiana-Reggiano cheese
Pinch of hot red pepper flakes (optional)

1. Heat the olive oil and add the onion, cooking until translucent. Add the garlic and brown lightly. Add the tomatoes, parsley and basil and simmer over moderate heat.

2. Remove the sausage from its casing, crumble and cook with 2 to 3 ounces water in a frying pan over moderate heat. Brown, stirring occasionally and cooking until all the pink is gone. Remove from pan with a slotted spoon and add to the tomato sauce. Add salt and pepper to taste.

3. Prepare the polenta, adding salt and pepper to taste, and when done, pour it into a lightly buttered deep baking dish. Pour half the sauce over the polenta and sprinkle with half of the grated cheese. Cover with remainder of polenta followed by sauce and cheese. Add hot red pepper flakes if desired.

4. Bake uncovered in 350-degree oven for 20 minutes.

Serves 6-8

POLENTA BOSCAIOLA

Forest-style Polenta

In this variation, we have incorporated the flavors that remind one of the sylvan forest, thus the name, which has its root in the word, "bosco" meaning the forest.

Ingredients:

1 recipe basic Polenta (page 102)
1 Tbs. olive oil
3 cloves garlic, finely chopped
1 medium onion, chopped
4 oz. smoky bacon, diced
½ cup black calamata olives, pits removed and coarsely chopped
1 lb. Porcini mushrooms, cleaned and thinly sliced
½ cup dry white wine
1 beef bouillon cube
1 pinch red pepper flakes
1 can (28-oz) of plum tomatoes
3 sprigs flat leaf parsley, chopped
1 Tbs. butter
Salt and freshly ground pepper to taste
½ cup grated Parmigiana-Reggiano or Romano cheese

1. Heat the olive oil and add the onion, garlic and bacon and brown them. Add the mushrooms and sauté until golden.

2. Add the wine and let sizzle and evaporate. Add the bouillon cube, tomatoes and pepper flakes, if desired. Let simmer over moderate heat. Add salt and pepper to taste.

3. Prepare the basic polenta recipe. When done, pour into a lightly buttered serving dish.

4. Add the olives and tablespoon of butter to the Boscaiola sauce and stir well. Pour the sauce over the polenta and sprinkle with Pecorino Romano or Parmesan cheese and serve immediately.

Serves 6-8

POLENTA ALLA GORGONZOLA

Polenta with Gorgonzola Cheese

A true comfort food and it is so simple to prepare as well.

Ingredients:

1 recipe basic Polenta (page 102)
¾ lbs. plus 3 Tbs. Gorgonzola cheese, crumbled
¾ stick (6 Tbs.) butter

1. Soften the butter and ¾ lbs. of the cheese. Place in a bowl and cream the butter and cheese together with a wooden spoon. Set aside.
2. Cook the basic polenta recipe. When done, pour half into a large and deep serving dish. Pour the gorgonzola mixture over the polenta, spreading evenly. Pour the remaining polenta on top, spreading evenly over the mixture. Garnish with the remaining 3 Tbs. of gorgonzola. Let rest, uncovered, for 10 minutes, cut into slices and serve.

Serves 6-8

POLENTA AL PESTO

Polenta with Pesto Sauce

Just a lovely taste of basil is added to help to enhance the polenta. It gives a depth of flavor to what can be a plain dish otherwise. Our dear Franca came up with this delight.

Ingredients:

1 recipe basic Polenta (page 102)
1 recipe pesto sauce
1 sprig of fresh basil for garnish

1. Prepare pesto sauce and set aside.

2. Cook the basic polenta recipe. When done, pour half into a large and deep serving dish. Spread all the pesto evenly over the polenta and cover with the remaining polenta. Let rest 10 minutes and garnish with fresh basil leaves before cutting into squares to serve.

Serves 6-8

POLENTA CON SPEZZATINO DI VITELLO

Polenta with Veal Stew

The veal stew is tender and fragrant and goes well when served over the polenta. It can also be served over pasta or rice and also as a main course with mashed potatoes as a side dish.

Ingredients:

1 recipe basic Polenta (page 102)
2 Tbs. olive oil
2 Tbs. butter
1 small onion, finely chopped
1 sprig flat leaf parsley, finely chopped
2 basil leaves, finely chopped
2 lbs. Veal, cut in chunks
2 Tbs. flour, for dredging
1 lb. mushrooms of your choice, thinly sliced
4 oz. dry white wine
1 Tbs. tomato paste
2 cups beef broth
1 sprig fresh rosemary
1 fresh sage leaf
Salt and freshly ground pepper to taste
½ cup Parmigiana-Reggiano cheese

Prepare stew as follows:

1. Use one Tbs. each of the oil and butter, place in a saucepan and sauté the onion until golden. Add the garlic, parsley and basil and stir quickly over moderate heat for a few seconds. Add the cleaned and sliced mushrooms and sauté. Lower heat.

2. Put the remaining oil and butter in a skillet over moderate heat. Dredge the veal in the flour and sauté over a high flame in the skillet, stirring until golden. Add the white wine and let it evaporate. Add the vegetables to the meat and stir well. Add the tomato paste and mix well. Add the broth and the rosemary and sage and simmer over low heat until the mixture is of a thickened consistency and the meat is tender – about 2 to 2 and ½ hours. Add salt and pepper to taste.

3. While the meat is cooking, prepare the basic polenta recipe. When done, pour into a large and deep serving dish and let rest for 10 minutes. Slice and add the veal stew on top. Sprinkle with Parmesan cheese.

Serves 6-8

POLENTA RUSTICA

Rustic Polenta

This recipe is inspired from the north of Italy which is close to the Swiss border. That land is rich with a variety of dairy products and we have incorporated the creamy taste of the Brie to enhance the polenta.

Ingredients:

1 recipe basic Polenta (page 102)
3 heads of garlic
1 small Brie cheese, approximately 2 lbs.
2 Tbs. olive oil
Salt and pepper to taste

1. Prepare the basic polenta recipe. When done, place in a large, deep serving dish to cool.

2. Preheat oven to 400 degrees. Trim off the tip of the garlic and place in an ovenproof container. Drizzle with olive oil and cover tightly with foil. Bake for 35 to 40 minutes or until soft.

3. Place the Brie in an ovenproof container and bake, uncovered, for the last 7 to 8 minutes of the cooking time of the garlic. While the garlic is baking, cut the cooled polenta into slices approximately 5 inches by ¾ inches.

4. Brush an outside or stovetop griddle lightly with oil. Place the polenta slices on the grill and roast both sides until golden in color. Place on a serving dish.

5. Remove the garlic from the oven and press the roasted cloves out of their skins. Spread evenly over the polenta.

6. Remove the melted Brie from the oven. Using a large, flat spoon or knife, spread the Brie over the polenta and serve.

Serves 6

POLENTA FRITTA

Fried Polenta

This can also be considered a side dish and can even be used to accompany the veal stew in a previous recipe... that is, if any of them make it to the table!

Ingredients:

1 recipe basic Polenta (page 102)
½ cup olive oil
4 Tbs. butter
1 sprig fresh rosemary
3 sage leaves
2 unpeeled garlic cloves

1. Prepare the basic polenta recipe. When done, place on a wooden board or inside a deep baking dish. Allow to cool to room temperature.

2. Cut polenta into slices approximately 6 inches long and ½ inch thick.

3. If using a frying pan, place oil and butter in the frying pan along with rosemary, sage and unpeeled garlic cloves and heat. Place polenta slices in the pan and fry until golden on each side.

4. If using a griddle, heat the butter, oil, garlic, rosemary and sage in a small saucepan. Dip the polenta in this mixture before placing on the griddle. Grill each side until golden. Place on a serving dish and serve with your meal.

Serves 6-8

ZUPPE *(Soups)*

BRODO DI POLLO

Chicken Stock

This is what many a mother would call good old "Italian penicillin." Perfect for all that ails you, and the base for many other soups.

Ingredients:

3-4 sprigs flat-leaf parsley
2-3 fresh basil leaves
1 medium Chicken, approximately 2 and ½ lbs, cut in pieces and cleaned
5 quarts (20 cups) cold water
Salt to taste, approximately 3 teaspoons
1 large onion, washed, unpeeled and cut in quarters
2 medium carrots, peeled and halved
2 stalks celery, cleaned and halved
1 medium leek, cleaned and halved
1 fresh tomato, quartered and seeded (optional)
2 large garlic cloves, unpeeled and lightly crushed
1 bay leaf
4-5 peppercorns, optional
1 chicken bouillon cube, optional

1. Tie parsley and basil leaves together with kitchen twine. Place all ingredients in a large soup stock pot and bring to a boil over moderate heat. When boiling, reduce heat to simmer and cook for 45 minutes to an hour.

2. Skim the foam that rises to the top several times. If desired, add bouillon cube for additional flavor. Add salt and pepper to taste.

3. Turn off heat and let broth rest for 30 to 45 minutes. Skim off fat that rises to the surface.

4. Remove chicken and vegetables from broth and reserve for other use.

5. Strain broth through a fine mesh strainer.

Serves 8-10

BRODO DI MANZO

Beef Broth

A variation on the chicken broth, but here the main flavor is beef.

Ingredients:

3 to 4 sprigs flat-leaf parsley
2-3 basil leaves
2 ½ to 3 lbs. lean Beef, preferably with bone
1 lb. veal bones, if desired
5 quarts (20 cups) cold water
3 teaspoons salt
1 large onion, washed, unpeeled and quartered
2 medium carrots, peeled and halved
2 stalks celery, halved
1 medium leek, cleaned and halved
1 fresh tomato, quartered and seeded (optional)
2 large garlic cloves, unpeeled and crushed
1 bay leaf
4-5 peppercorns
1 beef bouillon cube

1. Tie parsley and basil leaves together with kitchen twine. Place all ingredients in a large stock pot and bring to a boil over moderate heat. Once boiling, reduce heat and simmer for 1 to 1 ½ hours.

2. Skim the foam that rises to the top several times. If desired, add bouillon cube for additional flavor. Add salt.

3. Turn off heat and let broth rest for 30 minutes. Skim off fat that rises to the surface.

4. Remove beef and vegetables from broth and reserve for later use

5. Strain broth through a fine mesh strainer.

Serves 8-10

BRODO BASE DI POLLO E MANZO

Basic Chicken and Beef Broth

Referring to the preceding recipes for chicken broth and beef broth, use half the quantity of chicken and half the quantity of beef.

Use remaining ingredients as listed for one soup, for example: 5 quarts water.

Proceed as listed in directions.

BRODO VEGETALE

Vegetable Broth

A vegetable version of a broth, which can also be called a stock, that is versatile and can be used alone, with boiled pastina added, or in various recipes.

Ingredients:

Bouquet garni consisting of:

- 4 sprigs flat-leaf parsley
- 2-3 fresh basil leaves
- 3-4 sprigs fresh chives

2 Tbs. olive oil
2 Tbs. butter
2 large onions, peeled and quartered
2 leeks, cleaned and quartered
3 medium carrots, peeled and quartered
2 stalks celery, cleaned and quartered
2 large garlic cloves, unpeeled and lightly crushed
1 bay leaf
6 peppercorns
3 teaspoons salt or to taste
5 quarts (20 cups) cold water
1 vegetable bouillon cube (optional)

1. Tie bouquet garni ingredients kitchen twine and set aside.

2. Place the oil and butter in a large stock pot and heat until butter is melted. Add all the ingredients except the water and bouquet garni to the pot and stir well with a large wooden spoon until all ingredients are coated.

3. Let cook over moderate heat until vegetables begin to turn a light golden color, stirring occasionally.

4. Add the water and bouquet garni and bring the pot to a boil.

5. Reduce heat and simmer for 45 minutes to one hour. You may add a vegetable bouillon cube to enhance taste, if desired. Add salt to taste.

6. Strain the vegetables and broth is ready for use.

Serves 8-10

ZUPPA DI POLLO

Chicken Soup

This is the hearty version where the cooked chicken and vegetables are returned to the broth and the pastina of your choice is added. It is perfect on a cold or rainy night.

Ingredients:

1 recipe Chicken broth (page 111)
1 cup small dried pasta of your choice, such as Tubettini or Ditalini
1/3 cup freshly grated Parmigiana-Reggiano cheese

1. Prepare chicken broth as directed.

2. After cooked and cooled, remove chicken and vegetables and place in a large bowl.

3. Take each piece of cooked chicken, remove skin and bones and cut the meat into small pieces. Return to broth.

4. Remove skin from onion and dice it into small pieces. Cut the carrot, celery and leek into small pieces and return all vegetables to the broth. Bring to a boil and add the pasta, so it can absorb the flavor of the broth.

5. Cook the pasta for about 8 minutes or until al dente. Serve hot with grated cheese.

Serves 8-10

MINESTRA DI SCAROLA E POLPETTINE

Escarole and Meatball Soup

This has also been called "Italian Wedding Soup" over the years.

Using preceding recipe for Zuppa di Pollo, proceed in same way.

Eliminate the tubettini pasta and add the following: 3 cups escarole or Swiss chard, washed and cut.

For the Meatballs (Polpettine):

½ lb ground Beef
1 egg, beaten
¼ cup breadcrumbs
1 sprig parsley, chopped
2 Tbs. grated Parmigiana-Reggiano cheese
Dash of garlic powder
Salt and pepper to taste

To make the polpettine: Place all ingredients in a bowl and mix well. Shape into tiny meatballs. Place meatballs and escarole in the soup and cook for 30 to 40 minutes. Serve with grated Parmesan cheese.

Serves 8-10

TORTELLINI IN BRODO

Tortellini Soup

This is a very tasty and delightful soup, typical of a first course in the Reggio-Emilia region.

Ingredients:

1 recipe basic Chicken and Beef broth
½ recipe Tortellini (page 85)
½ cup grated Parmigiana-Reggiano cheese

Bring the broth to a boil and add the fresh tortellini. Allow to cook for 2-3 minutes or until al dente. Serve hot with freshly grated Parmesan cheese.

Serves 8

BRODO CON GNOCCHETTI DI SEMOLINA

Semolina Dumplings in Broth

These have been called Abruzzese style dumplings, since they originated in the Region of Abruzzo, which is outside of Rome and very well known for their delicious cooking.

Ingredients:

1 recipe Beef broth (page 112)
3 eggs
12 oz. semolina
Nutmeg to taste

6 oz. (1 and ½ stick) butter, softened
Pinch of salt

1. Beat the eggs and softened butter together. Add the semolina, salt and nutmeg and mix well. Let rest for 15 minutes.

2. Bring a pot of salted water to boil. Using a ½ teaspoon measure, form the semolina mixture into little dumplings and drop into the boiling water. Continue until all ingredients are finished. Simmer over moderate heat for 20 minutes.

3. When cooked, drain and add into the hot beef broth. Serve immediately sprinkled with Parmesan cheese. **Serves 8**

STRACCIATELLA ALLA ROMANA

Roman-style Egg Drop Soup

This is very easy and as well as light and nutritious.

Ingredients:

1 recipe Chicken broth
3 eggs
5 Tbs. grated Parmigiana-Reggiano cheese

¼ teaspoon ground pepper
4-5 sprigs flat leaf parsley, chopped

1. In a bowl, combine eggs, pepper, cheese and parsley and beat well.

2. Bring broth to a lively boil and add egg mixture slowly. Stir thoroughly and reduce heat and let simmer for 2-3 minutes

3. Turn off stove, cover and let rest for one minutes. Stir again before serving. Serve with additional grated cheese sprinkled on top. **Serves 6-8**

MINESTRONE AL GIARDINO

Garden Minestrone Soup

An enjoyable vegetarian Minestrone soup, at first, we wished to call it "nostrana" meaning "ours," since both Franca and Fr. Matt composed the ingredients.

Ingredients:

6 quarts (24 cups) cold water
3 medium zucchini, finely diced
¾ lbs. string beans, washed and cut in ½-inch pieces
4 carrots, peeled, diced into small pieces
3 stalks celery, diced
2 medium onions, finely chopped
3 medium potatoes, peeled and diced into small pieces
¾ lbs. fresh or dried beans*
¾ lbs peas, fresh or frozen
1 lb. spinach, cleaned and coarsely chopped
1 cup basil, chopped
½ cup flat leaf parsley, shopped
1 bunch asparagus, cut in ½-inch pieces
2 cloves garlic, finely chopped
½ cup olive oil
3 Tbs. butter
Salt and freshly ground pepper to taste
1 cup freshly grated Parmigiana-Reggiano cheese

*If using dried beans, clean, soak in cold water overnight and rinse.

1. Place all ingredients except garlic, oil, basil, parsley and asparagus in a large stock pot and place over high heat. Bring to a boil, then reduce heat to a simmer and cook for one hour.

2. Meanwhile, sauté the finely chopped garlic in the oil until light golden in color. Do not allow to burn. Add garlic to the stock pot.

3. Add the chopped basil, parsley and asparagus the last 15 minutes of the cooking time. Add the salt and pepper to taste and stir well.

4. When cooking time is complete, turn off the heat and add the butter. Cover and allow to rest at least 20 minutes before serving. May be served at room temperature in the summer. Serve with grated cheese sprinkled on top.

Serves 8-10

MINESTRONE TRADIZIONALE

Traditional Minestrone

Here is a more typical and well-known version of minestrone soup. Be sure to drizzle a bit of fruity extra virgin olive oil on each dish to enhance the taste.

Ingredients:

½ cup dried navy or kidney beans* or one 19-oz. can of beans
2 cups cold water
6 quarts (24 cups) cold water
2 medium zucchini, diced
3 medium carrots, chopped
½ lb. string beans, cut into 1-inch pieces
3 stalks celery, chopped
2 medium onions, chopped
3 cloves garlic, finely chopped
2 medium potatoes, peeled and diced
4 fresh tomatoes, peeled and seeded, or 4 canned seeded tomatoes
3-4 sprigs flat leaf parsley, chopped
3-4 basil leaves, chopped
½ lb. dried pasta, such as small shells or Ditalini
8 oz. fresh or frozen peas
1 beef bouillon cube
½ cup olive oil
Salt and pepper to taste.

1. *If using dried beans, clean, wash and place in stock pot with 2 cups water and bring to a boil. Boil for 2 to 3 minutes. Remove from heat, cover and let rest for one hour. Add enough water to cover the beans if necessary.

2. Meanwhile, heat oil in a saucepan, add the onions and sauté until translucent. Add garlic and cook about one minute longer. Add to stock pot.

3. Add the tomatoes and 6 quarts of water to the stock pot and all the remaining ingredients except the pasta, basil and parsley.

4. Bring stockpot to a boil and then reduce to a simmer and cook for 1 to 1 and ½ hours or until all ingredients are tender. Add salt and pepper to taste.

5. Add the pasta the last 10 minutes and the chopped basil and parsley.
   Cook until the pasta is al dente. Serve with grated Parmesan or grated Pecorino Romano cheese.   **Serves 8**

MINESTRA DI LENTICCHIE

Lentil Soup

A great Lenten dish and lentils are known for their content of iron and very nutritious. Tubettini or Ditalini pasta can be substituted for the broken spaghetti if desired. Many a grandchild fondly remembers his or her grandmother breaking the spaghetti by hand over a large bowl.

Ingredients:

4 quarts basic vegetable stock (page 113) or cold water
1 lb. dried Lentils
2 large carrots, chopped
3 large celery stalks, chopped
2 medium potatoes, peeled and diced
1 large onion, chopped
1-2 to ¾ lbs. Spaghetti broken into 1 to 1 and ½-inch pieces
3-4 sprigs flat leaf parsley, chopped
3-4 basil leaves, chopped
3 cloves garlic, finely chopped
1 Tbs. olive oil
Salt and pepper to taste
¾ cups grated Parmigiana-Reggiano or Romano cheese

1. Pick over, clean and rinse the lentils. Place in a stock pot with water and bring to a boil.

2. Add all ingredients except parsley, basil, onion, garlic and oil.

3. While lentils and vegetables are cooking, sauté the onion and garlic until softened and add to the lentil soup, stirring well. Reduce heat to simmer and cook for one to 1 and ½ hours.

4. Add the spaghetti the last 10 minutes of the cooking time as well as the parsley, basil and the salt and pepper.

5. Serve hot with grated Parmesan or Romano cheese.

Serves 6-8

Minestra di Piselli Secchi

Ham and Pea Soup

This is our version of an American classic.

Ingredients:

3/4 lb. dried yellow split Peas
3/4 lb. dried green split Peas
3 medium carrots, chopped
3 celery stalks, chopped
½ lb. ham bone, ham steak or chopped smoked bacon
6 quarts (24 cups) cold water
2 medium onions, chopped
2 cloves garlic, finely chopped
3 Tbs. olive oil
3-4 sprigs flat leaf parsley, chopped
3 basil leaves, finely chopped
Salt and freshly ground pepper to taste

For garnish:

4 oz. frozen or fresh peas
1 sprig parsley, finely chopped
1 basil leaf, finely chopped
2 teaspoons butter

1. Pick over the peas and wash in a strainer. Place in stock pot with water and bring to a boil. Turn off heat and let rest, covered, for 30 minutes.

2. Meanwhile, cut all the vegetables and set aside. In a small saucepan, sauté the onion in the oil for approximately 5 minutes, until transparent. Add the garlic and cook for another minute or two. Add all ingredients to the peas.

3. Return to heat and simmer for 1 to 1 and ½ hours. Add salt and pepper to taste.

4. Before serving soup, remove the ham steak, discard bone, cut meat coarsely and return to soup.

5. While soup is cooking, prepare the garnish:

6. Bring ½ cup water to a boil and cook fresh peas until tender or frozen peas according to package instructions.

7. When cooked, add chopped basil and parsley and one Tbs. butter. Mix ingredients and add one Tbs. on each dish of pea soup as a garnish. **Serves 6-8**

PASTA E FAGIOLI

Pasta and Bean Soup

This is the more "wet" or soupy version, as opposed to the one found in the Pasta section.

Ingredients:

1 lb. dry cannellini Beans or one 19 oz. can
¼ cup olive oil
1 medium onion, chopped
3 cloves garlic, chopped
3-4 sprigs flat leaf parsley, chopped
Salt and freshly ground pepper to taste
¼ teaspoon red pepper flakes (optional)
1 lb. Ditalini pasta
6 cups vegetable stock (page 113) or cold water
2 Tbs. olive oil
½ cup grated Parmigiana-Reggiano cheese

1. If using dried beans, soak in cold water overnight.

2. Sauté the onion in the oil until translucent – approximately 8 to 10 minutes. Add garlic and cook an additional minute. Place in stock pot with beans and six cups cold water. Cook for 1 and ½ hours if using dried beans.

3. If using canned beans, reduce water to 2 cups and simmer for 10 minutes. When beans are near completion, bring a pot of salted water to a boil. Add the pasta and cook until al dente. Drain pasta and add to beans and stir well.

4. Add freshly chopped parsley, salt and pepper and 2 Tbs. olive oil and stir. Serve with grated cheese. **Serves 6**

PASTA E FAGIOLI IN ROSSO

Pasta and Bean Soup with Tomatoes

Using the above recipe, substitute red kidney beans (dried or canned) for the white cannellini beans.

Add one 28-oz. can of crushed tomatoes to the sautéed onion and garlic mixture before adding the beans into the stock pot. Reduce water by 2 cups. **Serves 6**

PASSATO DI CAROTE

Cream of Carrot Soup

This is a very healthy soup, since there is no flour or heavy cream used to thicken it. That is done by the potato that is blended with the other ingredients. The priests in the rectory always looked forward to lunch when this was on the menu.

Ingredients:

3 quarts (12 cups) cold water
6 large Carrots, peeled and chopped
2 medium potatoes, peeled and cut
1 large onion, chopped
3 sprigs flat leaf parsley, finely chopped
4 basil leaves, finely chopped
Salt and freshly group pepper to taste
1 chicken bouillon cube
1 Tbs. butter

For garnish:

1 small carrot, shredded

1. Pour water into stock pot, add carrots, potatoes, onions and bouillon cube. Bring to a boil and reduce heat to medium. Cook until vegetables are tender – approximately 30 minutes.

2. When vegetables are done, remove from pot in batches and place in a blender or food processor. Blend until smoother.

3. Return to pot and bring to a boil again. Add the basil, parsley, butter and the salt and pepper to taste and stir well.

4. Turn off heat, let rest for 5 minutes.

5. Serve in bowls garnished with shredded carrot and Parmesan cheese sprinkled on top, if desired.

Serves 6

PASSATO DI ASPARAGI

Cream of Asparagus Soup

Another delicious and healthy soup, but this time, asparagus is the featured taste.

Ingredients:

2 bunches Asparagus
1 large potato, peeled and cut
3 quarts (12 cups) vegetable stock (page 113) or cold water
2 medium onions, chopped
2 cloves garlic, finely chopped
1 Tbs. olive oil
1 Tbs. butter
Salt and pepper to taste

1. Prepare the asparagus by discarding the hard ends. Cut off approximately one inch from the flower end and set aside. Cut remainder of asparagus into 2-inch pieces and put in a stock pot with water, potato and onion. Bring to a boil and reduce heat to medium.

2. Meanwhile, heat oil and add garlic. Let cook until a light golden color. Remove from heat and set aside.

3. When vegetables are done, remove in batches and place in a blender or food processor. Pour blended soup through a fine strainer before returning to pot. Discard any fibers caught in the strainer. When all soup is blended and in the pot, add the asparagus tips and the oil and garlic mixture. Bring to a boil and cook for an additional 3 minutes. Add the butter and stir. Add salt and pepper to taste.

4. Turn off heat, let rest 5 minutes before serving. May be served with Parmesan cheese sprinkled on top.

Serves 6

PASSATO DI BROCCOLI

Cream of Broccoli Soup

Using the preceding recipe for Cream of Asparagus, substitute 1 bunch broccoli for the asparagus and use same directions.

ZUPPA DI FINOCCHIO

Fennel Soup

Fennel can be often overlooked, but adds a great taste dimension and can be a real surprise from time to time. We hope that you will find this a delightful change.

Ingredients:

4 quarts (12 cups) vegetable stock (page 113) or cold water
2 medium onions, chopped
2 Leeks, cleaned and finely chopped
4 Fennel bulbs, finely chopped, reserving tops for garnish
1 chicken bouillon cube
1 Tbs. butter
1 Tbs. flour
3-4 basil leaves, finely chopped
2-3 sprigs flat leaf parsley, finely chopped
Salt and pepper to taste

1. Place the water, onions, leeks and fennel in the stock pot. Add bouillon cube and bring to a boil. Reduce heat to medium and cook for 30 minutes. Test vegetables for tenderness. Remove one cup of liquid from pot and reserve.

2. When done, remove vegetables from pot in batches, place in blender or food processor and pour through a fine mesh strainer before returning to pot. Discard any solids caught in the strainer.

3. In a small saucepan, melt the butter, add the flour and stirring constantly, then add the reserved cup of liquid until it is of a creamy consistency. Add to the soup and stir well.

4. Add basil, parsley and the salt and pepper and bring to a boil. Turn off heat, cover and let rest a few minutes before serving.

Serves 6-8

ZUPPA DI SPINACI

Spinach Soup

We all need our spinach! This is a fun way to enjoy it and the tasty bacon adds a new flavor dimension.

Ingredients:

2 packages (10 oz. each) fresh spinach
1 large onion, chopped
2 garlic cloves, finely chopped
2 Tbs. olive oil
4 Tbs. butter
3 basil leaves, finely chopped
3-4 sprigs parsley, finely chopped
1/3 cup flour
1 cup 2% milk
9 cups chicken broth (page 111)
Salt and pepper to taste

For garnish:

4 slices bacon, fried to a crisp and crumbled

1. Wash spinach well and cook in 2 cups boiling water for three minutes. Drain, reserving the liquid. Let cool, squeeze out excess liquid, cut coarsely and set aside.

2. Sauté the chopped onion in 2 Tbs. butter and oil until light golden. Add chopped garlic and cook briefly. Add spinach, basil and parsley and sauté several minutes.

3. Meanwhile, in a small saucepan, melt 2 Tbs. butter, add flour and stir. Add one cup milk, stir and bring to a boil. Add the reserved spinach liquid and the chicken broth slowly and continue to cook for an additional 10 minutes until thickened.

4. Add sautéed spinach mixture, stir well and serve hot. Season with salt and pepper. Sprinkle with the crumbled bacon for garnish.

Serves 6

CREMA DI PATATE E AGLIO

Potato and Garlic Soup

When October arrives each year, besides the golden leaves that dance in the sunlight, this is an annual treat that we look forward to seeing once again on our tables for several months.

Ingredients:

5 large potatoes, peeled and diced
1 large onion, chopped
2 celery stalks, chopped
12 cloves garlic, peeled and halved
¼ cup olive oil
2-3 sprigs fresh flat-leaf parsley, chopped
2 basil leaves, finely chopped
12 cups (3 quarts) cold water
Salt and pepper to taste
2 Tbs. butter
1-2 fresh scallions, chopped

1. Place the oil in a stock pot and heat. Crush the garlic halves with a mallet or the back of your hand to accentuate flavor. Place in oil and heat over medium heat until fragrant, not allowing them to brown.

2. Remove from heat and add the onion, celery and potatoes and stir to coat.

3. Return to heat, add the water and bring to a boil. Reduce heat to medium and cook 30 minutes or until vegetables are tender.

4. Place in a blender or food processor in batches and puree until smooth. Return to pot and bring to a boil. Add the parsley, basil, salt, pepper and butter and stir.

5. Cover and turn off heat and let rest a few minutes before serving. Garnish each bowl with chopped fresh scallion.

Serves 6

ZUPPA DI CIPOLLA ALLA CONTADINA

Farmers' style Onion Soup with Toasted Crostini

The French Onion soup is a true classic, but this is the rustic version, from the Alto Adige-Trentino region of northern Italy.

Ingredients:

6 large onions, cut in half lengthwise and sliced thinly
2 cloves garlic, peeled and crushed
3 Tbs. olive oil
2 Tbs. butter
2 Tbs. flour
2 quarts (8 cups) Beef stock (page 112)
2 sprigs parsley, chopped
3 basil leaves, chopped
Salt and fresh ground pepper to taste
¾ cup grated Parmigiana-Reggiano cheese

For crostini:

8 slices Italian bread
8 thin slices Fontina cheese
1 clove garlic, peeled
1 Tbs. softened butter

1. In a large stockpot, heat the butter and oil together. Add the onion and garlic and sauté until golden brown, mixing constantly. Sprinkle in the flour and stir well.

2. Add beef stock and the salt and pepper and bring to a boil. Reduce heat to medium and cover. Simmer for 30 minutes.

3. Meanwhile, make the crostini: Toast bread until light golden in color. Brush with the softened butter and rub with the garlic clove. Place the Fontina cheese on each of the crostini and lay on the bottom of each serving dish.

4. When the soup is done, pour with a ladle into each bowl, covering the crostini. Garnish with a pinch of the basil and parsley and ½ teaspoon of the Parmesan cheese.

Serves 6-8

ZUPPA DI VONGOLE AL POMODORO

Clam and Tomato Soup

This is called Manhattan Clam Chowder in most circles and is well-loved by many.

Ingredients:

2 Tbs. butter
2 Tbs. olive oil
2 carrots, peeled and diced
1 stalk celery, chopped
1 potato, peeled and diced
1 medium onion, minced
2 garlic cloves, minced
1 28-oz. can whole plum tomatoes
2 Tbs. flour
8 cups basic vegetable stock (page 113)
3-4 lbs. fresh Clams in shells

For garnish:

3 stalks fresh chives, thinly sliced

1. In a large stock pot, heat the butter and olive oil. Add all the vegetables, onion and garlic, and sauté for about 15 minutes, stirring occasionally, not allowing to burn.

2. Remove seeds from the canned tomatoes, chop into medium pieces and set aside.

3. Add the flour to the stock pot and stir well. Add the chopped tomatoes and the strained tomato juice and the vegetable stock and incorporate all ingredients. Add salt and pepper to taste and let boil for 30 to 40 minutes.

4. Meanwhile, wash and scrub the clams and soak them in cold water for 30 minutes to allow any remaining sand to fall to the bottom of the bowl.

5. In a large frying pan, pour ½ cup water, bring to a boil and add the clams. Cover and cook over low heat for 10 minutes or until open. Remove clam meat from shells, discarding shells. Chop the clam meat and add to the soup along with all liquids from the frying pan passed through a strainer.

6. Stir soup and serve in bowls with sprinkled chives as garnish.

Serves 6

CHAPTER IV: SECONDI/SECOND COURSES

In a traditional Italian Meal, the "Secondo" is the main Entrée and usually consists of Meat, Fish, Poultry or Meatless Dish such as Eggplant or Frittata.

Beef and Veal:

- Polpette di Salsiccia al Ragu
- Polpette di Manzo e Vitello
- Polpettone Ripieno al Don Matteo
- Polpettone ai Funghi
- Verze Ripiene
- Spezzatino di Manzo con Patate e Piselli
- Involtini di Manzo alla Napoletana
- Arrosto di Manzo ai Profumi di Erbe
- Brasato di Manzo
- Bistecca alla Fiorentina
- Filetto di Manzo alla Griglia con Salsa Robusta
- Manzo alla Pizzaiola
- Trippa con Verdure
- Arrosto di Vitello al Rosmarino
- Arrosto di Vitello al Forno
- Petto di Vitello Ripieno
- Osso Buco Classico
- Osso Buco Rosso
- Vitello Saltimbocca la Romana
- Cotoletta alla Milanese
- Cotolette di Vitello alla Parmigiana
- Cotolette di Vitello Primavera
- Cotolette al Prosciutto e Fontina
- Scallopine di Vitello alla Piccata
- Medaglioni di Vitello alla Marsala
- Medaglioni di Vitello al Vino Bianco
- Medaglioni di Vitello a l'Ortolana
- Medaglioni di Vitello ai Piselli
- Nodini di Vitello Valdostana
- Nodini di Vitello Balsamico
- Nodini di Vitello alla Gorgonzola
- Vitello Tonnato
- Fegato alla Veneziana
- Fegato di Vitello alla Milanese
- Arrosto di Maiale Toscano
- Arrosto di Maiale Agrodolce
- Arrosto di Maiale Tirolese

- Arrosto di Maiale alla Salsa Forte
- Prosciutto Arrosto
- Costolette di Maiale alle Cipolle
- Costolette di Maiale Milanese
- Costolette di Maiale Piccante
- Costolette Ripiene
- Involtini di Maiale al Pomodoro
- Salsiccia e Pepperoni

Lamb:

- Cosciotto di Agnello Arrosto al Vino Bianco
- Cosciotto di Agnello al Pesto
- Cosciotto di Agnello Ripieno
- Abbacchio o Capretto Arrosto di Pasqua
- Corona di Agnello Arrosto
- Agnello con Carciofi
- Agnello alla Greca
- Costolette di Agnello alla Peperonata
- Costolette di Agnello alla Fiorentina
- Osso Buco di Agnello ai Fagioli

Chicken:

- Pollo Arrosto Tricarico
- Pollo Ripieno alla Salsiccia
- Pollo Arrosto Gourmet
- Pollo Arrosto ai Profumi
- Pollo Arrosto al Limone
- Pollo Arrosto con Patate
- Pollo alla Zia Concetta
- Pollo alla Cacciatora
- Pollo alla Cacciatora Stile Cremonese
- Pollo alla Salsa Agrodolce
- Pollo alla Tetrazzini
- Petto di Pollo Ripieno
- Petto di Pollo con Spinaci
- Pollo alla Pescatora
- Pollo Buongustaio
- Cotolette di Pollo Milanese
- Cotolette di Pollo Francese
- Cotolette di Pollo Sorrentino
- Pollo al Pesto Verde
- Arrosto di Tacchino Ripieno
- Cotolette di Tacchino alla Crema con Funghi
- Coniglio alle Verdure con Barolo
- Coniglio Arrosto al Forno

Fish:

- Baccala' Marinara
- Baccala' Fritta con Salsa Verde
- Insalata di Baccala'
- Salmone con Rucola
- Salmone con Salsa Bianca
- Salmone Cardinale
- Trota al Cartoccio
- Sogliola alla Milanese
- Sogliola Ripiena alla Marinara
- Sogliola Ripiena di Spinaci
- Calamari Farciti
- Tonno Arrabbiato
- Pesce Spada Marinato
- Aragosta Ripiena
- Aragosta con Intingolo
- Gamberi Ripieni alla Pescatora
- Gamberi all' Italiana
- Scampi alla Griglia
- Spiedini di Pesce
- Fritto Misto di Pesce in Pastella
- Gamberi fra Diavolo
- Pesce Festaiola
- Zuppa di Pesce
- Mussels Arrabbiata
- Cape Sante alla Veneziana

Meatless Entrees:

- Frittata di Zucchini
- Frittata di Patate
- Frittata di Asparagi
- Frittata di Spinaci
- Frittata di Funghi Trifolati
- Frittata ai Carciofi
- Frittata di Formaggio
- Quiche di Zucchini
- Quiche di Zucchini
- Pizza Margherita
- Rollatine di Melanzana
- Melanzane alla Parmigiana
- Melanzana Ripiena alla Napoletana
- Vegetali Ripieni Misti
- Pomodori Ripieni con Riso
- Peperoni Ripieni

Beef and Veal

POLPETTE E SALSICCIA AL POMODORO

Meatballs and Sausage in Tomato Sauce

This is the traditional Sunday afternoon meal in many Italian-American homes that have their roots from the south of Italy. The pasta is served as the first course and the "gravy meat" is served after that, as the second course.

Ingredients:

4 28-oz. cans crushed Tomatoes	4 cloves garlic, finely chopped
2 lbs. Italian Pork Sausage (sweet, with fennel seeds)	One cup olive oil
½ cup of water	2 and ½ lbs. ground chuck Beef
4 eggs	4-5 sprigs flat-leaf parsley, finely chopped
¼ cup grated Parmigiana-Reggiano cheese	1 and ½ cups breadcrumbs
½ cup milk	Salt and freshly ground pepper

1. In a large pot, pour ½ cup of olive oil and sauté half of the garlic. Add the crushed tomatoes and place over medium heat, stirring occasionally.

2. For the meatballs, place ground beef in a bowl, make a well in the meat and add the eggs, remaining chopped garlic, bread crumbs, cheese, parsley, ½ cup milk, salt and pepper. Mix ingredients well. To form meatballs, use 3 lightly heaped Tbs. of meat mixture and form by hand into a ball. This mixture will form about 20 meatballs.

3. Fry meatballs in ½ cup of olive oil for two to three minutes on each side, turning 3 to 4 times so that the meatballs are completely browned. Drain on paper towels for a few minutes and add to the tomato sauce to continue cooking. If desired, meatballs can also be baked by placing them on an ungreased cookie tray in a 350-degree oven for 15 minutes.

4. To cook the sausage, place in a frying pan and prick with the tines of a fork. Add ½ cup water over medium to high heat and bring to a boil. Reduce heat, let water evaporate and allow sausage to brown. Let brown on one side then turn to brown on the other. Then done, cut in 3- to 4-inch pieces and add to the tomato sauce to continue cooking.

5. Reduce tomato sauce with meatballs and sausage to a simmer over low to medium heat and cook for 40 minutes. This recipe may also be halved for a smaller quantity.

6. If serving 8-10 people, boil 2 lbs. pasta of your choice until desired tenderness. Drain and add 3 cups sauce, mixing well. Serve meatballs and sausage as the second course.

Serves 8-10

POLPETTE DI MANZO E VITELLO

Beef and Veal Meatballs

This is a variation of the previous recipe, which is more typical of the north of Italy.

Ingredients:

1 lb. ground Beef*
1 lb. ground Veal*
1 medium onion, finely chopped
3 cloves garlic, finely chopped
2 sprigs flat-leaf parsley, finely chopped
¼ cup olive oil
2 eggs
1 cup breadcrumbs
½ cup grated Parmigiana-Reggiano cheese
Dash nutmeg
Salt and freshly ground pepper to taste
¼ cup milk

For the sauce:

2 cans 28-oz each, whole tomatoes
1 small onion, finely chopped
4 basil leaves
1 Tbs. butter

2 cloves garlic, finely chopped
3 sprigs flat-leaf parsley
¼ cup oil
Salt and pepper to taste

1. To prepare the meatballs, pour the oil into a small frying pan, add the chopped onion and garlic and sauté until softened but not browned and set aside to cool slightly, then blend in food processor and set aside.

2. Place the ground meat in a large bowl. Add the Parmesan cheese, breadcrumbs, eggs, milk and sautéed vegetables. Also add the salt, pepper and dash of nutmeg. Mix all ingredients well.

3. For each meatball, use two heaping Tbs. of the meat mixture, form into a ball and place on ungreased baking sheet, bake for 15 minutes in a 350-degree oven.

4. To prepare the sauce: In a large saucepan, sauté the onion and garlic in the oil until softened but not browned. Place the whole tomatoes, basil and parsley in a blender or food processor and blend until smooth.

5. Pour tomatoes into pan with garlic and onion and simmer over moderate heat. Add salt and pepper to taste. Add meatballs and cook for a total of 25 to 30 minutes. Turn off heat, add butter and cover. Stir well before serving.

6. To serve, boil 1 and ½ lbs. pasta of your choice. Drain and mix with 2 cups tomato sauce, sprinkling Parmesan cheese on top. Serve with meatballs and reserved tomato sauce.

Note: You may also substitute ground Chicken or Turkey for the Beef or Veal, if desired.

Serves 6-8

POLPETTONE RIPIENO AL DON MATTEO

Fr. Matt's Stuffed Meatloaf

This is one of Fr. Matt's early culinary experiments when he was just a teenager.

Ingredients

For the meatloaf:

1 and ½ lbs. ground Meat (mixture of Beef, Veal and Pork)
2 eggs
1 garlic clove, finely chopped
3 sprigs flat-leaf parsley, finely chopped
2 heaping Tbs. grated Pecorino Romano cheese
¾ cups breadcrumbs
¼ cups milk
Salt and pepper to taste

For the filling:

1 lb. Ricotta cheese
1 egg, beaten
1 sprig flat-leaf parsley, finely chopped

½ lb. mozzarella cheese, shredded
1 Tbs. Pecorino Romano cheese
Salt and pepper to taste

For the sauce:

One 28-oz. can crushed tomatoes
1 Tbs. olive oil
Salt and pepper to taste

1 clove garlic, finely chopped
3 basil leaves, torn

1. Begin the sauce by sautéing the garlic in the oil until softened. Add the tomatoes and basil and simmer over moderate heat, stirring occasionally. Add salt and pepper to taste.

2. For the meatloaf: Place the meat in a large bowl, make a well and add all listed ingredients. Mix well and set aside.

3. For the filling: mix all listed ingredients and set aside.

4. Form the meatloaf by placing half of the meat mixture in a glass baking dish approximately 8-inches by 12-inches. Press meat in bottom of baking pan covering completely.

5. Pour ricotta cheese filling on the meat layer and cover with remaining half of meat, covering completely.

6. Cover meatloaf with 1 and ½ cups of the tomato sauce and place, uncovered, in a 350-degree oven for approximately 45 minutes.

7. Cut in squares and serve with remaining tomato sauce over pasta if desired.

Serves 6

POLPETTONE AI FUNGHI

Meatloaf with Mushrooms

You have not tasted a meatloaf until you have tasted this. It is succulent, moist and full of delightful flavor. As it has been said, it is "love at first bite."

Ingredients:

¼ cup oil
3 garlic cloves, chopped
4 basil leaves, torn
1 lb. ground Veal
1 and ½ cups breadcrumbs
3/4 cups milk

1 medium onion, chopped
3 sprigs flat-leaf parsley, chopped
2 lbs. ground Beef
2 eggs
¾ cups grated Parmigiana-Reggiano cheese
Salt and freshly ground pepper to taste

For the mushroom sauce:

2 Tbs. butter
1 lb. Mushrooms, sliced
2 cloves garlic, finely chopped
3 sprigs flat-leaf parsley, minced
3 cups beef broth
Salt and pepper to taste

2 Tbs. olive oil
1 large onion, finely chopped
½ cup dry white wine
3 basil leaves, finely chopped
2 Tbs. flour

1. For the meatloaf: Sauté the onion and garlic in the oil until softened. Add the chopped basil and parsley and set aside to cool Blend in food processor and reserve.

2. Mix all remaining meatloaf ingredients and add the blended vegetable mixture as well. Form into a meatloaf and place into a lightly buttered baking dish. Brush top with 1 Tbs. softened butter.

3. Cover and place into a 350-degree oven for 30 minutes.

4. While meatloaf is baking, prepare the mushroom sauce:

5. Sauté the onion in the oil and butter until golden brown. Add garlic, mushrooms, parsley and basil and sauté over lively flame, mixing occasionally but do not allow to burn. Add the wine and allow to evaporate completely. Mix the 2 Tbs. flour with 2 Tbs. of the beef broth until smooth. Add to the mushroom mixture.

6. Add the rest of the broth, mixing constantly. Lower the heat and cook for 10 minutes. Add salt and pepper to taste if necessary. Pour all the sauce over the meatloaf and continue to bake, uncovered, for an additional 30 minutes. Slice and serve over fresh egg noodles.

Serves 6

VERZE RIPIENE

Stuffed Cabbage

Somewhat of a nod to the Polish and Slovak traditions, this recipe is actually a part of the repertory of northern Italian cuisine in the Alpine region.

Ingredients:

1 head of Cabbage
1 recipe Béchamel sauce (page 10)

1 lb. cooked Meat of your choice

For the stuffing:

2/3 cups milk, scalded
1 clove garlic, minced
Salt and pepper to taste
1 link Italian sausage
2 cups breadcrumbs

pinch of grated nutmeg
sprig of flat-leaf parsley, minced
1 Tbs. olive oil
2 to 3 eggs
1 cup grated Parmigiana-Reggiano cheese

For the tomato sauce:

1 clove garlic, minced
1 Tbs. butter
1 stalk celery, finely chopped
1 28-oz. can crushed tomatoes

2 Tbs. olive oil
1 medium onion, peeled and minced
1 carrot, peeled and minced
salt and pepper to taste

1. Prepare the béchamel sauce and set aside.

2. Cut the core from the cabbage and peel away the individual leaves. Parboil in salted boiling water for 4 to 5 minutes each. Drain on paper towels.

3. For the stuffing: in a large skillet over medium heat, sauté the garlic in the oil until softened. Add the sausage meat, removed from its casing, and brown well.

4. Finely chop the cooked meat, and place in a bowl. Add the cooked sausage meat, breadcrumbs, milk, eggs, grated Parmesan, chopped parsley and béchamel sauce. Mix all ingredients well. Place 2 to 3 heaping Tbs. of stuffing on each cabbage leaf. Fold the side over to cover, filling then roll the stalk end to the end of the leaf. Continue until all leaves are done and set aside.

5. To make the sauce: Sauté the onion in the oil over medium heat in a large skillet. Add the remaining vegetables and cook until softened, about 5 minutes. Add the tomatoes, stirring well, and add the salt and pepper to taste.

6. To complete: Add the stuffed cabbage and layer if necessary. Make sure the sauce covers all the cabbage bundles. Add a cup of broth if necessary. Cook, covered, for 45 minutes to an hour over moderate heat. Place cooked cabbage on a serving dish, cover with sauce and sprinkle with ½ cup chopped fresh parsley. **Serves 6-8**

Variation for the sauce: Place ½ cup dried porcini mushrooms in hot water for 10 minutes. Clean off all sand and add to the sauce.

Spezzatino di Manzo con Patate e Piselli

Meat with Potatoes and Peas

This is a typical American stick-to-your-ribs dish, but we have lightened it and as well added a few Italian flavors.

Ingredients:

2 Tbs. olive oil
2 Tbs. butter
1 small onion, finely chopped
2 cloves garlic, minced
1 Tbs. parsley, chopped
3 to 4 leaves basil, chopped
2 lbs. lean Beef, cut in chunks
2 Tbs. flour, for dredging
4 oz. dry red wine
2 Tbs. tomato paste
3 cups beef broth
2 cups fresh or frozen peas
3 large potatoes, peeled and cut
Salt and pepper to taste

1. Use one Tbs. each of oil and butter and place in a small saucepan. Sauté the onion until softened, add the garlic, parsley and basil and stir quickly over moderate heat for a few seconds. Set aside.

2. Put the remaining butter and oil in a large skillet over moderate heat. Dredge the beef in flour and sauté over a high flame in the skillet, stirring until golden. Add the red wine, let evaporate, then add the sautéed ingredients, tomato paste and beef stock, and mix well.

3. Simmer over moderate heat until the mixture is thickened and the meat is tender – approximately 45 minutes.

4. Add the potatoes and peas, stir well and cook for an additional 15 minutes, until the potatoes are tender. Add salt and freshly ground pepper to taste. Serve with mixed salad.

Serves 6-8

Involtini di Manzo alla Napoletana

Neapolitan-style Beef Rolls

What a treat for those of Italian-American heritage! Over the years, some cooks have put sliced hard-boiled egg, raisins or pignoli nuts in the filling, but this is the version that is preferred by the purists, where less is definitely more.

Ingredients:

3 cloves garlic, minced
5 sprigs flat-leaf parsley, finely chopped
2 cups breadcrumbs
1 cup grated Parmesan cheese
¾ cups olive oil
12 thin slices of Beef round steak
1 clove of unpeeled garlic, crushed
1 28-oz. can of whole tomatoes
1 28-oz.can of tomato puree
Salt and freshly ground pepper to taste

1. Mix the garlic, parsley, breadcrumbs, cheese, salt and pepper and ½ cup of the olive oil in a bowl and set aside.

2. Pound the beef slices between sheets of wax paper to make them thinner and more tender. Distribute the breadcrumb stuffing evenly on all 12 pieces. Spread the stuffing evenly on each steak, but allow space around the edges.

3. Roll each slice and secure ends with wooden toothpicks or tie with cooking thread. And place in a large frying pan with the remaining oil and unpeeled garlic clove.

4. Fry the involtini, turning several times until well-browned. Remove the garlic clove and discard. Pour in the tomato puree and stir. Add salt and pepper to taste.

5. Pour the whole tomatoes into a bowl and, using a potato masher, break into medium-size pieces and add to the frying pan. Reduce heat and continue to cook for about an hour until the meat is very tender.

6. Serve with tomato sauce and pasta of your choice.

Serves 6

Arrosto di Manzo ai Profumi di Erbe

Herb-scented Roast Beef

A true American treat for a special occasion, here it is enhanced by a variety of aromatic herbs that is reminiscent of those used when preparing a Florentine steak.

Ingredients:

3 lbs. Rump Roast, Eye of Round Roast or 5 lbs. of Prime Rib Roast with bones
1 and ½ Tbs. butter, softened
1 teaspoon grated lemon peel
1 teaspoon dried thyme
2 sage leaves, finely chopped
1 sprig rosemary, finely chopped
2 garlic cloves, minced
1 cup beef broth
½ teaspoon each of salt and ground pepper

1. Preheat oven to 450 degrees. In a bowl, mix all chopped herbs with softened butter. Coat the entire surface of the roast with herb paste.

2. Place meat in roasting pan and add beef broth. Cook for 15 to 20 minutes per lb. Calculate complete cooking time according to the weight. Cook uncovered for the first 30 minutes at 450 degrees, basting frequently.

3. Reduce heat to 300 and cook additional time as needed. For medium-rare meat should be 150 degrees on a meat thermometer. For medium to well-done, it should be 160 degrees.

4. Remove roast from oven, let stand several minutes before slicing thinly.

5. Serve with Parmesan potato wedges and string beans almondine.

Serves 8

BRASATO DI MANZO

Italian-style Pot Roast

Fr. Matt learned this recipe from his sister, Suzanne when he was visiting her and the family in Milano. It is a cold winter dish that can be served with either polenta or gnocchi as denoted below. Homemade fettuccine or mashed potatoes go well also.

Ingredients:

3 lbs. top round of Beef Roast
1/3 cups flour
¼ cup olive oil
4 Tbs. butter
2 onions, chopped
3 carrots, peeled and chopped
2 ribs celery, cleaned and cut in to medium-sized pieces
4 cloves garlic, minced
2 cups beef broth
1 bay leaf
2 fresh sage leaves
1 sprig fresh rosemary
2 tomatoes, peeled, seeded and chopped
3 cups Barolo or other good red wine
2 sprigs flat-leaf parsley, chopped
½ teaspoon thyme
Salt and pepper to taste

1. In a pot large enough to hold the beef, heat the oil, add the beef roast and brown on all sides to seal in the juices.

2. Add the butter and melt. Add all the vegetables and spices. Add all the red wine, one cup of the stock and salt and pepper to taste.

3. Simmer, covered over medium heat, turning the meat every ½ hour for 2 and ½ to 3 hours until meat is very tender.

4. Remove the beef roast and cover to keep warm. Discard the bay leaf and rosemary.

5. Puree all remaining ingredients and return to the pot.

6. Dissolve the flour into the remaining beef broth and add to the vegetable gravy and bring to a boil. Reduce heat to very low.

7. Slice the beef and place on a deep serving dish. Pour the gravy over it and serve.

8. Serve with polenta or gnocchi.

Serves 6-8

BISTECCA ALLA FIORENTINA

Steak Florentine

After the beautiful Uffizi museum, the Ponte Vecchio and a few other art treasures located in the Renaissance city of Florence, this steak is also one of the major attractions of the well-loved city of Florence.

Ingredients:

6 T-Bone Beef Steaks, approximately one-inch thick
1 sprig fresh rosemary, chopped, or ½ teaspoon dried
1 Tbs. chopped flat-leaf parsley
1 Tbs. chopped fresh basil
3 cloves garlic, minced
3 Tbs. butter
Salt and freshly ground pepper to taste

1. Preheat a heavy skillet or a charcoal grill.

2. Rub the steaks with the chopped rosemary and set aside.

3. Mix the chopped parsley, basil and garlic with the butter and season with salt and fresh ground pepper.

4. Place the steaks on the grill or in the pan over medium heat and cook each side to a golden brown as desired:

    - For rare, 5-6 minutes
    - For medium-rare, 7-8 minutes
    - For medium, 9-10 minutes
    - For medium well, 11-12 minutes
    - For well-done, 13-14 minutes

5. Remove steaks from the grill or pan, place on a serving platter and top each with one teaspoon of the herb butter mixture. Serve at once.

Serves 6

Filetto di Manzo alla Griglia con Salsa Robusta

Grilled Filet Mignon with Peppercorn Sauce

Many people enjoy Filet Mignon, which is so tender that you can cut it with a fork. This sauce will help to enhance the flavors and please the palate.

Ingredients:

8 Filet Mignon Steaks, 6 oz. each
1 Tbs. olive oil
2 Tbs. butter
1 small onion, finely chopped
1 clove garlic, minced
1 teaspoon flour
¼ cup sherry wine
1 cup beef stock
1 Tbs. whole crushed peppercorns, black or blended colors
1 cup heavy cream
Salt to taste
8 sprigs fresh rosemary to garnish

To prepare the sauce:

1. Melt one Tbs. of the butter with the oil and add the onions. Sauté over medium heat for approximately 4 minutes, until onions are softened, but not browned. Add the garlic, stir well and continue to sauté for an additional 4 minutes.

2. Add the sherry and allow it to evaporate. Mix the flour with 2 Tbs. of the beef stock to dissolve any lumps. Add to the pan, stir and add the remaining beef stock. Cook, stirring occasionally until mixture thickens, about 5 minutes.

3. Mix in the peppercorns and the cream and cook the sauce over medium heat for 7-8 minutes, until it is of a sauce consistency. Season with salt and add the remaining Tbs. of butter. Keep warm until ready to use.

Serves 8

To cook the beef:

1. Preheat charcoal grill or broiler. Brush steaks lightly with oil and cook to desired doneness, referring to chart in the previous recipe.

2. When done, place on a serving platter or plates and spoon sauce over meat. Serve remaining sauce on the side.

Manzo alla Pizzaiola

Steak Pizza-style

The word "pizzaiola" means in the style of pizza. Here the two main flavors of pizza sauce, tomato and oregano are featured.

Ingredients:

2 Tbs. olive oil
6 thinly sliced pieces of Beef Steak, such as chuck or flank
Flour for dredging
2 cloves garlic, minced
½ teaspoon oregano
3 basil leaves
1 28-oz. can crushed tomatoes
1 sprig flat-leaf parsley, chopped
Salt and freshly ground pepper to taste
1 lb. of your favorite pasta, such as Orecchiette or Farfalle

1. Pour the oil into a large, heavy skillet and heat.

2. Dredge the beef lightly in the flour and add to the skillet, cooking over a lively flame for just a minute on each side. Add the garlic and sauté lightly.

3. Pour in the tomatoes and add the parsley, oregano and basil. Reduce heat to a simmer and cover. Cook for 20 minutes, or until meat is tender. Season with salt and pepper to taste.

4. Meanwhile, boil pasta according to package instructions. When ready, place steak on a serving platter and use tomato sauce to mix with the drained pasta.

Serves 6

TRIPPA CON VERDURE

Tripe with Vegetables

This recipe was developed by Franca and it incorporates many textures of various vegetables and beans. Fr. Matt also consulted his mother for her input, since she would prepare tripe for his father over the years.

Ingredients:

3 lbs. fresh Tripe
5 carrots, peeled and cut coarsely
½ cup olive oil
3 sprigs flat-leaf parsley
1 lb. dried spotted kidney beans
2 onions, peeled and diced
3 celery stalks, coarsely chopped
3 cloves garlic, minced
2 bay leaves
6 cups chicken stock
1 cup grated Parmesan cheese
½ teaspoon red pepper flakes (optional)
1 28-oz. can crushed tomatoes
1 cup dry white wine
2 onions, quartered
2 cloves
3 Tbs. tomato paste
Salt and pepper to taste

1. Rinse the tripe very well in cold, salted water. Put in a strainer and let drain for 10 minutes. Place on a cutting board and cut tripe into strips measuring approximately 3 inches long and ½ inches wide. Put into a pot of cold water over medium heat and add the 2 bay leaves, one stalk of celery, cloves and one of the onions. Allow to boil for 3-4 minutes. Cover, remove from heat, and let sit for one hour.

2. Clean and rinse the dry beans and put them in a pot. Cover with water and allow to boil for 3-4 minutes. Cover, remove from heat, and let sit for one hour.

3. Meanwhile, in a large stockpot, warm the oil, add the other onion and sauté until transparent. Add the celery, carrots and stir. Chop the garlic and parsley together until very fine on a chopped board, and add and mix all ingredients together. Cook slowly until tender over low heat for 10 minutes.

4. Drain the tripe, remove the bay leaves and cloves and add to the vegetable mixture. Add the wine and bring to a simmer. Dilute the tomato paste in one cup of the chicken stock and add to the pot. Add the crushed tomatoes and stir well. Add salt and pepper to taste.

5. Drain the beans and add to the tripe as well as the remaining chicken broth. Cook for an additional hour until the beans and tripe are very tender. Serve with crostini or polenta and grated Parmesan cheese.

6. *For a variation of this recipe, try Trippa in Bianco (tripe in white sauce). Using the preceding recipe, omit the tomato paste and crushed tomato and add one medium sprig of rosemary and two finely chopped sage leaves at step 3.

Serves 6-8

ARROSTO DI VITELLO AL ROSMARINO

Veal Roast with Rosemary

In Italy, the veal roast is more typically served than the roast beef. Although it is called a roast, it is actually cooked on the stove top. The sage and other herbs perfectly complement the delicate taste of the veal.

Ingredients:

1 and ½ lbs. Veal Roast
Flour for dredging
2 Tbs. olive oil
2 Tbs. butter
1 sprig fresh rosemary
2 sage leaves
1 cup dry white wine
2 cups chicken broth
2 cloves garlic, chopped

1. Place the oil in a deep pot large enough to hold the roast and place over medium heat. Put the butter in the oil to melt.

2. Dredge the roast in the flour and brown on all sides to seal in the juices. Add the garlic, rosemary, sage and white wine. Reduce heat to a simmer and partially cover the pot.

3. Add the chicken broth a little at a time and turn the roast often to make sure it does not burn.

4. Cook for 1 to 1 and ½ hours until the meat is very tender when pricked with a fork. Add salt and freshly ground pepper to taste.

5. Remove veal and let rest a few minutes before slicing. Serve with fried potatoes and a green salad.

Serves 6

ARROSTO DI VITELLO AL FORNO

Oven-baked Veal Roast

As opposed to the previous recipe that is cooked on the stovetop, this veal roast is cooked in the oven. Once again, the fresh herbs help to underline the delicate taste of the veal. We suggest this be served with mashed potatoes, so that the fragrant gravy can add flavor to them as well.

Ingredients:

One 6-bone Veal Rib Roast – about 4 lbs.
2 Tbs. grated lemon peel
2 garlic cloves, chopped
2 teaspoons chopped fresh rosemary
1 sprig fresh rosemary
1 Tbs. unsalted butter, cut into small pieces
1 cup beef broth
1 cup chicken broth
1/3 cup fresh lemon juice
1/3 cup dry white wine
Salt and freshly ground pepper to taste

1. Rub veal roast with the lemon peel, garlic and rosemary. Let stand at room temperature for 15 minutes.

2. Preheat oven to 425 degrees. Place veal in a roasting pan elevated on a rack. Season lightly with salt and pepper and dot with the butter.

3. Roast, uncovered, for 30 minutes. Reduce temperature to 375 and continue to roast for an additional 40 to 45 minutes.

4. Meanwhile, combine the lemon juice, wine, chicken and beef broths in a heavy saucepan and boil for about 25 to 30 minutes until reduced to one cup.

5. Remove the roast from the pan and discard the grease, reserving pan juices. Stir the broth mixture in to the juices in the roasting pan, scraping the bottom well.

6. Return the mixture to a saucepan and reduce by boiling for an additional five minutes. Slice meat and serve with sauce.

Serves 6-8

PETTO DI VITELLO RIPIENO

Stuffed Veal Breast

This is a bit of an unusual cut of meat and has been enjoyed for its stuffing as well as the buttery and tender meat.

Ingredients:

3 lbs. fresh spinach or 8 oz. frozen spinach, thawed
2 lbs. Ricotta
3 eggs
3 Tbs. fresh chives, chopped
1 sprig fresh rosemary
2 Tbs. softened butter
One 6-lb. breast of Veal, with pocket
2 cups beef broth

½ cup plain breadcrumbs
½ cup grated Parmigiana-Reggiano cheese
2 sage leaves
2 cloves garlic, minced
1 large Portobello mushroom
8 oz. dry white wine
Salt and pepper to taste

1. If using fresh spinach, trim stems, clean well and boil in lightly salted water for several minutes until wilted. Drain, refresh under cold water and squeeze out all the liquid. Finely chop and reserve. If using thawed spinach, squeeze out water and finely chop.

2. In a bowl, place the ricotta, breadcrumbs, eggs, Parmesan cheese, spinach and chives. Mix all ingredients well and adjust seasonings with the salt and pepper to taste.

3. Fill the veal pocket with the stuffing and seal it with cooking thread or toothpicks.

4. Preheat the oven to 450 degrees. Meanwhile, mince the sage, rosemary and garlic and mix with the softened butter. Spread this mixture over the entire surface of the veal breast and place in a large baking pan. Add salt and pepper to taste.

5. Clean and slice the Portobello mushroom and place in the pan around the veal. Place veal in the oven and roast until light golden in color – about 15 to 20 minutes. Stir the mushrooms occasionally. Add the wine and the broth and reduce heat to 350 degrees and roast for 2 and ½ to 3 hours. Baste occasionally.

6. Remove the roast from the pan and let rest 20 to 30 minutes before carving. Meanwhile, strain the mushrooms over a bowl, reserving the gravy, and use the mushrooms later as a garnish. Skim the fat from the gravy and keep warm. If it is not of a desired thickness, make a paste with one Tbs. of flour and three Tbs. of water, and add to the gravy. Bring to a boil, stirring frequently and boil for one minute.

7. Carve about one-inch thick slices and serve with desired vegetable and a tossed green salad.

Serves 8-10

Osso buco Classico

Classic Veal Shanks

This recipe originates in the region of Lombardy, wherein lies the northern Italian city of Milan. It is best served accompanied by Risotto Milanese and with a bright Chianti wine.

Ingredients:

Flour for dredging
6 Veal Shanks, cut 2 and ½ inches thick
½ cup olive oil
1 cup dry white wine
1 Tbs. chopped lemon peel
3 Tbs. butter
1 Tbs. chopped flat-leaf parsley
1 Tbs. chopped basil
2 cloves garlic, chopped
2 medium onions, finely chopped
2 celery ribs, finely chopped
2 carrots, finely chopped
3 cups beef stock
Salt and freshly ground pepper to taste

1. Dredge the veal in the flour and shake off the excess.

2. Heat ¼ cup of the olive oil in a heavy large pan and brown the veal shanks for five minutes on each side over medium heat. Add the lemon peel and the wine to deglaze the pan and reduce heat to simmer.

3. In another skillet, add the remaining oil and 2 Tbs. of the butter. Add all the remaining chopped ingredients. Sauté over moderate heat until tender, approximately 15 minutes, stirring frequently.

4. Add the vegetables to the veal and half of the beef stock. Cook, covered, over low heat until the meat is very tender – about 1 and ½ to 2 hours. Add additional stock throughout the cooking time to keep moist. Stir frequently while cooking, making sure the meat does not stock to the pan.

5. Meat is tender when tested with a fork. Remove from the pan and keep warm. The sauce should be thick. If not, turn up the heat and reduce until thickened to a desired consistency. Pour over veal and serve.

Serves 6

Note: This recipe is best served with Risotto Milanese on page 94.

Osso buco in Rosso

Veal Shanks with Tomato

A variation of the prior recipe, but here is featuring the flavor of tomato.

Proceed using the preceding recipe, adding 1 Tbs. tomato paste and one cup crushed tomatoes when adding the chopped vegetables and broth to the veal shanks at step 4.

This variation is best served with polenta on page 102.

Vitello Saltimbocca alla Romana

"Jump-into-the-mouth" Veal, Roman-style

This is a specialty of the Eternal City of Rome and combines a variety of flavors. It is enjoyed all year long and through not just Italy, but the world.

Ingredients:

12 Veal scallops
12 thin slices of prosciutto
12 fresh sage leaves or 1 teaspoon dried sage
Flour for dredging
6 Tbs. (3/4 stick) butter
1 cup dry white wine
Salt and ground pepper to taste

1. Place the veal scallops between layers of wax paper and pound to make thin and tenderize.

2. Lay a slice of prosciutto and a sage leaf on each slice of veal and affix with a toothpick. You may also roll the veal out with the prosciutto and sage on the inside. Dredge the veal in flour and set aside.

3. Place half the butter in a large skillet and melt and cook the veal for approximately two minutes on each side season with salt and pepper.

4. Add the wine and allow to evaporate by half. Remove the veal and keep warm add the remaining butter to the wine and melt, stirring to make a glaze. Pour over the veal and serve. Remove toothpicks before serving.

5. Serve with Potato Croquettes and Spinach Aglio e Olio.

Serves 6

COTOLETTA ALLA MILANESE

Breaded Veal Cutlets Milan Style

This basic veal cutlet is pure and unadulterated and allows the delicate taste of the veal to come through. The squeeze of the lemon accentuates the flavors.

Ingredients:

12 Veal cutlets
2 eggs, lightly beaten, more if needed
2 Tbs. milk, more if needed
1 teaspoon fresh rosemary, finely chopped
Oil for frying, either olive or vegetable oil
2 to 3 cups breadcrumbs
1 Tbs. Parmigiana-Reggiano cheese
1 Tbs. flat-leaf parsley, finely chopped
Salt and pepper to taste
6 lemon wedges for garnish
1 clove garlic, unpeeled

1. Combine the breadcrumbs with the cheese, parsley, rosemary and salt and pepper to taste and reserve.

2. Combine the egg with the milk and mix well.

3. If not already done by the butcher, pound the veal by placing between two sheets of plastic wrap or wax paper and flatten with a rolling pin or mallet.

4. Dip the veal in the egg mixture and then coat with seasoned breadcrumbs.

5. Pound the unpeeled garlic clove and place in the frying pan with the oil. Heat over a lively fire and when garlic begins to sizzle, add the veal cutlets.

6. Fry on each side until golden. Serve hot with lemon wedges and green vegetable of your choice.

Serves 6

Cotolette di Vitello alla Parmigiana

Parma-style Veal Cutlet

This very famous veal cutlet is well known and originated in the Province of Parma, home to the well known Parmigiana-Reggiano cheese. Over the years, mozzarella has also been incorporated into the dish.

Ingredients:

1 recipe Veal cutlet Milanese (see previous recipe)
1 recipe Tomato and fresh Basil Sauce (page 8)
1 lb. mozzarella cheese cut in 12 slices
3 Tbs. grated Parmigiana-Reggiano cheese

1. Prepare the sauce and set aside.

2. Prepare the veal cutlets as directed in above recipe, omitting the lemon wedges.

3. Cover bottom of a baking dish with the sauce. Place the breaded cutlets in the pan. Do no overlap – use an additional baking pan if needed.

4. Spoon sauce over the cutlets, covering them well. Sprinkle the grated cheese over them and place a slice of mozzarella on each cutlet.

5. Bake in a preheated, 350-degree oven for approximately 15 to 20 minutes, or until cheese has melted. Serve hot with the pasta of your choice.

Serves 6

Cotolette di Vitello Primavera

Spring-style Veal Cutlets

Here, the refreshing salad is placed on top of the cutlet and there is an interesting interplay of hot and cool. What a delightful summer dish that Fr. Matt first sampled with his sister and brother-in-law at a trattoria in Milano twenty years ago.

Ingredients:

1 recipe Veal cutlet Milanese (see page 150)
2 bunches arugula salad
6 medium ripe tomatoes
1 peeled garlic clove, mashed
Salt and freshly ground pepper to taste
1 lb. mozzarella or Fontina cheese cut in 12 pieces
10 fresh basil leaves, torn
¾ cup extra virgin olive oil

1. Wash tomatoes, remove stems, and dice. Place in a glass or ceramic bowl and add the mashed garlic, basil, ½ cup of the oil and the salt and pepper. Mix well, cover and set aside. Let rest for at least an hour so that the flavors blend well.

2. Prepare the arugula by washing and drying the leaves. Cut with a scissor and mix with the reserved ¼ cup oil, salt and pepper. Place on a serving platter.

3. Prepare the veal cutlets according to the recipe, omitting lemon wedges. Place in a baking dish, cover with the cheese slices and bake in a preheated 350-degree oven until cheese is melted but not browned.

4. Place veal cutlets over arugula and top with the tomato mixture and serve immediately.

Serves 6

COTOLETTE RIPIENE AL PROSCIUTTO E FONTINA

Veal stuffed with Parma Ham and Fontina Cheese

This is the Italian version of Veal Cordon Bleu and enjoyed by many. Here we try to incorporate the traditional ingredients, but with an Italian flair.

Ingredients:

8 Veal cutlets, thinly sliced
½ lb. prosciutto
½ lb. Fontina cheese
2 eggs, lightly beaten
2 Tbs. milk
Salt and pepper to taste
Oil for frying (either olive or vegetable)
Breadcrumbs
1 unpeeled garlic clove

1. Cut the cheese into eight pieces.

2. Place veal cutlets on a flat surface. Cover with the slices of prosciutto and place a piece of cheese in the middle. Fold each cutlet in half, overlapping the edges. Seal with a toothpick if desired.

3. Dip in egg, coat with breadcrumbs, trying to seal around the edges.

4. Pound the garlic clove, place it in a heavy skillet with the oil. When the garlic begins to sizzle, add the veal pockets. Fry until golden brown on each side. Lower heat and continue to cook one additional minute on each side to allow cheese to melt.

5. Veal can be served with roasted potatoes and fresh spinach salad with lemon-vinaigrette dressing.

Serves 8

Scallopine di Vitello alla Piccata

Veal Scallopine with Lemon Sauce

This has also been called "alla Francese," because Caterina de' Medici brought her Italian cooks to France when she moved there to become queen in 1547. There has been a combination of flavors across the borders. This recipe carries the Italian name.

Ingredients:

18 Veal scallopine, thinly cut (approximately 3-inch squares)

Flour for dredging

6 Tbs. butter

2 Tbs. olive oil

4 Tbs. fresh lemon

6 oz. dry white wine

1 Tbs. capers

2 sprigs flat-leaf parsley, finely chopped

Salt and freshly ground pepper to taste

1 teaspoon flour (if needed)

1 lemon, sliced

1. Dredge the veal in flour, shaking off excess.

2. Heat the 4 Tbs. of the butter and oil in a skillet until they begin to sizzle. Place the veal scallopine. in the skillet and fry the meat quickly. This will take only a few minutes. Remove veal and place on a heated serving platter. Keep hot.

3. Into the same skillet, add the lemon juice, wine, capers and parsley. If it is necessary to thicken the sauce, mix the teaspoon of flour with one Tbs. of the meat broth to make a paste and add to skillet. Stir well until it begins to bubble. Add salt and pepper to taste. Remove from heat, stir in the remaining butter and mix until incorporated. Pour sauce over scallopine.

4. Garnish with lemon slices and serve immediately.

Serves 6

MEDAGLIONI DI VITELLO ALLA MARSALA

Veal Medallions in Marsala Sauce

This is typical of the north of Italy, although the city of Marsala is on the west coast of Sicily. The wine from there has been used in cooking and baking because of its distinct flavor.

Ingredients:

18 Veal scallops, thinly cut (approx. 3-inch rounds)
3 Tbs. lemon juice
Flour for dredging
4 Tbs. olive oil
2 cups cleaned and thinly sliced mushrooms
Salt and pepper to taste
4 Tbs. butter
1 teaspoon flour (if needed)
4 oz. Marsala wine
4 oz. beef stock
1 unpeeled garlic clove, crushed

1. Sprinkle the veal with the lemon juice and let it marinate for about 15-20 minutes.

2. Heat 2 Tbs. of olive oil in a skillet and add the mushrooms. Sauté over moderate heat, stirring occasionally until tender. Add salt and pepper to taste and turn off heat.

3. Dry the veal, dredge in flour, shaking off excess.

4. Place the butter and remaining 2 Tbs. of the oil in a skillet with the unpeeled garlic clove and heat until the garlic begins to sizzle.

5. Add the veal and fry for 2 to 3 minutes on each side until lightly browned. When all are browned, add the Marsala wine and beef stock. If necessary to thicken the sauce, mix in the teaspoon of flour with a Tbs. of the stock to make a paste, then add it to the skillet. Add the mushrooms and sauté over a lively flame for an additional three minutes to reduce the sauce. Serve immediately.

Serves 6

Medaglioni di Vitello al Vino Bianco

Veal medallions in white wine sauce

Here we have a variation and are using a more delicate and much lighter wine than in the previous recipe.

Proceed, using the preceding recipes, substituting dry white wine for the Marsala. The mushrooms are optional.

Serves 6

Medaglioni di Vitello a L'Ortolana

Veal Medallions Garden-style

The word, "ortolana" refers to the lady who tends the garden, and this veal dish incorporates several vegetables. You can also substitute artichoke hearts in place of the asparagus for a different taste.

1. Proceed using the Veal Marsala recipe, substituting dry white wine for the Marsala.

2. Reduce sliced mushrooms to one cup, adding one cup asparagus tips cooked al dente.

3. Slice 3 garlic cloves, sauté in 1 Tbs. of olive oil until lightly browned and add during the last three minutes of cooking time.

Serves 6

MEDAGLIONI DI VITELLO AI PISELLI

Veal Medallions with Peas

This recipe has been well known over the years. The sweetness of the peas adds a characteristic flavor to the tender and delicate flavor of the veal.

Ingredients:

18 Veal scallops, thinly cut (approx. 3-inch rounds)
3 Tbs. lemon juice
Flour for dredging
1 small onion, finely chopped
1 sprig flat-leaf parsley, finely chopped
1 garlic clove, minced
12 oz. beef stock
Salt and fresh pepper to taste
5 Tbs. butter
5 Tbs. olive oil
1 unpeeled garlic clove, crushed
2 cups fresh or frozen peas
2 basil leaves, finely chopped

1. Sprinkle the veal with lemon juice and let marinate for 15-20 minutes.

2. Sauté the onion in one Tbs. each of the butter and oil until softened. Add the garlic and cook an additional minute or two, not allowing to burn. Add the peas, beef stock, parsley and basil and cook until the peas are tender. Add salt and pepper to taste.

3. Dry the veal dredge in flour, shaking off excess.

4. Place the remaining butter and oil in a skillet with the unpeeled garlic clove and heat until the garlic begins to sizzle.

5. Add the veal and fry on each side for 2-3 minutes until golden brown.

6. Add the peas with the stock, cook over a lively flame for three minutes. If necessary to thicken the sauce, add one teaspoon flour mixed with 2 teaspoons stock made into a paste to the cooking mixture before the final three minutes of cooking time.

7. Serve immediately with Potato croquettes.

Serves 6

NODINI DI VITELLO VALDOSTANA

Veal Chop from the Val d'Aosta region

This recipe is named for the region called Val d'Aosta, which borders France to the west and Switzerland to the north. The flavors incorporated in the recipe are typical from that region.

Ingredients:

6 Veal chops, approximately 8 oz. each
3 slices prosciutto ham
4 oz. Fontina cheese, thinly sliced
2 eggs, well beaten
Flour for dredging
½ cup breadcrumbs
1 package (10 oz.) fresh spinach
3 Tbs. butter
1 unpeeled garlic clove, crushed
1 teaspoon grated Parmigiana-Reggiano cheese
3 Tbs. oil
Lemon vinaigrette dressing

1. Slit each chop horizontally almost to the bone, making a pocket for the filling.

2. Cut the prosciutto slices in half and fill each chop with the prosciutto and cheese. Press the edges around the chop to seal in the filling. Dredge in the flour, then dredge in the egg and breadcrumbs mixed with the grated Parmesan.

3. Place the butter and oil in a skillet with the unpeeled garlic clove, heat until the garlic begins to sizzle.

4. Sauté the veal chops in the pan until golden brown on both sides – about 6 to 7 minutes on each side.

5. Drain on paper towels and serve over a bed of fresh spinach that has been tossed with lemon vinaigrette dressing.

Serves 6

Variazioni di Nodino di Vitello
Variations on the Veal Chop recipes

Milanese: Follow the Cotolette Milanese recipe, (page 150) allowing 4-5 minutes cooking time on each side due to thickness.

Primavera: Follow the Cotolette Primavera recipe, (page 152) allowing 4-5 minutes cooking time for each side of the veal chop.

Piccata: Follow the Scallopine di Vitello recipe, (page 154) allowing 4-5 minutes cooking time on each side of the veal chop.

Marsala: Follow the Medaglioni di Vitello recipe, (page 155) allowing 4-5 minutes cooking time on each side of the veal chop.

Vino Bianco: Follow the Medaglioni di Vitello in Bianco recipe, (page 156) allowing 4-5 minutes cooking time on each side of the veal chop.

Ortolana: Follow the Medaglioni di Vitello all'Ortolana recipe, (page 156) allowing 4-5 minutes cooking time on each side of the veal chop.

Piselli: Follow the Medaglioni di Vitello ai Piselli recipe, (page 157) allowing 4-5 minutes cooking time on each side of the veal chop.

NODINI DI VITELLO BALSAMICO

Veal Chop with Balsamic Glaze

This recipe is from Modena, in the region of Emilia-Romagna, where this sweet and sour vinegar originates.

Ingredients:

6 Veal chops, approximately 8 oz. each
1 and ½ lbs. small or pearl onions
1 Tbs. olive oil
½ cup balsamic vinegar
3 Tbs. sugar
1 Tbs. butter
1 teaspoon peppercorns (optional)

1. Peel the onions and add to the boiling salted water. Boil for five minutes, then drain.

2. Heat the oil and butter together and add the onions. Sauté over low heat for 10 to 15 minutes until a golden color.

3. Pour the sugar into a heavy saucepan. Heat over a high flame, stirring constantly until it begins to melt and turn a caramel color. Cook to a medium brown and then add in the vinegar and stir well. Pour the onions into this mixture and keep warm while grilling the veal chops.

4. To grill, you may use an outdoor grill or stovetop. When well-heated, place chops on the grill and cook 4-5 minutes on each side. Top with the onions and balsamic vinegar glaze and serve.

Serves 6

NODINI DI VITELLO ALLA GORGONZOLA

Veal Chop with Gorgonzola

This soft cheese is from a town in the region of Lombardy and is well known throughout the world. The American version is called Blue Cheese and the French version is called Roquefort. It has a very distinct flavor, which joins well with the sweet and delicate taste of the veal.

Ingredients:

6 Veal chops, approximately 8 oz. each
½ clove garlic, minced
2 oz. gorgonzola cheese, crumbled
1 sprig flat-leaf parsley, finely chopped
2 Tbs. butter, softened
Salt and pepper to taste

1. Mix the garlic, cheese, parsley and butter in a bowl with a wooden spoon. Season with salt and pepper. Form into six small balls, place on wax paper and chill.

2. Grill the veal chops on a very hot outdoor grill or a heavy frying pan for 5 to 6 minutes per side. Top with gorgonzola butter and serve.

Serves 6

VITELLO TONNATO

Veal in Tuna Sauce

This is a summer dish, typical of Piedmont in the north, but now enjoyed throughout all of Italy. It is usually served cold or at room temperature.

Ingredients:

2 lbs. of tenderloin of Veal, in one piece
1 carrot, peeled
1 stalk celery
1 small onion, peeled and quartered
1 clove
1 bay leaf
1 tsp. whole peppercorns

For the tuna sauce:

14 oz. canned Tuna, preferably in olive oil
4 anchovy filets
2 tsp. capers, rinsed and drained
3 Tbs. fresh lemon juice
1 ¼ cups mayonnaise
Salt and freshly ground black pepper
Capers, to garnish

1. Place the veal, vegetables and flavorings in a medium saucepan. Cover with water. Bring to a boil and simmer for 50-60 minutes. Skim off any scum that rises to the surface. Do not overcook, or the veal will fall apart when sliced. Allow veal to cool in its cooking liquid for several hours, or overnight.

2. Drain the tuna. Place it in a food processor and add the anchovies, capers and lemon juice. Process to a creamy paste. If it seems too thick, add 2-3 Tbs. of the cool veal stock and process again.

3. Scrape the tuna puree into a bowl. Fold in the mayonnaise. Check the seasoning and adjust as necessary. Slice the veal as thinly as possible. Spread a little of the tuna sauce over the bottom of a serving platter.

4. Arrange a layer of the veal slices on top of the sauce. Cover with a thin layer of sauce. Make another layer or two of veal slices and sauce, ending with the sauce. Garnish with the capers. Cover with plastic wrap and refrigerate until needed.

Serves 6-8

FEGATO ALLA VENEZIANA

Venetian-style Liver

This liver is a classic that originated in the city of Venice. It is enhanced here with our own addition of the garlic and parsley to add additional flavor.

Ingredients:

½ cup olive oil
5 Tbs. butter
4 to 5 large onions, peeled and thinly sliced
2 garlic cloves, finely chopped
2-3 sprigs flat-leaf parsley, finely chopped
6 slices of white bread, cut in quarters
2 and ½ lbs. Calves Liver, thinly sliced
Salt and pepper to taste
4 Tbs. beef stock
Flour for dredging

1. Place ¼ cup of the oil and 2 Tbs. of the butter in a large frying pan; add the onions and sauté until light golden – about 10 minutes. Add the garlic and parsley and stir well. Reduce heat and cover, cooking very slowly for an additional 20 minutes. Add salt and pepper to taste.

2. Place remaining butter in a frying pan and heat. When it begins to sizzle, add the bread and brown on each side. Place on paper towels when done.

3. Into the pan where the bread was browned, add the remaining ¼ cup olive oil. Turn up the heat and add the liver and cook for about 3 minutes on each side. Liver should be slightly pink inside. Add the cooked liver to the onions and deglaze the pan with the beef stock. Add this to the liver and onions. Stir quickly and serve, garnished with the fried bread crostini.

4. This can be served with mashed potatoes or hot polenta.

Serves 6

FEGATO DI VITELLO ALLA MILANESE

Veal Liver Milan Style

This was our own invention and we named it for the beautiful and stylish city of Milano. Dredging the liver in flour makes an outer crust and helps to seal in the moisture.

Ingredients:

2 lbs. Veal Liver, sliced 1/2 –inches thick
3 Tbs. butter
6 lemon slices for garnish
Flour for dredging
Salt and freshly ground pepper
Juice of ½ lemon
1 sprig parsley, chopped

1. Add salt and pepper to the flour. Dredge the liver in the flour and set aside.

2. Melt the butter in a heavy skillet over lively fire and add the liver, cooking for about 3 minutes on each side. Add the lemon juice and coat the liver in the sauce that forms.

3. Place on a serving dish and garnish with lemon slices. Serve with arugula or green salad of your choice.

Serves 6

MAIALE *(Pork)*

ARROSTO DI MAIALE TOSCANO

Tuscan Style Pork Roast

This recipe incorporates the flavors of Tuscany and in particular the herbs that are typically used for the Bistecca Fiorentina. The aromatic flavors are made more fragrant during the roasting.

Ingredients:

1 large rosemary sprig, finely chopped
2 sprigs flat-leaf parsley, finely chopped
3 garlic cloves, minced
1 Tbs. softened butter
4-5 lb. loin of Pork Roast
1 cup dry white wine or vermouth
Salt and pepper to taste
2 Tbs. olive oil
1 cup beef broth

1. Preheat oven to 375 degrees.

2. Mix the rosemary, parsley and garlic together and finely chop. Mix with the softened butter to make a paste.

3. With a sharp knife, cut small pockets in the pork roast about 2 inches deep and insert ½ teaspoon of the paste, using either your finger or the back of a spoon. Reserve one teaspoon of the herb paste for basting.

4. Spread the olive oil over the surface of the roast and sprinkle with the salt and pepper. Place in an ovenproof pan and roast all sides until golden – about 30 minutes.

5. Pour the wine or vermouth over the roast and lower the heat to 350 degrees, then spread with the reserved herb butter and roast uncovered for an additional 1 and ½ hours, basting with the beef broth occasionally but not allowing the bottom of the pan to dry out.

6. Remove the roast from the oven and place on a serving platter to rest for 5 minutes.

7. Degrease the pan juices and add the remainder of the beef broth to make a natural gravy. If necessary, dilute one Tbs. flour with 2 Tbs. broth or water and add to the pan juices. Bring to a boil in a saucepan and serve hot with the sliced meat.

Serves 6

ARROSTO DI MAIALE AGRODOLCE

Sweet and Sour Pork

There is something unique about the sweet and sour taste which has a certain complexity. Here we joined it to the heartiness of the pork.

Ingredients:

4-5 lb. loin of Pork Roast
1 Tbs. brown sugar
1 sprig fresh rosemary, chopped
4 Tbs. olive oil
2 medium onions, thinly sliced
1 cup balsamic vinegar
1 cup beef stock
2 garlic cloves, minced
Freshly ground pepper
Salt to taste

1. Generously coat the roast with the 2 Tbs. of the oil, the ground pepper and salt and brown on all sides over medium flame in an ovenproof pan.

2. Place the pan with the roast in a preheated 375-degree oven for 1 hour.

3. While the pork is baking, prepare the sweet sour sauce. Place the remaining 2 Tbs. of the oil in a heavy skillet and sauté the sliced onions until transparent. Add the chopped garlic, rosemary and the brown sugar. Add salt and pepper and stir well.

4. Add the balsamic vinegar and ½ cup of the beef stock. Bring to a boil then reduce heat and let simmer.

5. When the meat has baked the first hour, remove from the oven and pour the onion sauce over it and bake for an additional hour. Baste occasionally with the remaining beef broth.

6. When done, place meat on a serving dish, slice and top with the sweet sour sauce.

Serves 6

Arrosto di Maiale Tirolese

Tyrolean Style Pork Roast

The area of the Tyrol is in southern Austrian, very near to Belluno in northern Italy. Here the robust flavors of the Germanic lands are featured.

Ingredients:

4-5 lb. loin of Pork Roast
2 lbs. Sauerkraut
1 Tbs. oil
1 sprig rosemary, finely chopped
2 medium onions, chopped
6 slices smoked bacon
Freshly ground pepper and salt
1 Tbs. caraway seeds (optional)

1. Preheat oven to 375 degrees.

2. Coat the roast with the oil, pepper, salt and rosemary and place in oven for a total cooking time of two hours.

3. Cut the bacon into one-inch pieces and place in heavy skillet. Fry lightly for a few minutes, add the onion and sauté until onion becomes tender.

4. Drain the sauerkraut in a colander and add to the skillet with the caraway seeds, if desired. Stir, cooking until heated through.

5. Add to the pan with the roast for the last hour of the cooking time. Add salt and pepper to taste.

6. Slice the roast and serve with sauerkraut on the side and potato pancakes.

Serves 6

Arrosto di Maiale alla Salsa Forte

Pork Roast in "Strong sauce"

The word "forte" means strong, sturdy or stout and this sauce is just that.

Ingredients:

6 oz. beer
½ cup Dijon mustard
6 Tbs. honey
¼ cup olive oil
2 Tbs. chopped fresh rosemary
2 garlic cloves, minced
3-4 lb. loin of Pork Roast
½ cup whipping cream
Salt and pepper to taste
Fresh rosemary sprig for garnish

1. In a large bowl combine beer, mustard, honey, oil, chopped rosemary and garlic and mix well.

2. Place the roast in a deep baking dish and pour the marinade over it. Turn to coat well. Let stand at room temperature for one hour or in the refrigerator overnight.

3. Place the pork into the roasting pan, fitted with a rack. Reserve marinade. Place in a preheated 350-degree oven for 1 and ¾ hours. A meat thermometer inserted in the center should register 150 degrees.

4. Remove roast from oven and let rest for 15 minutes.

5. Meanwhile, strain the marinade into a heavy medium saucepan and add the cream and roasting pan juices. Boil the sauce until reduced to 1 and ½ cups, about 15 minutes, and then season with salt and pepper.

6. Slice pork roast and arrange on a serving platter. Drizzle some sauce over it and serve the remaining sauce on the table.

Serves 6

PROSCIUTTO ARROSTO

Baked Ham

This is the typical Baked Ham that many American households serve for special occasions. It is particularly associated with Easter the aromatic spices fill the air with a festive spirit.

Ingredients:

6-7 lb. fully cooked Smoked Ham with bone
1 teaspoon cinnamon
8 whole cloves
3 Tbs. butter
3 Tbs. brown sugar
6 oz. apple cider or orange juice

1. Place ham in a large pot of boiling water. Reduce to a simmer and cook for 30 minutes.

2. Remove the ham from the pot and place in a baking pan. Using a sharp knife, make slits to insert the whole cloves. Place into a preheated 350-degree oven for 1 hour and 15 minutes, allowing approximately 15 minutes per lb.

3. Pour one cup of the water in which the ham was boiled into the base of the pan.

4. To make the glaze, melt butter in a small saucepan. Add the apple cider or orange juice and cinnamon and stir in the brown sugar.

5. Remove the ham and cover with the glaze and return to the oven for the last 20 minutes of the cooking time.

6. Take the pan drippings, remove the fat and place into a saucepan. Mix one Tbs. flour with 2 Tbs. water and add to pan. Bring to a boil to thicken. Serve over the sliced ham.

Serves 6 -8

COSTOLETTE DI MAIALE ALLE CIPOLLE

Pork Chops in Onion Sauce

We have incorporated the sweetness of the onions with the aromatic flavors of the other herbs to help enhance the pork chop. It is an interesting melding of flavors.

Ingredients:

Salt and pepper to taste

Flour for dredging

9 Pork chops

2 Tbs. olive oil

2 garlic cloves, minced

2 large onions, thinly sliced

3 sprigs flat-leaf parsley, finely chopped

1 and ½ cups beef stock

3 basil leaves, chopped

1 unpeeled garlic clove, crushed

1. Add salt and ground pepper to the flour and dredge pork chops in it.

2. Heat the oil in a heavy skillet and add the unpeeled garlic clove. When it begins to sizzle add the pork chops and brown over a high flame for a few minutes on each side. Reserve pork chops and discard the garlic clove.

3. Place the onions in the same skillet and cook about 10 minutes until softened. Add the chopped garlic, parsley, basil and stir well. Add the stock and bring to a simmer.

4. Return the pork chops to the pan and cook, covered, for an additional 30 minutes until tender.

Serves 6

Costolette di Maiale Milanese

Breaded Pork Chops

Here is the pork version of the classic breaded veal cutlet, complete with a tangy apple plum sauce to help compliment the flavor.

Ingredients:

Six Pork chops, ½-inches thick
1 Tbs. milk
1 Tbs. Parmigiana-Reggiano cheese
Oil for frying
2 egg, lightly beaten
2 to 3 cups breadcrumbs
1 sprig flat-leaf parsley, finely chopped
6 lemon wedges
1 unpeeled garlic clove, crushed
Salt and freshly ground pepper to taste

1. Combine the breadcrumbs with the parsley, Parmesan cheese, salt and pepper and set aside. In a separate bowl, add the eggs and milk and mix well.

2. Dip the pork chops in the egg mixture and then coat in the seasoned breadcrumbs.

3. Pound the unpeeled garlic clove and place in the frying pan with the oil. Heat over a lively fire and when the garlic begins to sizzle, add the pork chops.

4. Reduce heat to medium and fry on each side for about 2 to 4 minutes until golden in color.

5. Serve with apple-plum sauce.

Serves 6

Apple Plum Sauce

Ingredients:

4 apples, peeled seeded and cut in chunks
2 Tbs. sugar
5 small red plums, seeded and peeled
½ cup water
Peel of ½ a lemon

1. Mix the sugar and water in a saucepan. Add the fruit and peel and cook until tender

2. Remove peel and mash fruit with a potato masher. Serve room temperature or chilled, as desired.

COSTOLETTE DI MAIALE RIPIENE

Stuffed Pork Chops

Here we have a true delight and the savory flavors complement each other so well.

Ingredients:

6 loin Pork chops, approximately 1-inch thick
2 eggs, lightly beaten
3 and ½ cups breadcrumbs
½ cups grated Parmesan cheese
2 sprigs of flat-leaf parsley, finely chopped
3 basil leaves, finely chopped
2 cloves garlic, minced
1 Tbs. milk
1 recipe mushroom sauce
Oil for frying
Salt and freshly ground pepper to taste

Ingredients for the mushroom sauce:

2 Tbs. butter
2 Tbs. olive oil
1 lb. mushrooms, sliced
1 large onion, finely chopped
2 cloves garlic, finely chopped
½ cup dry white wine
3 sprigs flat-leaf parsley, finely chopped
3 basil leaves, finely chopped
3 cups beef broth
2 Tbs. flour
Salt and pepper to taste

To prepare the mushroom sauce:

1. Sauté the onion in the oil and butter until golden brown. Add garlic, mushrooms, parsley and basil and sauté over lively flame, mixing occasionally, but do not allow to burn. Add the wine and allow to evaporate completely. Mix the 2 Tbs. flour with 2 Tbs. of the beef broth until smooth. Add to the mushroom mixture.

2. Add the rest of the broth, mixing constantly. Lower the heat and cook for 10 minutes. Add salt and pepper to taste if necessary.

To prepare the pork chops:

1. Cut a deep pocket in each pork chop from one side only.

2. Prepare stuffing by mixing 1 and ½ cups of the bread crumbs with the parsley, basil, garlic, Parmesan cheese, salt, pepper and olive oil.

3. Distribute stuffing evenly, filling each pork chop. Use a wooden toothpick to close each pocket.

4. Mix the beaten egg with the milk in a bowl. Dip each pork chop in this mixture and then in the remaining breadcrumbs.

5. Fry each pork chop over moderate heat for about 3-4 minutes on each side.

6. Cover the bottom of a baking dish with some of the mushroom sauce. Place the stuffed pork chops in the pan, cover with remaining sauce and then with foil.

7. Bake in 350-degree oven for 20 to 25 minutes. **Serves 6**

INVOLTINI DI MAIALE AL POMODORO

Pork Rolls in Tomato Sauce

Follow the recipe for Involtini di Manzo Napoletana (page 138) and substitute Pork cutlets for the thinly sliced beef.

COSTOLETTE DI MAIALE PICCANTE

Spicy Spare Ribs

These are just perfect for the summer barbeque or any time of the year, whenever you feel that these tasty spare ribs may fit the occasion.

Ingredients:

2 racks of Pork spare ribs, approximately 6 lbs.
2 cloves garlic, finely chopped
1 small sprig of fresh rosemary, finely chopped

For the sauce:

½ cup red wine vinegar
Juice of ½ lemon
4 Tbs. soy sauce
2 cloves garlic
5 apricots, fresh (pitted) or dried or 5 Tbs. apricot preserves
3 Tbs. brown sugar
3 Tbs. tomato paste
¼ teaspoon hot red pepper flakes
1 small sprig rosemary
¼ cup water
½ cup ketchup

1. Rub the spare ribs with the garlic and rosemary and place in a baking dish in a preheated 375-degree oven. Roast, uncovered, for 20 minutes.

2. Meanwhile, make the sauce by combining all ingredients in a food processor or blender. You may also mix in a bowl, being sure to finely chop the apricots, garlic and rosemary.

3. Remove the spare ribs from the oven and drain and discard the fat. Coat them with the glaze, cover with foil and return to the oven for an additional 25 to 30 minutes. Test with a fork. The ribs should be very tender. Serve hot.   **Serves 6**

Salsiccia e Peperoni

Sausage and Peppers

Please note that there is no tomato sauce in this recipe, but just the subtle and natural flavors that meld together from the peppers, fresh tomatoes and onions.

Ingredients:

2 lbs. Italian Pork sausage, sweet or hot as desired
1 and ½ cups water
2 garlic cloves, minced
4 large bell peppers
5 fresh plum tomatoes
2 medium onions
½ cup olive oil
3-4 basil leaves, coarsely chopped
3 sprigs flat-leaf parsley, finely chopped
½ teaspoon sugar
Salt and pepper to taste

1. Prick the sausage all over with a fork. Place in a heavy skillet and brown over moderate heat, adding ½ cup of the water at little at a time to prevent sausage from burning. Brown well on all sides – about 15 minutes.

2. Add the garlic, stir quickly and add the remaining cup of water. Reduce heat to a simmer and cook until very tender – about 30 minutes.

3. Meanwhile, prepare the vegetables: Cut the peppers in half. Remove the stem and seeds and cut into ½-inch strips. Peel and slice the onions. If desired, peel the tomatoes by plunging into boiling water until the skins burst. Cut the tomatoes into medium sized chunks and place in a bowl with the basil and parsley.

4. Pour ½ cup olive oil into a heavy frying pan. Add the peppers and onions and place over a lively fire. Fry, stirring frequently, until tender but not overcooked, about 10 to 15 minutes.

5. Add the tomatoes, parsley and basil and ½ teaspoon sugar. Stir well and continue to cook for an additional five minutes. Turn off the heat and cover.

6. Remove the sausage from the frying pan and cut diagonally into 2 to 3-inch pieces, or as desired.

7. Skim the fat off the sausage pan juices and reserve the brown juice. Add the sausage, and its brown juices, to the pepper mixture. Combine ingredients well, add salt and pepper to taste, heat for about 5 additional minutes and serve. **Serves 6-8**

AGNELLO *(Lamb)*

COSCIOTTO DI AGNELLO ARROSTO AL VINO BIANCO

Roast leg of Lamb with White Wine

This is the centerpiece for another great festive holiday meal, mostly associated with Easter Sunday dinner, but it is just perfect for any occasion.

Ingredients:

6-8 lb. Leg of Lamb with bone
8 sprigs flat-leaf parsley, finely chopped
8 oz. dry white wine
1 cup chicken stock
3 Tbs. olive oil
4 garlic cloves, minced
2 Tbs. butter, softened
2 sprigs fresh rosemary
Salt and freshly ground pepper to taste

1. Preheat oven to 450 degrees.

2. Wash leg of lamb and pat dry. In a small bowl, combine the parsley, garlic and butter and salt and pepper to make a paste. With a small, sharp knife, make 12 pockets, about 1 and ½-inch to 2-inch deep into the roast. With a small spoon or your finger, insert the paste into the pockets, distributing evenly.

3. Coat the roast with the oil and sprinkle with salt and pepper. Place in a large baking dish.

4. Cook the roast 25 minutes per lb. for well-done and 20 minutes per lb. for medium-rare. Calculate complete cooking time according to the weight. Roast for the first 30 minutes at 450 degrees. Then, open the oven, baste with the wine and add the rosemary. Reduce oven to 375 degrees and roast for additional time as needed. For medium rare, thermometer should be at 150 degrees; for medium to well-done, it should read 160 degrees.

5. Baste occasionally with the chicken stock while roasting so it does not dry out. When done, remove from oven and let rest 10 minutes before carving.

6. Serve with natural pan juices.

Serves 6-8

Cosciotto di Agnello al Pesto

Roast Leg of Lamb with Pesto

Refer to the previous recipe and use the following variations: Cut the garlic into thin slivers and substitute the parsley with 5 to 6 coarsely chopped basil leaves. Place in lamb pockets as directed.

Pesto recipe:

4 garlic cloves
8 basil leaves
½ cup olive oil
¾ cup grated Parmigiana-Reggiano cheese

1. Mix ingredients in food processor until a creamy paste consistency.

2. Spread the pesto on the roast for the last 10 minutes of baking time.

3. Proceed with recipe as directed above.

Cosciotto di Agnello Ripieno

Stuffed Leg of Lamb

Here is a very interesting combination of flavors that accentuate the flavor of the lamb from within since they are in the stuffing. This preparation is a longstanding tradition in both Italy and in Italian-American homes.

Ingredients:

1 boned Leg of Lamb, approximately 6 lbs.
3 garlic cloves, minced
½ cup olive oil
8 oz. thinly sliced prosciutto
½ lb. Fontina cheese, thinly sliced
1 cup dry red wine

¾ cup grated Parmigiana-Reggiano cheese
Salt and freshly ground pepper to taste
4 fresh sage leaves
8 sprigs flat-leaf parsley, coarsely chopped
1 cup breadcrumbs
1 cup chicken stock

1. Preheat oven to 450 degrees. Place boned lamb, skin side down, on work surface. Leave one inch border without stuffing. Layer the prosciutto evenly over the lamb, followed by the garlic, parsley, Parmesan cheese, Fontina and breadcrumbs.

2. Roll, starting from one end and after rolling, tie with cooking twine every 2 to 3 inches. Coat with olive oil and sprinkle with freshly ground pepper and salt.

3. Roast for 30 minutes. Open oven and add wine and sage leaves. Baste with chicken stock as needed to keep moist. Reduce heat to 350 degrees and continue to roast for an additional 2 hours.

4. Let rest 15 minutes before slicing thinly. Serve with natural pan juices.

Serves 8-10

ABBACCHIO O CAPRETTO ARROSTO DI PASQUA

Roasted Baby Lamb or Baby Goat for Easter

A tradition in Italy for Easter, Fr. Matt learned this from his sister and then Franca and he added their own touches. It is usually served with oven-roasted potatoes.

Ingredients:

4 lbs. Lamb or young Goat, cut in pieces
9 unpeeled garlic cloves, crushed
8 oz. dry red wine
½ cup olive oil
6 sprigs fresh rosemary
4 fresh sage leaves
1 cup chicken stock
Salt and pepper to taste

1. Be sure that the lamb or goat is cut into small, even-sized pieces.

2. Preheat oven to 375 degrees. Pour the olive oil into a heavy skillet with one of the crushed garlic cloves. Heat over high flame and when garlic clove begins to sizzle add the lamb pieces, browning quickly on each side.

3. Place all browned meat into a large baking dish and add the rosemary, sage, wine and salt and pepper and half the chicken stock.

4. Cover and bake for one hour. Uncover and return to oven for an additional 30 minutes to brown, adding more chicken stock if necessary, to keep moist.

5. Serve with natural pan juices.

Serves 6-8

CORONA DI AGNELLO ARROSTO

Crown Roast of Lamb

This crown roast is a triumph when beautifully prepared and presented during a special meal. The individual ribs are usually carved and served at the table. You can put cherry tomatoes on each bone to make a festive garnish.

Ingredients:

1 Crown Roast of Lamb, about 6 lbs. total
1/3 cup olive oil
1 large sprig fresh rosemary or 3 Tbs., dried, crumbled
2 sprigs fresh flat-leaf parsley, finely chopped
3 garlic cloves, minced
Salt and freshly ground pepper to taste
1 cup beef stock

1. Preheat oven to 450 degrees.

2. Mix all chopped herbs with the oil, add salt and pepper, and rub over the lamb roast. Place lamb in a large baking dish and roast uncovered for 20 minutes. Add the stock as needed to prevent the bottom from burning.

3. Reduce oven temperature to 350 degrees and roast for an additional 20 minutes for medium rare.

4. Serve with Risotto con Verdura (see page 95) placed into the center of the roast. Slice between ribs to serve.

Serves 8-10

AGNELLO CON CARCIOFI

Lamb with Artichokes

Artichokes are enjoyed all year round, but the new crop is available in the springtime throughout Italy. Lamb can also be considered a spring specialty, since it is served for Easter, so we have combined these two enjoyable spring flavors in this dish.

Ingredients:

1 package frozen artichoke hearts (20 oz), defrosted
2 cloves garlic, minced
1 small onion, coarsely chopped
4 Tbs. butter
1 cup chicken stock
4 lbs. Lamb stew meat (from shoulder)
Juice of one lemon
1 sprig rosemary
¾ cup white wine
¼ cup olive oil
Flour for dredging
Salt and pepper to taste

1. Make a marinade, mixing the lemon juice, wine garlic, onion, rosemary and the salt and pepper. Add the lamb pieces, mix well and let marinate for three hours at room temperature or refrigerated overnight.

2. Heat 2 Tbs. of the butter and oil together in a heavy skillet. Remove the lamb from the marinade and dry with paper towels. Dredge in flour and brown in the skillet.

3. Drain the vegetables from the marinade and add them to the skillet, reserving the liquid. Sauté the vegetables over moderate heat.

4. Add the chicken stock to the reserved marinade and add half to the stewing lamb. Reduce heat to a simmer and cook slowly until meat is very tender, approximately 1 to 1 and ½ hours. Add more liquid as needed to keep moist.

5. Melt the remaining butter in a medium-sized skillet and add the artichoke hearts, cooking them until tender over moderate heat – about 10 minutes. Cover and set aside.

6. When lamb is tender, remove the meat with a slotted spoon and keep warm. Strain the juice and combine with the artichokes. Bring to a boil and pour over lamb stew. Serve immediately.

Serves 6

AGNELLO ALLA GRECA

Greek-style Lamb

The Greek people are well-known for their love of lamb. This dish is reminiscent of Moussaka, with the various elements and flavors included; however, here it is presented as a stew.

Ingredients:

4 Tbs. olive oil
2 red bell peppers, chopped
2 medium onions, chopped
1 eggplant, peeled and cut into 1-inch cubes
3 cloves garlic, minced
2 lbs. lean, boneless Lamb, cut in ¾-inch pieces
Flour for dredging
½ cup grated Parmesan cheese
Salt and freshly ground pepper to taste
6 fresh tomatoes, peeled, seeded and chopped
4 sprigs flat-leaf parsley, coarsely chopped
1 teaspoon oregano, fresh or dried
1 cup chicken stock

1. Heat 2 Tbs. of the oil in a large skillet. Add the bell pepper, onion, eggplant and garlic. Cook and stir until tender and crisp, about 10 to 15 minutes. Remove vegetables with a slotted spoon and place in a bowl and cover.

2. Add remaining oil to the skillet. Dredge the lamb in flour and brown over medium to high heat in the oil. Lower the heat and add one cup of the chicken stock and cook until tender and the stock reduces to a thick sauce – about an additional 15 to 20 minutes.

3. Add the reserved vegetables, tomatoes and the salt and pepper and cook over medium heat for an additional 10 minutes.

4. Pour over cavatelli or mostaccioli pasta, sprinkle with Parmesan and garnish with the parsley and serve hot.

Serves 6-8

COSTOLETTE DI AGNELLO ALLA PEPERONATA

Lamb Chops with Peppers

This is the well-known and enjoyed throughout all of Italy and we have given our own version here. The pepper medley is typical of the Marche region on the Adriatic coast.

Ingredients:

10 loin Lamb chops, approximately 1-inch thick
2 yellow bell peppers
1 large garlic clove, minced
½ cup olive oil
4 to 5 hot cherry peppers (optional)
2 red bell peppers
2 large onions, sliced
2 sprigs flat-leaf parsley, finely chopped
Salt and freshly ground pepper to taste

1. Wash and dry the peppers and place them on a charcoal grill. Turn each side until pepper is completely charred and looks black. Remove from the grill, place in a paper bag and let rest for 10 minutes. Peel off the charred skin and discard stems and seeds. Slice peppers lengthwise and place in a bowl and set aside.

2. Pour ¼ cup oil into a heavy skillet. Add the onions and sauté over medium heat, stirring frequently, until they are softened and lightly browned. Add the garlic, parsley and reserved peppers and stir well. Cover and turn off heat.

3. Grill the lamb chops over a charcoal fire for 3 to 4 minutes on each side.

4. Reheat the onion and pepper mixture briefly, add salt and pepper to taste, place in the center of a large serving platter. Arrange grilled lamb chops around the peppers and serve.

Serves 6

Costolette di Agnello alla Fiorentina

Florentine-style Lamb Chops

These are lamb chops that are typically served on a bed of spinach that is widely used in Florentine dishes.

Ingredients:

10 loin Lamb chops, approximately 1-inch thick
1 Tbs. butter
2 unpeeled garlic cloves, crushed
1 sprig flat-leaf parsley, finely chopped
Two 10-oz. bags of fresh spinach
Salt and freshly ground pepper to taste
4 Tbs. olive oil
1 sprig fresh rosemary
8 oz. dry white wine
1 basil leaf, finely chopped
2 cloves garlic, minced
Flour for dredging

1. Prepare the spinach first. Rinse in cold water to remove any dirt. Heat 3 Tbs. of the olive oil over moderate heat in a large pot. Add the 2 chopped garlic cloves and stir until browned. Add the spinach with any water clinging to the leaves into the pot. Cover and allow to steam for about 5 to 7 minutes. Add salt and pepper to taste, set aside and keep warm.

2. Prepare the lamb chops by heating the remaining Tbs. of olive oil with the unpeeled garlic cloves until they begin to sizzle.

3. Dredge the lamb chops lightly in the flour, shaking off the excess. Place them in the frying pan and cook over a lively flame until golden brown in color – about 3 to 4 minutes on each side.

4. Make a bed with the spinach on a large serving platter. Arrange the lamb over the spinach. Meanwhile, add the white wine to the skillet and over a high flame, let it reduce by half, making a blonde colored sauce. Pour over the chops and sprinkle with the chopped parsley and basil and serve immediately.

Serves 6

OSSO BUCO DI AGNELLO AI FAGIOLI

Lamb Shank with Beans

This recipe is similar to the Veal Osso Buco and the beans are very typical of the cuisine of northern Italy. Here we have lovely aromatic vegetables to round off the flavors.

Ingredients:

4 Tbs. olive oil
2 carrots, peeled and cut into ½-inch diagonal strips
2 large onions, coarsely chopped
3 cloves garlic, chopped
6 Lamb Shanks, cut 2 and ½ inches thick
1 cup dry red wine
One 28-oz can of Italian tomatoes, chopped
Grated zest of one lemon
Salt and freshly ground pepper to taste
4 cups white beans, freshly cooked or canned
6 sprigs flat-leaf parsley chopped coarsely
3 basil leaves, chopped coarsely
Flour for dredging

1. In a heavy large skillet, add 2 Tbs. oil, carrots, onion and garlic and cook over low heat until vegetables are soft but not browned – about 4 to 6 minutes.

2. Heat remaining oil in a large frying pan. Dredge lamb shanks in flour and shake off excess. Brown the shanks in the oil on each side and add to the pan with the softened vegetables.

3. Remove any fat remaining in the frying pan. Add wine and deglaze the pan over high heat. Pour wine mixture over lamb and add the tomatoes, lemon zest and salt and pepper. Bring to a boil and let cook for a few minutes.

4. Transfer all ingredients to a baking dish and place, covered into a preheated, 350-degree oven for 2 hours, turning meat over after the first hour.

5. Gently fold beans and parsley into the baking dish and continue to cook, uncovered, for an additional 30 minutes. Serve with green vegetable of your choice.

Serves 6

POLLO ARROSTO TRICARICO

Tricarico-style Stuffed Roast Dhicken

This is the stuffed chicken that Fr. Matt's Mom would typically make. She had learned it from her own mother, who was born and raised in southern Italy in the hill town of Tricarico in the region of Basilicata.

Ingredients:

2 Tbs. olive oil
1 medium onion, finely chopped
1 clove garlic, minced
3 eggs, beaten
2 Tbs. pignoli (pine nuts), slightly crushed
2 Tbs. golden raisins
3 sprigs flat-leaf parsley, coarsely chopped
¼ cup grated Parmigiana-Reggiano or Pecorino cheese
1 and ½ cups breadcrumbs
One 4-5 lb. roasting Chicken
1 Tbs. paprika
Salt and pepper to taste

1. Begin the stuffing by heating one Tbs. of the oil in a skillet. Add the onion and sauté over moderate heat for about 5 to 7 minutes, until softened but not browned. Add garlic, stir well and heat for another minute.

2. Pour mixture into a bowl and add the egg, pignoli, raisins, parsley, Parmesan cheese, salt and pepper, and breadcrumbs and mix well.

3. Preheat the oven to 350 degrees. Wash and pat dry the chicken. Fill the cavity with the stuffing and affix 3 to 5 toothpicks or as needed to close the cavity.

4. Coat the stuffed chicken with the remaining oil and sprinkle with paprika and salt. Place in a roasting pan with 1 cup water and cover. Roast for 1 hour, remove cover, baste and continue to roast for an additional 45 minutes, uncovered, basting occasionally. The total time for cooking should be 20 minutes per lb., with an additional 30 minutes for stuffing. The chicken is done when the thigh is tested with a fork and the juices run clear.

5. Remove stuffing from chicken and slice. Carve chicken and serve with pan juices.

Serves 4-6

POLLO RIPIENO ALLA SALSICCIA

Roast Chicken with Sausage Stuffing

This is a very savory stuffing that adds a great flavor to the poultry, and it is used both in the north and south of Italy. It can also be used as the stuffing for the turkey for Thanksgiving Day dinner.

Using the preceding recipe for Pollo Arrosto Tricarico, substitute the following for the stuffing:

Ingredients:

1 lb. Italian sweet Pork sausage
1 stalk celery, finely chopped
3 scallions, cut thinly
1 and ½ cups breadcrumbs
½ cup milk
1 medium onion, finely chopped
1 carrot, finely chopped
2 sprigs flat-leaf parsley, chopped
2 eggs, beaten
Salt and freshly ground pepper to taste

1. Remove the sausage from its casing and crumble. Place in a skillet, add all the chopped vegetables and sauté over moderate heat for about 10 to 15 minutes until sausage is well browned, but not burned, and vegetables are softened. Remove contents from pan with a slotted spoon and place in a bowl.

2. Add the breadcrumbs, milk and egg and mix. Add parsley, Parmesan cheese, salt and freshly ground pepper.

3. Stuff chicken and continue recipe as indicated.

POLLO ARROSTO GOURMET

Gourmet-style Roast Chicken

This recipe was created by both Franca and Fr. Matt and it has a delicate stuffing of various herbs and vegetables, and the ham adds an extra special rich flavor.

Ingredients:

For the stuffing:

2 Tbs. butter
1 large onion, finely chopped
2 cloves garlic, minced
3 fresh basil leaves, finely chopped
3 eggs, beaten
1 cup grated Parmesan cheese
1 cup dry white wine

2 Tbs. olive oil
2 cups white mushrooms, cleaned & thinly sliced
2- 10-oz. bags fresh spinach, cleaned & chopped
3 sprigs flat-leaf parsley, finely chopped
1 cup diced ham
1 cup breadcrumbs
Salt and pepper to taste

For chicken:

One 5-6 lb boneless Chicken
2 Tbs. butter
2 Tbs. oil

3 sage leaves
1 sprig rosemary
1 tsp. thyme
Salt and freshly ground pepper to taste

1. In a heavy large skillet, heat the butter and oil together. Add the onion and sauté until transparent. Add the mushrooms and garlic and sauté together for 10 minutes. Add the spinach, basil and parsley and sauté an additional 10 minutes until softened. Remove the pan from the stove and let cool for 10 minutes.

2. Add the eggs and mix well. Add the ham, cheese and breadcrumbs and mix all these ingredients. Add salt and pepper to taste. The consistency should be such that it can form a ball. If the mixture is too soft, add more breadcrumbs, ¼ cup at a time. If too hard, moisten with a little milk.

3. Stuff inside the deboned chicken, pushing the stuffing through the leg wings and body cavity. Close by bringing the two breasts together and sew closed at the center with cooking thread or use toothpicks that will be removed after the chicken cooked.

4. Grease the chicken with one Tbs. of softened butter and sprinkle with the thyme, rosemary and sage, salt and pepper. Place chicken in a roasting pan with the garlic in a preheated, 350-degree oven. Roast for 30 minutes covered. Add the wine and continue to bake covered for an additional 30 minutes, then uncover and bake for the last 30 minutes, basting occasionally. Serve with rosemary and garlic fried potatoes.

Serves 6-8

POLLO ARROSTO AI PROFUMI

Herb-scented Roast Chicken

The various aromatic herbs in this recipe make the roasted chicken very tasty. In particular, the flavor of the rosemary helps to enhance the dish.

Ingredients:

One 7-8 lb. roasting Chicken
3 leaves fresh sage
1 large onion, sliced
1 Tbs. butter, softened
2 cups chicken broth
1 sprig fresh rosemary
1 sprig fresh thyme
3 cloves garlic, chopped
Salt and freshly ground pepper

1. Preheat oven to 400 degrees.

2. Slice onions and place on the bottom of a roasting pan. Wash and pat the chicken dry with paper towels, then place it on the bed of onions in the pan, breast up. Sprinkle in and out with salt and pepper.

3. Remove stems from the herbs and chop coarsely. Add to the chopped garlic. Sprinkle half of this mixture on the outside and the other half inside the cavity. Spread the softened butter on the entire surface of the chicken.

4. Place chicken in the oven and roast uncovered. After the first hour, pour one cup of the broth over the entire chicken. Continue to roast uncovered for an additional hour to hour and a half, basting occasionally if necessary. It should make a rich and flavorful golden gravy.

Serves 6-8

POLLO ARROSTO AL LIMONE

Lemon-roasted Chicken

This roasted chicken features the taste of lemon which gives it a flavor that is very appropriate for enjoying during the summer months, when you want to take a break from grilling.

Ingredients:

One 4-lb roasting Chicken
1 lemon, cut in halves
Salt and pepper to taste
2 cloves of garlic, chopped
1 Tbs. olive oil
Fresh spinach leaves for garnish

1. Preheat oven to 425 degrees.

2. Squeeze half the lemon and mix with the chopped garlic and the oil and salt and pepper. Baste the chicken with this mixture and place in a large baking dish.

3. Roast chicken uncovered for 1 hour and 30 minutes, basting every 15 minutes with the pan juices until skin is crisp. Add chicken stock if needed to prevent bottom of pan from drying out.

4. Continue roasting until the juices run clear when the chicken is pierced in the thickest part of the thigh.

5. Remove chicken from pan. Deglaze juices with ¼ cup chicken stock. Place on a bed of fresh spinach leaves and cut remaining lemon half into wedges as a garnish. Serve immediately with deglazed juices.

Serves 4-6

Pollo Arrosto con Patate

Roasted Chicken with Potatoes

Here the potatoes are included with the chicken to be oven roasted and absorb some of the aromatic flavors.

Using the preceding recipe for lemon roasted chicken, omit lemon juice and add 1 medium sprig of fresh rosemary or ½ Tbs. dried crumbled rosemary. Peel and quarter six potatoes. Mix them in a bowl with one Tbs. olive oil, salt and pepper to taste and 1 teaspoon paprika. Place in a roasting pan with the chicken and continue recipe as directed.

Pollo alla Zia Concetta

Chicken Aunt Connie's style

This is named after one of Fr. Matt's paternal aunts and he always enjoyed this dish at her home. His mother would duplicate it at their house and we want to have you try it as well. We are sure that you will enjoy it.

Ingredients:

2 broiler Chickens, approximately 3 to 4 lbs. each
¾ cup red wine vinegar
2 garlic cloves
Salt and pepper to taste
3 stalks celery, with leaves
1 Tbs. oregano

1. Preheat broiler on stove. Cut each chicken into quarters. Wash and pat dry and sprinkle with salt and pepper.

2. Place on broiler tray and broil each side 15 to 20 minutes. Place garlic cloves through a press and into a bowl. Combine with oregano and vinegar. Use the leaves of the celery stalk to baste the chicken with the vinegar mixture after the first 10 minutes of cooking time on each side.

3. Continue to broil and after 40 minutes cooking time, test the thigh by piercing with a fork to see if juices run clear.

Variation: Make a marinade of the following ingredients:

½ cup fresh lemon juice	*¼ cup olive oil*
1 sprig rosemary, finely chopped	*3 sage leaves, finely chopped*
1 teaspoon thyme, fresh or dried	*2 cloves garlic, thinly sliced*
Salt and freshly ground pepper to taste	*½ tsp. hot red pepper flakes (optional)*

1. Place chicken in a large bowl. Cover with marinade and refrigerate at least 4 hours or overnight.

2. Place chicken in a broiler tray and follow directions as in Pollo Alla Zia Concetta, basting with the marinade.

Serves 6-8

POLLO ALLA CACCIATORA

Hunter's-style Chicken

This dish is usually served with polenta or gnocchi, although many serve it with pasta. It is in the wild game style that the hunters would use to cook the birds that they caught.

Ingredients:

5-6 lbs Chicken pieces	*½ cup olive oil*
1 large onion, coarsely chopped	*2 carrots, chopped*
½ cup dry white wine	*Salt and freshly ground pepper to taste*
2 basil leaves, torn	*½ cup flour*
3 cloves garlic, chopped	*1 lb mushrooms, cleaned and sliced*
3 sprigs parsley, chopped	*One 28-oz. can crushed tomatoes*
1 garlic clove, unpeeled and crushed	

1. Mix flour with salt and pepper and dredge chicken pieces in this mixture.

2. Place unpeeled garlic clove and oil in a heavy skillet and heat until clove begins to brown. Add chicken and brown on all sides. When chicken is done, place in a covered dish and keep warm. Discard garlic clove.

3. In the oil remaining in the skillet, add the onion, garlic, mushrooms and carrots and brown for about 10 minutes. Add the wine, crushed tomatoes, parsley and basil, stir well and simmer for about five minutes. Add salt and pepper to taste.

4. Return the chicken to the skillet and continue to cook over low heat for an additional 45 minutes or until very tender when tested with a fork. Serve with cappellini, polenta ot gnocchi. **Serves 4-6**

Pollo alla Cacciatora Stile Cremonese

Hunter's-style Chicken, Cremona style

This recipe is from the part of Italy where Franca was born, Cremona, which is very famous for the Stradivarius violins, and this was handed down from her family over the years.

Ingredients:

6-7 lbs Chicken pieces
Flour for dredging
1 and 1/2 cups fresh porcini mushrooms, sliced or ½ cup dried
¼ cup olive oil
2 onions, chopped
1 stalk celery, chopped
1 carrot, chopped
1 cup dry white wine
2 Tbs. tomato paste
2-3 cups chicken broth
1 bay leaf
3 juniper berries (optional)
3 sprigs flat-leaf parsley, chopped
1 Tbs. butter
2 cloves garlic, chopped
Salt and pepper to taste

1. Wash and pat dry the chicken pieces and dredge in flour. If using dried mushrooms, soak in warm water for 10 minutes.

2. Heat the oil in a heavy skillet over moderate heat, brown the chicken pieces on each side. Add all of the vegetables and sauté, mixing occasionally about 10 minutes, or until tender.

3. Add the wine, stir and cook until evaporated. Mix the tomato paste with one cup of the broth and add to the chicken. Add the bay leaf and add the juniper berries, if desired. Cover and stir occasionally and cook about 40 minutes, or until the chicken is very tender. Add salt and pepper to taste.

4. Add more broth if necessary, so the gravy does not dry out.

5. Then, with a spoon, remove the excess grease at the top of the gravy. Add the Tbs. of butter. Cover and let the flavors amalgamate.

6. Serve with pasta of your choice, gnocchi or polenta. Garnish with parsley.

Serves 6-8

POLLO ALLA SALSA AGRODOLCE

Chicken with Sweet and Sour Barbecue Sauce

This is a delightful grilled chicken with our own sweet and sour sauce that we developed and gives the chicken a summery and perky taste.

Ingredients:

5-6 lbs Chicken pieces
1 sprig rosemary, finely chopped
1 clove garlic, minced
Salt and pepper to taste

For the sauce:

1 medium onion, finely chopped
2 garlic cloves, minced
½ cup ketchup
¼ cup brown sugar
2 Tbs. soy sauce
Salt and pepper to taste
2 Tbs. olive oil
½ cup tomato paste
1/3 cup pineapple juice
¼ teaspoon hot red pepper flakes
½ cup cider vinegar

1. Wash and pat dry the chicken and coat with the chopped rosemary, garlic, salt and pepper and set aside.

2. Prepare the sauce by sautéing the onion in the oil in a heavy skillet until softened but not browned. Add the chopped garlic and, stirring, cook an additional two minutes. Place in a bowl to cool for a few minutes. When cooled, add all the remaining sauce ingredients and mix well.

3. Preheat oven to 450 degrees or prepare barbecue grill.

4. Place chicken in a baking pan and place in oven uncovered for 15 minutes. If using grill, place on the grill for five minutes on each side.

5. Brush chicken with sauce and continue to bake or grill for an additional 10 minutes. Test the thigh with a fork to see if juices run clear. Continue to bake or grill, if needed, until cooked through.

6. Serve with fresh pineapple slices as garnish.   **Serves 4-6**

POLLO TETRAZZINI

Chicken Tetrazzini Style

Fr. Matt always enjoyed this recipe since his childhood and the creamy sauce is the perfect comfort food.

Ingredients:

One 5-6 lb. stewing Chicken, cut in pieces
1 recipe Béchamel sauce (page 10)
1 cup Parmigiana-Reggiano cheese
1 red bell pepper, roasted and cut into strips (page 36)
1 and ½ lbs. fresh or dried Fettuccine
1 small onion, halved
1 bay leaf
1 lb. mushrooms, cleaned and thinly sliced
Salt and freshly ground pepper to taste
2 sprigs of flat leaf parsley for garnish

1. Place the chicken pieces in a stock pot with the onion, bay leaf and salt and pepper. Cover with water and cook slowly 2 and ½ to 3 hours until meat loosens from the bones. Remove bones and skin from the chicken and discard along with onion and bay leaf. Cut the meat into medium sized pieces and set aside. Reserve chicken stock.

2. Prepare the béchamel sauce and set aside.

3. Heat the butter in a large skillet and add the mushrooms, cooking over moderate heat, stirring occasionally until they exude their juices and cook until tender – about 5 minutes.

4. Lower heat, add the béchamel sauce and chicken pieces and strips of red bell pepper. Mix all ingredients well and keep warm.

5. Boil the fettuccine in the chicken stock until tender or according to package instructions.

6. Drain pasta, place in a large serving bowl, mix in half of the chicken mixture and ½ cup of the cheese.

7. Pour the remaining chicken mixture on the top and garnish with parsley sprigs and serve with additional cheese for sprinkling.

Serves 6-8

PETTO DI POLLO RIPIENO

Stuffed Chicken Breast

This is our version of Cordon Bleu and the delicate chicken meat is well complimented by the ham and cheese stuffing.

Ingredients:

4 whole skinless, boneless Chicken breasts
8 slices of prosciutto
½ lb. Fontina cheese
Oil for frying
Breadcrumbs
2 eggs, lightly beaten
2 Tbs. milk
Salt and pepper to taste

1. Divide the four whole breasts at the center, making eight individual slices. To make the filet, use a sharp knife and cut the breast, beginning from the thicker end and cut across almost to the end. Lb. to make thinner, if desired.

2. Top each flattened breast with a piece of prosciutto and a piece of the Fontina. Fold the left and right sides of the chicken breast over about an inch on each side. Then overlap the front and back, making a pocket. It should look like a miniature meatloaf.

3. Mix the beaten egg in a bowl with the milk, salt and pepper. Dip the stuffed breasts into the egg mixture and then the breadcrumbs, being sure to cover each side and the seams.

4. Fry each piece in a heavy skillet, beginning with the seam side down first. Fry on each side until golden.

Serves 8

Variation:

Prepare one recipe Mushroom sauce (see recipe for Costolette di Maiale Ripiene on page 171).

Cover the bottom of a baking dish with sauce, place chicken pockets in the pan and spoon the remainder of the sauce over them. Bake uncovered in a 350-degree oven for 15-20 minutes.

PETTO DI POLLO CON SPINACI

Spinach-stuffed Chicken Breast

Here the featured ingredient for the stuffing of the chicken breast is spinach that is enhanced by the flavor of the sautéed onion.

Ingredients:

4 whole, skinless, boneless Chicken breasts
4 Tbs. olive oil
1 Tbs. grated Parmesan cheese
2 eggs, beaten
1 Tbs. butter
1 cup dry white wine
1 cup chicken stock

1 package frozen spinach or two bags fresh
1 small onion, chopped
½ lb. Fontina cheese, shredded
Salt and pepper to taste
Flour for dredging
Juice of ½ lemon

1. Slice chicken breasts into 8 filets as in prior recipe and keep refrigerated until ready to stuff.

2. Prepare the spinach for the stuffing. If using fresh spinach, wash, cook in a cup of boiling water for one minute, drain, let cool, squeeze out all the water and chop coarsely. If using frozen spinach, follow the package instructions for cooking and proceed as above.

3. To prepare stuffing, heat 2 Tbs. of the oil in a small frying pan, sauté the onion in this mixture until softened but not browned. Pour mixture into a bowl and let cool for a few minutes.

4. Add the spinach, cheeses and the salt and pepper and mix well. Spoon the stuffing equally in the center of each breast. Following step 3 in the previous recipe, close each breast to form a pocket.

5. Heat the remaining oil and the butter in a heavy skillet over moderate heat. When it begins to sizzle, dip each breast in the egg, then the flour, being sure to seal the edges. Fry, beginning with the seam side down, and brown to a light golden color on each side.

6. Add the wine and lemon juice once all the breasts are browned. Reduce the liquid to half. Add the broth and reduce heat to low and cook for 15 to 20 minutes until breast is cooked. Season with salt and pepper as desired.

Variation I: Add two cups sliced fresh mushrooms to the skillet after browning the breasts and sauté lightly for a few minutes before adding the liquid.

Variation II: Add 1 cup frozen or canned artichoke hearts to the skillet after browning the breasts and before adding the liquid.   **Serves 8**

POLLO ALLA PESCATORA

Chicken Stuffed with Seafood

This is a delicate crabmeat stuffing that is a perfect balance to the flavor of the chicken.

Follow either of the preceding two recipes: Stuffed chicken breast, which is breaded and fried, or the Spinach-stuffed chicken breast, which is cooked in a light gravy, and substitute the following ingredients for the stuffing as a variation:

16 oz. lump Crabmeat, fresh or canned
1 cup chicken broth
1 Tbs. chopped fresh chives
1 Tbs. butter
3 Tbs. flour
3 sprigs flat-leaf parsley, chopped
Salt and freshly ground pepper to taste

1. Melt the butter in a small saucepan, add the flour, remove from flame and mix quickly. Add the chicken stock, gradually mixing well with a wire whisk. Return to stove and bring to a boil over medium heat until it thickens, about 2-3 minutes. Remove from heat and place in a bowl to cool.

2. When cooled, mix in the crabmeat, chopped herbs and the salt and pepper.

3. Spoon the stuffing in the center of each breast and proceed as on previous pages.

Serves 8

POLLO BUONGUSTAIO

Delicious Stuffed Chicken Breast

The expression "Buongustaio" refers to someone who appreciates good tasting food. We hope that you will agree.

Follow the preceding recipe for seafood stuffed chicken breast, replacing the lump crabmeat with coarsely chopped artichoke hearts. Add 2 Tbs. crumbled gorgonzola cheese to the stuffing mixture and proceed as above

COTOLETTE DI POLLO MILANESE

Milan-style Breaded Chicken Cutlets

We have the cuisine of the city of Milan to thank for the Milanese style. Here the chicken cutlet is featured as the main ingredient and the typical squeezing of the fresh lemon wedge can be replaced by the sauce below.

Ingredients:

4 whole, skinless, boneless Chicken breasts

Wash, dry and trim the breasts of any fat. Cut each whole breast in half, then make two cutlets out of each individual breast by cutting across the thicker side and through to the other side, dividing it in two cutlets. You will have sixteen individual cutlets.

Follow the recipe for Veal Cutlet Milanese style.

Dish can be served with the honey mustard sauce. To prepare:

Ingredients:

¼ cup prepared mustard

¼ cup mayonnaise

3 tbs. honey

Mix all ingredients together with a fork and blend well. May also add ½ teaspoon fresh lemon juice.

Serves 8

COTOLETTE DI POLLO FRANCESE

French-style Chicken Cutlets

This is actually very light and flavorful and the lemony taste and the wine accentuate the delicate flavor of the chicken.

Ingredients:

4 whole skinless, boneless Chicken breasts
Flour for dredging plus I teaspoon
1 Tbs. grated Parmigiana-Reggiano cheese
2 Tbs. butter
¼ cup water
¼ cup white wine
2-3 beaten eggs, as needed
1-2 sprigs flat-leaf parsley, coarsely chopped
olive oil for frying
juice of two lemons
Lemon slices for garnish
Salt and pepper to taste

1. Wash, dry and trim breasts of any fat. Cut each whole breast in half, then make two cutlets out of each individual breast by cutting across the thicker side and through to the other side, dividing it in two cutlets. You will have sixteen individual cutlets.

2. Beat the eggs in a bowl and add the parsley, grated cheese and the salt and pepper.

3. Heat the oil in a heavy skillet over moderate heat.

4. Dip the cutlets in the egg and then in the flour and sauté in the oil on each side for about 3-4 minutes, until golden brown. Place in a baking dish. When all are done, cover dish with foil and continue to cook in a preheated 350-degree oven for 15 minutes to keep warm while making the sauce.

5. For the sauce, melt the butter in a small saucepan. Add one Tsp. flour, remove from heat and mix well. Add ¼ cup water, ¼ cup wine and the lemon juice. Bring to a boil, stirring constantly with whisk, until thickened. Add salt and pepper to taste.

6. Arrange chicken cutlets in a large platter. Cover with sauce and garnish with lemon slices. Serve hot with rice.

Serves 8

COTOLETTE DI POLLO SORRENTINO

Sorrento-style Chicken Cutlets

The expression "Sorrentino" from the city of Sorrento always refers to the usage of eggplant as a special feature in the recipe. With the addition of the ham and cheese, this becomes a very satisfying and tasty dish.

Ingredients:

4 whole skinless, boneless Chicken breasts
1 large Eggplant
Half recipe Tomato Basil Sauce (page 8)
1 and ½ Tbs. olive oil
8 slices Prosciutto ham
1 lb. mozzarella cheese
Salt and pepper to taste

1. Arrange rack to about 6 inches from broiler and preheat oven to broil. Peel the eggplant and slice lengthwise into 16 thin slices about ¼ inch thick.

2. Pour the oil on a large cookie sheet. Place the eggplant slices on the cookie sheet in one layer and broil for approximately three minutes on each side. When all are done, set aside and set oven on bake to 350 degrees.

3. Prepare the chicken cutlets as described in the preceding Chicken Francese recipe, omitting lemon sauce.

4. Coat the bottom of a large baking pan with 1/3 of the sauce. Place the the chicken breast on top of the sauce and cover with a slice of the eggplant, ½ slice of ham and a slice of mozzarella. Reserve the remaining sauce and keep warm for the table

5. Place the chicken cutlets in the oven for approximately 15 to 20 minutes until the cheese is melted but not browned. Serve hot.

Serves 8

POLLO AL PESTO VERDE

Chicken in Green Pesto Sauce

Just as we have had the prior chicken recipes from Milan and Sorrento, this is the contribution from Genoa in the region of Liguria where pesto is the well-known and well-loved sauce used in many dishes. We decided to join it with the flavor of the chicken breast.

Ingredients:

4 whole skinless, boneless Chicken breasts cut in chunks
½ cup dry white wine
Salt and freshly ground pepper to taste
1 recipe Pesto sauce (page 7)
Flour for dredging
½ cup olive oil
½ cup chicken broth
½ cup grated Parmigiana-Reggiano cheese

1. Lightly sprinkle chicken chunks with salt and pepper. Dredge chicken pieces in flour, shake off excess and set aside.

2. Heat oil in a heavy skillet. Add chicken and brown until a light golden color on each side. Add wine and broth to skillet, reduce heat and continue to cook for about 10 minutes until chicken is fully cooked and tender.

3. Remove from heat, add pesto sauce, toss quickly and serve over your favorite pasta or rice. Serve Parmesan cheese for sprinkling.

Serves 6-8

ARROSTO DI TACCHINO RIPIENO

Roast Stuffed Turkey

This is a meal that is well-enjoyed in the fall and winter months and in particular at the holiday season. It is traditional at Thanksgiving.

Ingredients:

One 18-lb. Turkey
1 small sprig rosemary
Salt and pepper to taste
2 Tbs. olive oil
2 fresh or dried sage leaves
2-3 large onions, sliced

1 Tbs. butter, softened
2 sprigs fresh flat-leaf parsley
4 cups chicken broth
2 cloves garlic
Grated rind of one lemon, yellow part only

For the stuffing:

Double the recipe for either of the following: Pollo Arrosto Tricarico or Pollo Arrosto Ripieno alla Salsiccia.

1. Preheat oven to 350 degrees.

2. Remove giblets from cavity and wash turkey under running water, inside and out. Pat dry with paper towels. Sprinkle inside cavity with salt and pepper.

3. Finely chop all the herbs and place in a small bowl, mixing with the grated lemon rind and the oil and softened butter, making a soft paste, and set aside.

4. Prepare the stuffing of your choice and fill the cavity of the turkey, securing closed with cooking thread. Coat the turkey with herb butter paste.

5. Spread the sliced onions on the bottom of a roasting pan, cover with aluminum foil and place turkey in the pan. Place in oven. After the first hour, add ½ cup of broth and continue to do so gradually while turkey cooks to prevent burning.

6. Roast for approximately 15 minutes per lb., calculating complete cooking time. Add an additional 30 minutes since it is stuffed. Uncover for the last hour to allow to brown. Remove from pan, place on a large serving dish and let rest.

7. To make the gravy, degrease the pan drippings, pass through a strainer, pressing down on the onions and place in a saucepan. Mix two Tbs. flour in ½ cup cold water to avoid lumps. Mix into saucepan and bring to a boil for 10 minutes, until thickened, then remove from heat. Add salt and pepper to taste.

8. Remove thread, loosen stuffing with a large spoon, then set the stuffing on a separate plate and slice. Carve the turkey and serve with the warmed gravy and stuffing on the side. **Serves 8-10**

COTOLETTE DI TACCHINO ALLA CREMA CON FUNGHI

Turkey Cutlets in Cream and Mushroom Sauce

This is a very delicate and elegant dish that is perfect for that most special occasion. Although it has a French influence, we have added the Italian touch.

Ingredients:

2 oz. dried porcini mushrooms
8 sprigs flat-leaf parsley
8 Tbs. butter
12 Turkey breast cutlets
1/3 cups brandy
Salt and freshly ground pepper to taste

1 lb. fresh white mushrooms
2 garlic cloves, peeled
4 Tbs. olive oil
Flour for dredging
¾ cups heavy cream
½ lb. Fontina cheese, shredded

1. Soak dry mushrooms in bowl with 3 cups warm water for 15 minutes. Drain the mushrooms, filter the water through a paper coffee filter and reserve the liquid.

2. Wash the fresh mushrooms, place on a paper towel to dry and slice about ¼ inches thick and set aside.

3. Finely chop the parsley and garlic together on a board. Place 4 Tbs. butter in a heavy skillet and melt over moderate heat. Add the dried mushrooms, garlic and parsley mixture and lightly sauté for 5 minutes.

4. Add the fresh white mushrooms, and sauté an additional 5 minutes. Add ¼ cup of the strained mushroom water, and simmer for about 15 minutes, adding more water as needed to keep moist.

5. Heat the oil and remaining butter in a frying pan over medium heat. Dredge the turkey cutlets in flour and brown in the pan for about a minute or two until golden on both sides. Season with salt and pepper, add the brandy and let evaporate approximately 2 minutes.

6. Place the turkey cutlets in the skillet with the mushroom mixture. Add the heavy cream to the pan and incorporate slowly, approximately 10 minutes. Sprinkle with Fontina, cover and let rest until cheese melts.

7. Serve immediately.

Serves 6

Cotolette di Tacchino al Vostro Gusto

Turkey Cutlet of Your Choice

Substitute Turkey breast cutlets for Chicken or Veal in any of the following recipes either stuffed or plain:

Stuffed Chicken Breast (page 193)

Spinach Stuffed Chicken Breast (page 194)

Seafood Stuffed Chicken Breast (page 195)

Delicious Stuffed Chicken Breast (page 195)

Breaded Chicken Breast Milanese (page 196)

Veal Parmesan Style (page 151)

Veal Piccata (page 154)

Veal Primavera (page 152)

Veal Marsala (page 155)

French-Style Chicken Breast (page 197)

Sorrento-Style Chicken Breast (page 198)

Chicken in Pesto Sauce (page 199)

CONIGLIO ALLE VERDURE CON BAROLO

Rabbit with Vegetables and Barolo Wine

This was developed to cook wild game, similar to the "cacciatore." Rabbit has a very sweet meat that joins well with the combination of these ingredients.

Ingredients for the marinade:

4 cups water

Salt and pepper

1 sprig fresh rosemary, coarsely chopped

3 cups red vinegar

2 cloves garlic, sliced

For the rabbit:

1 Rabbit, cut in pieces

2 onions, chopped

2 cups Barolo wine

2 carrots, peeled and chopped

3 Tbs. tomato paste

Flour for dredging

2 cloves garlic, chopped

3 sprigs flat-leaf parsley, chopped

2 Tbs. butter

2 celery stalks, chopped

¼ cup olive oil

Salt and pepper to taste

To be done the night before:

1. Rinse rabbit very well under running water. Mix all marinade ingredients together, add the rabbit, cover and refrigerate overnight.

For the preparation:

1. Remove rabbit from marinade and wash under running water. Dry with paper towels. Dredge in flour and set aside.

2. Heat oil and butter in a heavy skillet. Brown rabbit until golden on all sides. Add all chopped vegetables and sauté for about 10 minutes, stirring occasionally to avoid burning.

3. Add the tomato paste and mix. Add the wine and stir. Add broth as needed to keep moist. Add salt and pepper to taste.

4. Reduce heat and cook slowly, covered, for about 1 and ½ hours until tender. Serve with polenta.

Serves 4-6

CONIGLIO ARROSTO AL FORNO

Roast Rabbit

This is another way to cook rabbit meat and here the usage of the fresh herbs very much help to enhance the flavors of this dish.

Ingredients:

2 Rabbits, cut in pieces
1 sprig fresh rosemary, finely chopped
½ cup dry white wine
2 garlic cloves, finely chopped
Salt and pepper to taste
½ cup extra virgin olive oil

To be done the night before:

1. Rinse the rabbit pieces under running water and pat dry.

2. Mix together the garlic, rosemary, wine, oil and salt and pepper to taste. Marinate the rabbit pieces in this mixture in the refrigerator overnight, turning occasionally.

For the preparation:

1. Preheat the oven to 400 degrees. Place the rabbit pieces in a roasting pan and pour the marinade over them.

2. Roast for 25 minutes, basting frequently. Turn the rabbit pieces over and roast an additional 15 to 20 minutes, and continue basting.

3. To serve, place the rabbit pieces on a serving dish, degrease the fat from the gravy and pour over. Serve with oven roasted rosemary potatoes.

Serves 6-8

BACCALA' MARINARA

Codfish in Tomato Sauce

This well-known fish first arrived though the south of Italy. It had been used extensively throughout most of Europe, especially in Portugal. This preparation was from Franca's mother, Caterina, who would prepare it on the wood-burning stove.

Ingredients:

3 lbs. dried boneless Codfish
One 28-oz. can crushed tomatoes
3 garlic cloves, chopped
1 small onion, chopped
3 sprigs flat-leaf parsley, chopped
5 basil leaves, chopped
Pinch of oregano
Freshly ground pepper to taste
¼ cup olive oil

1. Cut fish into 4-inch pieces and soak in plenty of cold water, refrigerated, for at least 4 days before cooking. Change water twice each day.

2. Heat oil in large skillet. Add onion and sauté until tender, but not browned. Add the garlic, parsley and basil and stir quickly 2 to 3 times.

3. Add crushed tomatoes, bring to a boil, then reduce heat, add fish and sprinkle the oregano and cook for 30 minutes.

4. Check for seasonings. Add freshly ground pepper and salt only if necessary. Serve with polenta or pasta of your choice.

Serves 6

Baccala' Fritto con Salsa Verde

Codfish in Green Sauce

These sauces are actually two options to accompany the fried Codfish to help make it more interesting and tasty. The green sauce is more typical of northern Italy and red sauce comes from the sunny south.

Ingredients:

3 lbs. dried boneless Codfish
Flour for dredging
Oil for frying

Prepare the fish by soaking as described in preceding recipe.

On day of cooking remove fish from water and place on paper towels to absorb excess water. Dredge in flour and fry in oil over moderate heat until golden, about 5 to 6 minutes on each side.

For the sauce:

One garlic clove, finely chopped
1 hard-boiled egg, very finely chopped
1 tsp. capers, finely chopped

1 cup white vinegar
½ cup chopped parsley
salt and pepper to taste

¾ cups olive oil
2 slices white bread

Break bread into small pieces and soak in vinegar for 5 minutes or until soft. Remove bread and squeeze out all vinegar.

Place bread in bowl, add chopped garlic, egg, parsley, capers and stir well. Add oil and blend all ingredients with a whisk. Let the sauce sit for two hours at room temperature for flavors to amalgamate before using.

Variation: Salsa Rossa

1 onion, chopped
1 Tbs. oil
1 Tbs. capers

12 oz. canned whole tomatoes, chopped
½ cup pitted green olives
salt and pepper to taste

Soften onion in oil. Add tomatoes and bring to a boil. Reduce heat to simmer, add capers and olives, continue to cook an additional few minutes.

Serves 6

INSALATA DI BACCALA'

Codfish Salad

This is typically served as the appetizer on Christmas Eve in many households thought both the north and south of Italy. This tradition has also become a part of the festive table for many Italian-Americans as well.

Ingredients:

3 lbs. dried, boneless Codfish
2 tsp. capers
¾ cups olive oil
Pinch of oregano
2 cloves garlic, finely chopped
3 stalks celery, chopped
½ cup green olives, chopped
Salt and pepper to taste

1. Cut the baccala' into four-inch pieces. Refrigerate and soak in cold water for 4 days, changing water twice daily.

2. Boil fish until tender for 30 minutes. Remove any skin or bones. Rinse under cold water to refresh. Flake the fish with a fork.

3. Place the fish in a bowl and mix with all other ingredients. Mix well and let the flavors amalgamate for 2-3 hours before serving. Serve well chilled on a bed of lettuce.

Serves 6

SALMONE CON RUCOLA

Salmon with Arugula

This is the perfect summer entree and the distinct peppery taste of the arugula and other flavorful ingredients adds great interest to the mild flavor of the fish.

Ingredients:

1 lb.fresh plum tomatoes, seeded and chopped
1 bunch fresh arugula, washed and coarsely chopped
3 to 4 basil leaves, chopped
2 sprigs flat-leaf parsley, chopped
1 shallot, chopped
2 Tbs. lemon juice
1 Tbs. capers, drained
½ cup olive oil
6 medium-sized pieces of Salmon filet
Salt and freshly ground pepper to taste

1. Combine tomatoes, arugula, basil and parsley. Add shallot, lemon juice, capers and oil and mix well.

2. Preheat broiler. Brush both sides of fish with oil and season with salt and pepper. Broil fish until cooked, about 4-5 minutes on each side.

3. Transfer salmon to serving dish and place arugula salad over it. Serve with lemon wedges to garnish.

4. Variation: Substitute swordfish steaks for salmon.

Serves 6

Salmone con Salsa Bianca

Salmon with White Sauce

This is a very refreshing summer dish and can be enjoyed with a crisp glass of white wine.

Ingredients:

6 Salmon steaks, about 1-inch thick
Salt and pepper to taste
Flour for dredging
1 Tbs. butter
1 Tbs. olive oil
Juice of ½ lemon
2 garlic cloves, finely chopped
1 to 2 sprigs flat-leaf parsley, finely chopped

For the sauce:

1 cup sour cream
Juice of ½ lemon
2 sprigs flat-leaf parsley, finely chopped
Salt and pepper to taste
½ cup mayonnaise
1 Tbs. fresh chives, finely cut
2 to 3 basil leaves, finely chopped

Prepare the sauce by mixing all ingredients and beat together with a fork. Refrigerate until ready to use.

To prepare the fish:

1. Wash and dry salmon with paper towels, sprinkle with salt and pepper and dredge in flour.

2. Melt the butter in the oil in a heavy skillet over moderate heat. When it begins to sizzle, add the fish steaks and cook about 3 to 4 minutes on each side until lightly browned.

3. Add the garlic and sauté with fish for an additional minute, being sure not to burn it.

4. Mix the lemon juice with ½ cup water and pour over fish. Baste fish with juices and cook an additional 4-5 minutes.

5. Place fish on a serving dish and remove large center bone. Cover each steak with one heaping Tbs. of the white sauce and then pour the pan juices over all.

6. Serve hot with additional sauce on the side.

Serves 6

SALMONE CARDINALE

Cardinal-style Salmon

The bright red color is reminiscent of the beautiful bird, as well as the robes worn by the cardinals of the church. The festive color and taste in this dish accompanies the delicate poached salmon. We hope you will enjoy it.

Ingredients:

Six 6-oz. Salmon filets
3 garlic cloves, finely chopped
½ lemon, cut in round slices
2 packages, 10 oz. each, of fresh spinach
2 Tbs. olive oil
2 red bell peppers

For the sauce:

1. Roast the two bell peppers over a flame or in the oven under the broiler until charred on all sides. Place in a paper bag for 20 minutes to steam. Remove the skin, stem and seeds.

2. Cut peppers into strips, reserving 6 strips for garnish. Blend remaining roasted peppers with one Tbs. oil and reserve for later use as sauce.

To prepare the fish:

1. Poach salmon by seasoning with salt and pepper and placing in a heavy skillet. Cover with water and lemon slices.

2. Cook over medium heat. Bring water to simmer, reduce heat to low, cover and poach gently until salmon is cooked, about 8 minutes.

3. Meanwhile, prepare the spinach by washing and removing large stems. Heat oil in a large pot over moderate heat, add garlic and stir quickly. Do not allow garlic to brown. Add the spinach with the water attached to its leaves. Cover and steam for 2-3 minutes until wilted.

To serve:

Place sautéed spinach on a platter, top with poached salmon, red pepper sauce and one strip of roasted pepper on each fish filet as a garnish.

Serves 6

TROTA AL CARTOCCIO

Grilled Wrapped Trout

This is well-known and the lemon and herbs add a great taste to the trout. The charcoal grill taste also adds a touch of flavor.

Ingredients:

6 Trout, cleaned, about 10 oz. each
Juice of one lemon
1 lemon sliced in 12 round slices
4 Tbs. oil
12 medium sprigs rosemary
Salt and pepper to taste

1. Cut six sheets of foil, each large enough to wrap each trout. Brush sheets with oil.

1. Brush the inside of each fish with lemon juice and season with salt and pepper.

2. Put one sprig of rosemary inside each fish cavity. Place trout on foil, brush with oil and place two lemon slices on each.

3. Wrap well in foil and seal.

4. Place on preheated charcoal grill and cook for 5-6 minutes on each side. Serve immediately.

Serves 6

Sogliola alla Milanese

Filet of Sole, Milan style

This is very similar to the veal and chicken Milan-style; however this features the delicate flavor of the fish. We have enhanced the ingredients in the breadcrumbs in this version.

Ingredients:

6 filets of Sole, approximately 8 oz. each
2 eggs, lightly beaten
1 Tbs. milk
1 teaspoon fresh rosemary, finely chopped
Oil for frying, either olive or vegetable oil
2 to 3 cups breadcrumbs
1 Tbs. flat-leaf parsley, finely chopped
Salt and pepper to taste
lemon slices for garnish
1 clove garlic, unpeeled

1. Mix egg and milk and beat lightly with a fork. Add salt and pepper to taste.

2. Dip filets in egg mixture then dredge in breadcrumbs and set aside.

3. Heat oil and butter in a heavy skillet over a lively flame until melted and sizzling.

4. Place fish in the skillet and cook until golden on each side – about 1-2 minutes for each side.

5. Serve with lemon slices and sprinkle with chopped parsley.

Serves 6

SOGLIOLA ALLA FRANCESE

French-style Filet of Sole

This recipe is similar to the veal and chicken versions, but the emphasis here is on the delicate taste of the fish, that is enhanced by the lemon and wine flavors.

Ingredients:

6 filets of Sole, approximately 8 oz. each
1 Tbs. milk
2 eggs, beaten
Salt and freshly ground pepper to taste
Flour for dredging
½ cup dry white wine
1 Tbs. olive oil
1 Tbs. butter
Juice of one lemon
½ cup dry white wine
1 lemon, sliced
Chopped flat-leaf parsley for garnish
1 Tbs. caper

1. Mix egg and milk and beat lightly with a fork. Add salt and pepper to taste.

2. Dip filets in egg mixture, then dredge in flour and set aside.

3. Heat oil and butter in heavy skillet over a lively flame until melted and sizzling. Place fish in skillet and cook until golden on each side – about 1 to 2 minutes per side.

4. Mix the lemon juice and wine together and pour over the fish. Cook for an additional minute or two, shaking pan to incorporate juices.

5. Serve with lemon slices and sprinkle on top with chopped parsley and capers.

Serves 6

Variation: You can omit the egg and dredge the fish in just the flour and proceed the same. This recipe is called "Alla Mugnaia" meaning the way it would be prepared by the miller of wheat.

Sogliola Ripiena alla Marinara

Stuffed Filet of Sole, Fisherman style

Franca learned this recipe from a friend who came from Palermo, Sicily and it is enjoyed over a bed of thin pasta. You can also use orecchiette pasta.

Ingredients:

6 filets of Sole, approximately 6-8 oz. each
2 basil leaves, finely chopped
1 cup breadcrumbs
2 tbs. olive oil

1 garlic clove, finely chopped
1 Tbs. water
2 sprigs flat-leaf parsley, finely chopped
Salt and freshly ground pepper to taste

1. Make the stuffing by mixing the breadcrumbs, garlic, basil, parsley, oil, water and salt and pepper and reserve.

2. Rinse and dry the fish. Place on a working surface and distribute the stuffing equally. Roll up from the tail end to head and seal with a wooden toothpick.

For the sauce:

2 cups canned tomatoes, seeded & chopped
Pinch of oregano
2 Tbs. oil

2 basil leaves, finely chopped
2 sprigs flat-leaf parsley, finely chopped

1. Chop garlic, basil and parsley together and place in a bowl. Add the tomatoes, oil, salt and pepper and mix well.

To assemble:

1. Preheat oven to 350 degrees. Cover bottom of baking dish with half of the tomato mixture.

2. Lay the fish over the tomato sauce. Cover with the remaining sauce.

3. Bake for 30 minutes. Serve hot.

Serves 6

SOGLIOLA RIPIENA DI SPINACI

Filet of Sole stuffed with Spinach

This has the influence of the beautiful city of Florence, well-known for the use of spinach. Here we have added a delicate sauce.

Ingredients:

6 filets of Sole, approximately 6-8 oz. each
1 package fresh spinach
1 Tbs. olive oil
Salt and pepper to taste
1 cup breadcrumbs
1 garlic clove, finely chopped
1 small onion, finely chopped

For the stuffing:

1. Prepare spinach by cleaning, washing and steaming in a pot over moderate heat until wilted. Cool, squeeze out all liquid and chop. Set aside.

2. Sauté onion in oil until softened, add garlic and spinach and stir. Cool, add salt and pepper to taste. Stuff filet with spinach filling and roll up from tail to head. Seal with wooden toothpick.

For the sauce:

½ cup dry white wine
2 sprigs flat-leaf parsley, chopped
Juice of one lemon
2 Tbs. butter

1. Melt butter in a sauce pan, add other ingredients and keep warm.

To assemble:

1. Preheat oven to 350 degrees. Cover bottom of baking dish with half of the mixture.

2. Lay the fish over the sauce. Cover with the remaining sauce.

3. Bake for 30 minutes. Serve hot.

Serves 6

CALAMARI FARCITI

Stuffed Squid

This is a recipe from the Bay of Naples and is seen particularly on Christmas Eve, but can be enjoyed all year through. We have enhanced it by adding additional herbs such as basil and parsley to the more traditional oregano.

Ingredients:

2 lbs. Calamari
½ cup olive oil
2 cloves garlic, finely chopped
4 sprigs flat-leaf parsley, finely chopped
2 and ½ cups flavored breadcrumbs
2 basil leaves, finely chopped
Pinch of oregano
Salt and freshly ground pepper to taste
½ cup dry white wine
6 cups Marinara sauce (page 8)

1. Prepare calamari by peeling off the thin outer skin. Cut off the head just below the eyes. Cut off tentacles, wash, dry, chop finely and reserve. Squeeze out the inside and discard the thin bone. Wash in cold water, drain and set aside.

2. Preheat oven to 350 degrees.

3. Pour half the oil in a heavy skillet and heat. Add garlic, parsley and stir. Add chopped tentacles and sauté for 3 minutes.

4. Remove from heat and add the breadcrumbs, remaining oil, basil, oregano and the salt and pepper to taste.

5. Stuff squid loosely and fasten opening with wooden toothpicks.

6. Place in baking dish. Add the wine to the marinara sauce, pour over the fish and bake uncovered for 45 minutes.

7. Serve over a bed of linguini.

Serves 4-6

TONNO ARRABBIATO

Tuna Steaks in Peppercorn Crust

This is a very simple recipe and easy to prepare after a long day at work. The flavor is unique and the light crust we have added helps to seal in some of the juices.

Ingredients:

6 Tuna steaks, approximately 6 oz. each
1 Tbs. peppercorns
1 cup breadcrumbs
1 Tbs. fennel seeds
Salt to taste
Oil as needed

1. Coarsely crush peppercorns and fennel seeds with a mortar and pestle. Place in a bowl with breadcrumbs and salt and mix well.

2. Rinse and dry tuna steaks. Coat with crumb mixture.

3. Lightly grease skillet with olive oil and heat over lively flame

4. Sear the tuna steaks, cooking 5-6 minutes on each side. Serve hot.

Serves 6

PESCE SPADA MARINATO

Marinated Swordfish

This is very healthy and delicious. You can prepare the marinade that morning or the night before. It is a fast and perfect summer dish for the grill.

Ingredients:

½ cup extra virgin olive oil
Juice of 2 lemons
½ cup dry white wine
2 tsp. fresh rosemary, finely chopped
1 clove garlic, chopped
6 Swordfish steaks, 6 oz. each
Salt and freshly ground pepper to taste
Lemon slices and mint leaves to garnish

1. In a bowl, whisk oil, lemon juice, wine, rosemary, chopped garlic and the salt and pepper.

2. Arrange the swordfish in a shallow dish in one layer and sprinkle with salt and pepper

3. Pour marinade over the fish and marinate at least 4-6 hours, turning occasionally.

4. Cook over charcoal or under the broiler for 3 minutes on each side.

5. Cover with half of the remaining marinade and garnish with lemon slices and mint leaves.

Serves 6

ARAGOSTA RIPIENA

Stuffed Lobster

A real treat! The savory stuffing helps to compliment the delicate and sweet lobster meat. It is always well received and enjoyed by all.

Ingredients:

4 live Lobsters, about 1 ¼ lbs. each
4 garlic cloves, finely chopped
¼ cup olive oil
Salt and freshly ground pepper to taste
2 lbs. Bay Scallops
4 sprigs flat-leaf parsley, chopped
2 cups unflavored breadcrumbs

1. Preheat oven to broil. Bring large pot of salted water to a boil. Plunge in the lobsters and cook for 5-6 minutes each. Remove from pot and let cool until able to handle.

2. Heat oil in a heavy saucepan, add the garlic and cook for 2 minutes, stirring constantly. Add the scallops and parsley and continue to cook over moderate heat for 4-5 minutes. Add the breadcrumbs, stir well, check for seasoning and add salt and pepper as needed.

3. Cut the lobsters top to bottom on the stomach side, from below the head to the top of the tail. Remove interior organs and discard, leaving only the meat.

4. Fill empty cavity with scallop stuffing, distributing evenly.

5. Arrange lobsters on a cookie sheet and place under the broiler for 10-12 minutes. Serve hot with melted butter and lemon wedges.

Serves 4

Variation: Substitute fresh, shelled and deveined shrimp for the scallops in the stuffing.

ARAGOSTA CON INTINGOLO

Lobster in Dipping Sauce

This is the typical and simple way that many people enjoy eating lobster. In this recipe, we have added additional flavors to the drawn butter that is used for the dipping.

Ingredients:

4 live Lobsters, about 1 ½ lbs. each
2 garlic cloves, finely chopped
Salt and pepper to taste
½ lemon
Juice of ½ lemon
1 and ½ sticks of salted butter
2 sprigs flat-leaf parsley, chopped
1 lemon, cut in 4 wedges

1. Fill a large pot with water, add ½ lemon and 1 Tbs. salt and bring to a boil. Plunge the lobsters into the pot and boil for 15 minutes. Add more time if lobsters are larger.

2. Place the butter in a small saucepan and melt slowly over very low heat. Add the garlic, parsley and some fresh ground pepper and lemon juice and stir. When butter begins to sizzle, pour into four individual cups and serve with boiled lobster.

Serves 4

GAMBERI RIPIENI ALLA PESCATORA

Fisherman-style Stuffed Shrimp

This is a great dish that Fr. Matt first tasted in Formia, in the lower region of Lazio, below Roma. He and Franca added their own particular special touch.

Ingredients:

30 jumbo Shrimp
½ cup butter
2 garlic cloves, very finely chopped
3 sprigs flat leaf parsley, finely chopped
4 Tbs. olive oil
2 cups breadcrumbs
Juice of one lemon
1 cup fish stock
Lemon wedges
1 Tbs. flour
½ cup dry white wine
Parsley for garnish
Salt and pepper to taste

1. Remove shells and devein shrimp, leaving tail. Cut back almost in half and pound each shrimp between two sheets of wax paper to flatten.

2. To make filling, melt ¼ cup of the butter in a small saucepan, add garlic, parsley and the 2 Tbs. olive oil and stir. Cook over medium heat to soften the garlic, about 2 minutes.

3. Remove from heat, add the breadcrumbs, half the lemon juice and salt and pepper.

4. Preheat oven to 375 degrees. Place all the flattened shrimp on a lightly greased, large baking dish. Distribute the stuffing evenly on each shrimp and set aside.

5. Melt the remaining butter and 2 Tbs. olive oil in a small saucepan add the flour and mix very quickly to incorporate well. Add the fish stock, white wine and remaining lemon juice. Bring to a boil to thicken. Add salt and pepper to taste. Pour over the shrimp and bake uncovered in a preheated oven for 10 to 15 minutes.

6. Serve very hot with lemon wedges and parsley for garnish.

Serves 6

GAMBERI ALL' ITALIANA

Italian Style Shrimp

This is a light summertime meal that can be accompanied by a green tossed salad and a glass or two of refreshing white wine like Frascati or Orvieto.

Ingredients:

2 lbs. large Shrimp
2 Tbs. olive oil
6 cloves garlic, finely chopped
1 tsp. finely grated lemon peel
Salt and freshly ground pepper to taste
½ cup butter
1/4 cup dry white wine
3-4 sprigs flat-leaf parsley, finely chopped
Juice of ½ lemon

1. Clean shrimp by peeling off shells, leaving the tail. Devein and rinse under cold water. Place on paper towels to dry.

2. In a heavy skillet, heat the butter and oil together, add the garlic and parsley and stir well.

3. Add the shrimp and sauté over a lively flame for 2-3 minutes on each side. Sprinkle with the lemon peel. Add the lemon juice and wine, reduce heat to medium and cook an additional 4-5 minutes or just until tender.

4. Check for seasoning, and add salt and pepper to taste. Arrange on a serving platter and pour over the juices.

5. Serve hot with lemon wedges and rice.

Serves 6

SCAMPI ALLA GRIGLIA

Grilled or Broiled Shrimp

This is perfect for a light luncheon, enjoyed outdoors called "al fresco" meaning eaten on the veranda, outside in the fresh air. We suggest that it be accompanied by a refreshing Fennel Salad as the side dish.

Ingredients:

2 lbs. large Shrimp
2 sprigs flat-leaf parsley, finely chopped
Salt and freshly ground pepper to taste
½ cup olive oil
Juice of one large lemon
1 garlic clove, finely chopped

1. Remove shells and devein shrimp. Rinse in cold water.

2. Mix the oil, salt, pepper, lemon juice and parsley in a bowl. Add the shrimp in this mixture and refrigerate for 15 minutes.

3. Preheat broiler. Broil the shrimp on a pan or cookie sheet 2 inches from heat for 2 minutes on each side. You can also place the cookie sheet, covered with foil, on a charcoal grill to cook.

4. Remove and place shrimp on a baking dish and keep warm. Pour the marinade onto the broiler dish to mix with the shrimp juices. Pour over broiled shrimp and serve.

Serves 6

SPIEDINI DI PESCE

Fish Skewers

Here we have a mixture of various fish that is marinated and can be either broiled or placed on the grill similar to the previous recipe. It is a very healthy and delightful summer dish.

Ingredients:

1 lb. medium Shrimp
1 lb. Swordfish, cut in cubes
3 cloves garlic, finely chopped
2 basil leaves, finely chopped
Juice of ½ lemon
1 lb. large Sea Scallops
½ cup olive oil
4 sprigs flat-leaf parsley, finely chopped
Pinch of oregano
Salt and freshly ground pepper to taste

1. Shell and devein the shrimp, leaving tails on. Rinse under cold water. Wash scallops and swordfish under cold water and pat dry with paper towels.

2. Combine the oil, garlic, lemon juice and spices. Add the fish and marinate for 15-20 minutes, refrigerated.

3. Place fish on 6 metal skewers, alternating types. These can be broiled for 2-3 minutes on each side in a preheated broiler or placed on a charcoal grill.

Serves 6

Fritto Misto di Pesce in Pastella

Batter-dipped Seafood

Here we have two options for enjoying fried fish, one is the more typical version, in the light batter and the other is the alternate, with breadcrumbs that you can flavor with parsley and chopped rosemary. We suggest a fresh string bean salad as the side dish.

Ingredients:

1 and ½ lbs. Shrimp   *2 lbs. Calamari*
1 and ½ lbs. Sea Scallops   *Oil for deep frying*

For the Pastella batter:

3 eggs, lightly beaten   *2 cups flour*
Salt to taste   *2 cups milk*
1 tsp. baking powder

1. Mix all pastella ingredients together to make the batter. Let rest at room temperature. Meanwhile, shell, devein and remove tails of shrimp. Clean calamari and cut into ½-inch rings. Wash and dry all fish on paper towels.

2. Heat oil in a deep pot over medium to high heat. Dip fish in the pastella batter and fry in batches until golden brown.

3. Serve hot with lemon wedges.

Variation:

Omit pastella and use the following to dip fish:

2 eggs, lightly beaten   *2 Tbs. milk*
Flour for dredging   *Flavored breadcrumbs for dredging*

1. Combine egg and milk and mix well. Dip cleaned, washed and dried fish in flour, then egg and milk mixture

2. Dredge in breadcrumbs and fry as described above.

Serves 6-8

GAMBERI FRA DIAVOLO

Shrimp in Spicy "Devil" Sauce

Refer to Cappellini Fra Diavolo in Pasta Section for this recipe (page 63).

PESCE FESTAIOLA

Festival Fish

Refer to this recipe in the Pasta Section under Tagliatelle Festaiola (page 56).

ZUPPA DI PESCE

Fish Soup

Franca learned this recipe from her sister Angiolina, who lives in Forte dei Marmi, in the province of Lucca in upper Tuscany, on the Mediterranean Sea. In America, this is called Cioppino and it is a well-known and famous dish that comes from San Francisco, California.

Ingredients:

Two 28-oz. cans whole tomatoes
3 Tbs. olive oil
2 stalks celery, chopped
2 onions, finely chopped
3 cloves garlic, crushed
½ tsp. fresh thyme, chopped
3 sprigs flat-leaf parsley, chopped
1 cup fish stock
1 lb. Calamari, cleaned and cut in rings
1 lb. Bay Scallops
8 slices Italian bread, browned in butter
½ tsp. oregano
3-4 basil leaves, chopped
1 cup dry white wine

2 lbs. mussels, scrubbed
1 lb. Shrimp, shells removed, deveined
2 lbs. Clams, scrubbed
Salt and pepper to taste
½ tsp. red pepper flakes (optional)

1. Remove seeds from tomatoes. Chop coarsely and reserve liquid.

2. Heat oil in a large saucepan. Add onion, celery and garlic and sauté for 5-7 minutes. Add herbs, tomatoes and reserved liquid. Add salt and pepper to taste. You may also add the red pepper flakes, if desired.

3. Cook for an additional 5-7 minutes, then add the wine and cook over moderate heat until tomatoes are reduced to a pulp. Add the fish stock and stir.

4. Add the calamari, shrimp, mussels and clams together in the pot. Mix well and cover. Cook for approximately 10 minutes or until shells open up.

5. Serve in large bowls over fried bread or linguini.

Serves 6-8

MUSSELS ARRABBIATA

Hot, Spicy Mussels

This recipe is found on page 26 in the "Antipasti" chapter and can also be served as an entrée.

CAPE SANTE ALLA VENEZIANA

Venetian-Style Scallops

Venice is a well-known and much visited city. It brings us many treasures and among them its seafood recipes. Here we have one of them that is typically enjoyed in this floating city of love and art.

Ingredients:

24 large Sea Scallops
3 Tbs. olive oil
1 clove garlic, finely chopped
2-3 sprigs flat-leaf parsley, finely chopped
Bread crumbs for dredging
3 Tbs. butter juice of one lemon
½ cup dry white wine
Salt and pepper to taste

1. Wash the scallops under cold water and dry them with paper towels. Coat with breadcrumbs and set aside.

2. Heat the oil and butter together in a heavy skillet. Sauté the garlic and parsley. Add the scallops and fry them gently over moderate heat until browned.

3. Moisten with the lemon juice and wine, salt and pepper to taste, and continue cooking gently until wine has reduced.

4. Serve hot, garnished with lemon wedges and parsley sprigs.

Serves 6

Meatless Entrées

FRITTATA DI ZUCCHINI

Zucchini Frittata

The word frittata comes from the Italian word, "fritto" meaning to fry. It is fried in a skilled as a torte, on both sides. They are truly "comfort food," but this one is especially so.

Ingredients:

8 large Eggs, beaten
3 medium Zucchini, cleaned and thinly sliced
1/3 cup olive oil
3 Tbs. butter
Salt and pepper to taste
½ cup grated Parmigiana-Reggiano cheese
2 medium onions, thinly sliced
2 sprigs flat-leaf parsley, finely chopped
2-3 basil leaves, finely chopped

1. In a large bowl, beat eggs with salt and pepper and the grated cheese.

2. In heavy skillet, melt the butter and add 2 Tbs. of the oil. Add the onion and sauté over medium heat until softened and a light golden color.

3. Add the zucchini, garlic and parsley and sauté until just tender. Remove the zucchini with a slotted spoon and let cool slightly.

4. Pour the remaining oil into a clean skillet and heat. Mix zucchini mixture into bowl with eggs and pour into the skillet. Cook over medium heat for 5-6 minutes until the bottom is light brown.

5. Place a large plate on top of the skillet and turn frittata onto plate. Slide inverted frittata back into the skillet. Cook 4-5 minutes longer.

6. Slide frittata onto a heated platter and cut into serving pieces, as a pizza. Serve hot or at room temperature.

Serves 4-6

FRITTATA DI PATATE

Potato Frittata

This is a typical Friday night main course in many a household, especially during the season of Lent. Most likely this would follow the "Pasta and Fagioli," or another meatless first course. In Spain, it is known as the Tortilla Española.

Ingredients:

8 Eggs, beaten
3 Potatoes, peeled
½ cup olive oil
2 onions, thinly sliced
½ cup grated Parmigiana-Reggiano cheese
Salt and pepper to taste

1. Cut the potatoes into small cubes and set aside.

2. In a heavy skillet, heat the oil, add the potatoes and brown until almost cooked. Add the onions and cook until tender. Remove with a slotted spoon and cool in a bowl.

3. Beat the eggs well in a bowl, add the potato and onion mixture and grated cheese, salt and pepper and mix well.

4. Pour ¼ cup of the oil into a clean skillet, heat the oil, add the egg and potato mixture and continue from step 4 of zucchini frittata recipe.

Serves 4-6

FRITTATA DI ASPARAGI

Asparagus Frittata

Here the featured ingredient is asparagus and the cheese and parsley helps to add a distinct flavor.

Ingredients:

8 large Eggs, beaten
Salt and pepper to taste
I sprig flat-leaf parslty, chopped

½ cup grated Parmigiana-Reggiano cheese
1 lb. fresh Asparagus
½ cup olive oil

1. Steam or parboil asparagus until crisp, but tender. Cool slightly and cut into 1-inch pieces.

2. In a bowl, beat eggs, grated cheese, salt and pepper. Add asparagus.

3. Pour ¼ cup olive oil in a heavy skillet and heat over moderate flame. Pour in egg mixture and continue from step #4 of zucchini frittata recipe.

Serves 4-6

FRITTATA DI SPINACI

Spinach Frittata

This is a delightful and healthy combination, once again from the Florentine tradition, where they feature and enjoy spinach in many of their dishes.

Ingredients:

8 large Eggs, beaten
Salt and pepper to taste
½ cup olive oil

½ cup grated Parmigiana-Reggiano cheese
1 lb. fresh Spinach
1 large onion, finely chopped

1. Clean and cook the spinach in lightly salted boiling water. Drain well, squeezing out excess water, and chop.
2. Heat ¼ cup of the oil over medium heat in a heavy skillet. Add the onion and sauté until softened and a light golden color. Add the spinach and stir well to absorb the flavors. Place in a bowl and cool slightly.
3. Add the Parmesan cheese, salt, pepper and the beaten eggs.
4. Refer to step #4 of the preceding zucchini frittata recipe to continue.

Serves 4-6

FRITTATA DI FUNGHI TRIFOLATI

Mushroom Frittata

This is a true treat, with the flavors of the forest, especially if you select wild Porcini mushrooms with its distinguished taste, which are almost like truffles.

Ingredients:

8 large Eggs, beaten
2 garlic cloves, finely chopped
1 lb. Mushrooms of your choice
2-3 sprigs flat-leaf parsley, finely chopped
½ cup olive oil
Salt and pepper to taste

1. Clean, wash and slice mushrooms. Dry on paper towels.

2. Sauté mushrooms in ¼ cup oil over high heat until water evaporates and they are a golden color.

3. Add the chopped garlic and parsley, stir well and cook for an additional minute. Let cool slightly.

4. Beat eggs in a bowl and add the cooked mushroom mixture. Add salt and pepper to taste.

5. Pour ¼ cup oil into a clean skillet and heat over moderate flame. Add the egg and mushroom mixture and continue from step #4 of the zucchini frittata recipe.

Serves 4-6

FRITTATA AI CARCIOFI

ArtichokeFrittata

This frittata has an abundance of flavors from the distinct taste of the artichoke, unlike any other vegetable, to the combination of the garlic and the chopped parsley.

Ingredients:

8 large Eggs, beaten
1 garlic clove, chopped
½ cup olive oil
1 package frozen Artichoke hearts, defrosted and sliced thin
2 sprigs flat-leaf parsley, finely chopped
3 basil leaves, finely chopped
Salt and pepper to taste

1. Heat ¼ cup of the oil over moderate heat. Add the garlic and sauté one minute until softened. Do not allow to burn.

2. Add the artichoke hearts, parsley and basil and sauté 4 to 5 minutes. Place in a bowl and cool slightly.

3. Add the beaten eggs to the artichoke mixture. Add salt and pepper to taste.

4. Pour ¼ cup oil in heavy skillet and heat. Add the egg mixture and refer to step #4 of the zucchini frittata recipe to continue.

Serves 4-6

Variation: You may also use 4-5 fresh artichokes. However, they need to be cleaned, sliced and boiled, and then sautéed as in step 2.

233

FRITTATA DI FORMAGGIO

CheeseFrittata

A very simple yet satisfying frittata, you can vary the cheese to your liking. However, we suggest a semi-hard cheese, so please do not use ricotta or anything too soft.

Ingredients:

8 large Eggs, beaten

½ cup grated Parmigiana-Reggiano cheese

Salt and pepper to taste

½ lb. Fontina cheese, thinly sliced

½ cup olive oil

1. Beat eggs with salt and pepper in a large bowl.

2. Pour the oil in a heavy skillet and heat. Add the eggs and cook over moderate heat for 3-4 minutes.

3. Place a large plate on top of the skillet and turn frittata onto plate. Slide inverted frittata back into the skillet. Cover with the cheese. Cover with the lid and continue to cook for an additional 2-3 minutes, until the cheese is melted.

Serves 4-6

QUICHE DI ZUCCHINI

Zucchini Quiche

This was developed by Franca over the years. In the same way that the previous frittatas have a variety of flavors, we have included several options here as well. It is a very satisfying and well-received meal and can be perfect for luncheon.

Ingredients:

1 recipe Basic Quiche crust, chilled (page 12)
4 medium Zucchini, cleaned and sliced ¼-inch thick

2 sprigs flat-leaf parsley	1 clove garlic, chopped
2 Tbs. butter	3 Tbs. oil
1 medium onion, thinly sliced	2-3 basil leaves
3 large eggs, lightly beaten	Salt and freshly ground pepper to taste

2/3 cup light cream
1 cup shredded cheese: choice of Gruyere, Mozzarella, Muenster or Fontina

1. Chop garlic, parsley and basil together until very fine and set aside.

2. Melt butter and oil together over a lively flame. Add zucchini and onion and sauté until crisp but tender. Remove from fire, add garlic, parsley, basil and cool together.

3. Roll out pastry and line 9 ½-inch to 10-inch pie pan, letting the dough overlap one inch.

4. Place the zucchini mixture in the shell, distributing evenly. Cover with the shredded cheese of your choice. Pour the egg and cream mixture over this.

5. Overlap the dough and bake in a preheated, 375-degree oven until golden for 45 minutes. Let set for 5 to 10 minutes to set before serving.

Serves 6

Variations:

Onion Quiche:

1. Follow zucchini quiche recipe, but omit zucchini.
2. Thinly slice 5-6 large onions, sliced in rings. Mix with 1/3 cup olive oil and 3 Tbs. butter and cook over medium heat until softened until tender.
3. Add chopped garlic, parsley and basil and continue from step #3 above.

Mushroom Quiche:

1. Follow, zucchini quiche recipe, omitting zucchini.

2. Add 1 lb. mushrooms of your choice. Clean and slice mushrooms and sauté in oil and butter.
3. Continue from step #2 above

Spinach Quiche:

1. Follow, zucchini quiche recipe, omitting zucchini.
2. Use 2 packages frozen chopped spinach, thawed and squeeze of excess water
3. Add ¼ cup grated Parmesan cheese
4. Sauté one large chopped onion in oil, add spinach, and continue from step #2 above

Options for non-meatless quiche:

1. Add 1 cup cooked diced ham, diced bacon or crumbled Italian sausage as desired.

Makes a 9- to 10-inch pie

PIZZA MARGHERITA

Pizza Queen Margaret Style

This was developed in Naples in 1889 for the visit the Queen Margherita of Italy, wife of King Umberto I. The red, white and green colors represent the Italian flag.

Ingredients:

1 recipe Pizza Dough (page 14)	*½ recipe Tomato Basil Sauce (page 8)*
1 pound Mozzarella, shredded	*Pinch of oregano*
6 basil leaves, torn in pieces	*2 Tbsp. Grated Parmesan cheese*

1. Prepare dough, cover loosly with a damp cloth and let rise in a warm place. Meanwhile prepare sauce, adding oregano, let cool to room temperature.

2. Preheat oven to 375 degrees. Punch the dough down and stretch out to fit on a lightly greased rectangular cookie sheet. Place the sauce on the dough, add the mozzarella and grated cheese. Dot with the basil and let it rise for about 10-15 minutes.

3. Put in the oven and let it bake for 15-20 minutes or until the crust is golden, and the cheese is bubbling. Let cool slightly and cut into squares. **Serves 6**

    Variation: You can use fresh sliced tomatoes instead of the sauce and proceed. However, drizzle the tomatoes with 3 Tbspns. Olive oil and salt and pepper.

    You can also add the flavor of your choice such as Shrimp or Anchovies, or quickly sautéed vegetables such as Onions or Bell Peppers. For non-meatless: cooked Italian Sausage or Pepperoni. For additional ideas, also please check the Focaccia variations pg. 15-16.

ROLLATINE DI MELANZANA

Eggplant Rollatini

This is more typical of the south of Italy where Ricotta and Mozzarella originated, but has spread throughout Italy and is enjoyed for its unique combination, almost like Manicotti.

Ingredients:

2 large Eggplants	6 eggs
3 Tbs. milk	Salt and pepper to taste
Flour for dredging	Olive oil for frying
1 garlic clove, unpeeled	2 lbs. Ricotta cheese
1 lb. Mozzarella, diced	1 recipe Tomato & Basil sauce (pg. 8)
3-4 sprigs flat-leaf parsley, finely chopped	½ cup grated Parmigiana-Reggiano cheese

1. Wash and dry the eggplant, cut off the ends and discard them. Cut the eggplant lengthwise into thin slices. Remove the skin on the edge of each end piece.
2. Mix three eggs and milk together in a bowl and beat lightly. Add salt and pepper. Place the flour for dredging in another bowl.
3. Heat oil in a large skillet. Crush the unpeeled garlic and add to the skillet. When garlic begins to sizzle, dip each eggplant slice into the beaten egg mixture, then the flour, and place in the skillet.
4. Fry the eggplant on both sides until a light golden color. Place the slices of fried eggplant on paper towels to absorb excess grease. Continue until all eggplant slices are done.
5. In a bowl mix the ricotta with the diced mozzarella, ¼ cup grated Parmesan cheese, remaining three eggs, parsley and the salt and pepper to taste.
6. Cover the bottom of a deep baking dish with sauce.
7. Place a heaping Tbs. of the ricotta filling on the large end of the eggplant slices. Roll each slice to the other end and place in rows in the prepared baking dish.
8. Cover with sauce, reserving enough to serve at the table. Sprinkle with the remaining ¼ cup grated cheese. Bake uncovered in a 350-degree oven approximately 45-50 minutes. Remove from oven and let rest for a few minutes before serving.

Serves 6-8

Variation: Add 1 package defrosted, chopped spinach to the ricotta mixture.

MELANZANE ALLA PARMIGIANA

Eggplant Parmigiana

This world-famous dish actually comes from the city of Parma, in the region of Emilia-Romagna, where Donald, Franca's husband originated. It has often been duplicated, but this family recipe is very authentic, and we hope you enjoy it.

Ingredients:

2 large Eggplants
3 eggs, beaten
¼ cup milk
Flavored breadcrumbs for dredging
Flour for dredging

1 cup grated Parmigiana-Reggiano cheese
Oil for frying (1/2 vegetable and ½ olive)
1 garlic clove, unpeeled
1 and ½ lbs. Mozzarella cheese, shredded
1 recipe TOmato-basil sauce (pg. 8)

1. Wash and dry eggplants. Cut off the ends and discard them. Slice crosswise into round slices approximately ¼-inch thick.
2. Place all slices in layers on a plate and sprinkle each layer with a little salt. Place a weighted dish on the top and let rest for 15 minutes. Water will collect on the bottom of the plate.
3. Discard the water and rinse the salt off each eggplant slice and pat dry on a paper towel.
4. Take three bowls. Pour flour in the first, the beaten egg mixed with milk in the second and the breadcrumbs in the third.
5. Using a fork, dredge the eggplant slices in the flour one by one, then into the egg, then the breadcrumbs, until all are done.
6. Pour oil in a heavy skillet. Lightly crush the garlic clove and add to the skillet along with oil. Heat until the garlic begins to sizzle. Fry eggplant slices over moderate heat until golden brown on each side*. Place on paper towels to absorb excess grease.

* Please Note: you may have to add more oil or change it completely if the breadcrumb fragments collect at the bottom of the skillet and begin to burn.

To assemble:

1. Preheat oven to 350 degrees.
2. Cover the bottom of a deep baking dish with sauce. Place eggplant slices in one layer, cover with sauce, sprinkle with shredded mozzarella and Parmesan cheese. Continue layering in this manner until all eggplant slices are used, finishing top layer with sauce and grated Parmesan cheese.
3. Bake uncovered for 45-50 minutes in a preheated 350-degree oven. When done, let rest for a few minutes before serving. **Serves 6-8**

Melanzana Ripiena alla Napoletana

Neapolitan-style Stuffed Eggplant

This is one of Fr. Matt's favorite meatless meals. He hopes that you will try it and enjoy it as well and it will also become a favorite of yours.

Ingredients:

4 medium Eggplants
1 large onion, finely chopped
4-5 basil leaves, chopped
1 lb. ricotta cheese
¼ cup plus 1 Tbs. olive oil
3 cloves garlic, finely chopped
4-5 sprigs flat-leaf parsley, chopped
½ lb. Mozzarella, cubed
½ cup grated Parmigiana-Reggiano or Pecorino cheese
1 cup flavored breadcrumbs
Salt and pepper to taste

1. Cut the eggplant in half lengthwise. Scoop out pulp from the eggplant shells, reserving the shells.

2. Cut pulp into ½-inch cubes, place in a bowl and set aside.

3. Place ¼ cup of the oil in a heavy skillet over moderate heat and cook onion until softened, but not browned. Add garlic, basil and parsley and stir quickly. Add eggplant cubes and cook 2 to 3 minutes, stirring occasionally. Pour into bowl and cool.

4. Preheat oven to 350 degrees.

5. Mix the ricotta, mozzarella and half of the Parmesan cheese into the eggplant mixture and add salt and pepper to taste. Fill eggplant shells with the mixture.

6. Mix breadcrumbs, remaining Parmesan cheese and 1 Tbs. oil in a bowl. Sprinkle over the top of the stuffed eggplant. Place eggplants in a baking dish, over them with foil and bake for 45 minutes. Uncover and bake for an additional 15 minutes.

Serves 4-6

VEGETALI RIPIENI MISTI

Mixed Stuffed Vegetables

This is a tasty variety of stuffed vegetables, each having its distinct taste. It can be eaten warm or at room temperature in the summer eaten. They are featured in many of the trattorias in Rome and all of Italy.

Ingredients:

3 medium Zucchini
3 large Onions, peeled
2 medium Eggplants
1 lb. large Mushrooms (for stuffing)

1. Wash all vegetables. Cut off and discard the ends of the zucchini. Cut zucchini in half crosswise and then cut lengthwise in half. Do the same with the eggplants and set aside.
2. Remove stems from the caps of the mushrooms and set aside. Cut onion in half lengthwise from root to stem. Place in a pot of cold water and bring to a boil, and let cook for two minutes until tender but not soft. Drain and set aside to cool.

For the stuffing:

4 cups flavored breadcrumbs	*8 Tbs. milk*
8 sprigs flat-leaf parsley, finely chopped	*8 basil leaves, finely cut*
2 large onions, finely chopped	*4 garlic cloves, finely chopped*
1 cup grated Parmigiana-Reggiano cheese	*5 Tbs. Butter*
5 Tbs. olive oil	

1. Place 2 Tbs. each of the butter and oil in a heavy skillet over moderate heat. Add the chopped onion and sauté until softened. Add the garlic and stir well. Add the parsley and basil and stir. Cook an additional minute and remove from heat. Place in a bowl to cool and set aside.
2. Scoop the zucchini pulp out of the shell, leaving a ½-inch border around the sides and ends. Chop the pulp finely and sauté in the same skillet with one Tbs. each of oil and butter. Sauté until tender and pour into a separate bowl to cool. Repeat same procedure with the eggplant
3. Chop the mushroom stems finely and sauté in the same procedure as the zucchini and eggplant and set aside in a separate bowl.
4. Divide the sautéed onion mixture evenly into four parts. Add each part to the individual bowls for the sautéed vegetables, reserve one of the parts for the onions in their own bowl.
5. Add one cup of breadcrumbs and ¼ cup Parmesan cheese into each bowl. Add two Tbs. milk to each bowl. Beat the eggs and divide equally in each of the 4 bowls. Add salt and pepper to taste to each bowl.
6. Mix each separate bowl well and add a little more milk if the mixture seems dry.

To assemble:

1. Preheat oven to 350-degrees. Lightly grease a large baking dish.
2. Separate each layer of the cooled onion.
3. Fill each vegetable with its corresponding stuffing.
4. Bake, covered, for the first 30 minutes, remove cover and bake an additional 15 minutes or until tender and a golden color on top. Let rest for a few minutes before serving.

Serves 8-10

Variations:

1. Add 2 cups crumbled, cooked Italian sausage or chopped ham to the stuffing and divide accordingly.
2. Add 1 lb. ricotta or cream cheese to the recipe and divide accordingly.
3. Spread layer of tomato basil sauce on the bottom of the baking dish, place stuffed vegetables over it and bake.

POMODORI RIPIENI CON RISO

Rice-stuffed Tomatoes

This is another tasty summer dish. You can also substitute fresh mint for the basil for a unique and different taste.

Ingredients:

12 large, firm Tomatoes
¾ cup Arborio rice, uncooked
8 sprigs flat-leaf parsley, finely chopped
½ cup olive oil

6 basil leaves, finely chopped
½ cup grated Parmigiana-Reggiano cheese
3 garlic cloves, finely chopped
Salt and pepper to taste

1. Preheat oven to 350 degrees. Wash tomatoes, slice tops off and reserve. Scoop out the pulp and juices and press through a sieve into a large bowl, making sure not to include the seeds.

2. Sprinkle tomato cavity lightly with salt and set aside.

3. Meanwhile, combine garlic, basil and parsley to tomato pulp juice.

4. Add the rice and Parmesan cheese to bowl and mix well. Fill tomatoes with rice mixture, replace tops and transfer to a lightly oiled baking dish.

5. Cover with foil and bake 50 minutes. Remove foil and bake an additional 10 minutes. Serve warm or at room temperature. **Serves 4-6**

PEPERONI RIPIENI

Stuffed Peppers

This is for the person who enjoys peppers, and a perfect dish in cold weather that is very comforting and full of flavor.

Ingredients:

2 red bell Peppers
4 green bell Peppers
2 yellow bell peppers
1 medium Eggplant, peeled and diced
½ stick (4 Tbs.) butter
¼ cup olive oil

3 large onions, finely chopped
3 cloves garlic, finely chopped
½ cup grated Parmigiana-Reggiano cheese
1 cup milk
Salt and pepper to taste
4 cups breadcrumbs

For the topping:

1 garlic clove, finely chopped
4 ripe tomatoes, cubed
2 sprigs flat-leaf parsley, chopped
Salt and pepper to taste

1 Tbs. olive oil
2 basil leaves, finely chopped
pinch of oregano

1. Heat the oil in a heavy skillet over moderate heat. Add the onion and sauté, stirring until softened but not burned. Add the garlic, parsley, basil and stir well.
2. Add the diced eggplant, stir well and cook for 2-3 minutes until slightly softened.
3. Remove from heat, add breadcrumbs and mix. Add the Parmesan cheese, milk, salt and pepper, mix well and set aside.
4. Cut bell peppers in half from stem to bottom and remove core, stem and all seeds. Wash and drain.
5. Preheat oven to 350 degrees. Lightly grease a large baking dish.
6. Place a tiny slice of butter in the bottom of each pepper half. Fill with stuffing.
7. Mix all ingredients for topping together in a small bowl and spoon on the top of each pepper.
8. Add ¼ cup water to the bottom of the baking pan. Place stuffed pepper in pan, cover with foil and bake for 30 minutes. Uncover and bake an additional 30 minutes until tender. Serve hot or at room temperature. **Serves 6**

Variations:

1. Omit eggplant and add two bags of fresh spinach, cleaned cooked, chopped and with water squeezed out.
2. Add one lb. cleaned, sliced mushrooms to step #2 instead of eggplant
3. Substitute 3 cups cooked rice instead of the breadcrumbs

Note: Additional meatless entrees can be found in the Pasta, Pasta Ripiena, Polenta, Pasta al Forno and Risotti sections.

Chapter V: Contorni/Side dishes

In a traditional Italian Meal, the "Contorno" accompanies the Main Entrée

- Zucchini Trifolati
- Zucchini al Pomodoro Fresco
- Zucchini al' Aceto
- Zucchini Fritti Impannati
- Zucchini in Pastella
- Fiori di Zucchini Fritti
- Fritelle di Zucchini
- Zucchini Ripieni
- Melanzane Ripiene
- Zucchini all' Olio e Parmigiana
- Melanzane Fritte
- Frittelle di Melanzane
- Melanzane al Funghetto
- Ratatouille
- Peperonata
- Giardiniera di Peperoni
- Peperonata alla Mamma
- Peperonata in Padella
- Fagiolini al Burro e Formaggio
- Fagiolini alle Mandorle
- Fagiolini all' Estate
- Fagiolini all' Arcobaleno
- Fagiolini al Prezzemolo
- Insalata di Fagiolini
- Fagiolini al Prosciutto
- Asparagi Burro e Formaggio
- Asparagi al Volti in Prosciutto
- Carciofi Ripieni Meditteraneo
- Carciofi in Intigolo al Limone
- Spinaci Aglio e Olio
- Spinaci alla Parmigiana
- Sformata di Spinaci
- Sformata al Burro e Prosciutto
- Broccoli alla Romana
- Broccoli al Limone
- Broccoli all' Abbruzzese
- Broccoli Gratinee

- Cavolifiori Fritti
- Broccoli Rape Aglio e Olio
- Cavolini di Bruxelles alla Mamma
- Scarola Verde e Rossa
- Erbette Casalinghe
- Sedano col Profumo di Acciuga
- Finocchio col Profumo di Acciuga
- Finocchio in Padella alla Suzanna
- Insalata Finocchio
- Cipolline Agrodolce
- Cipolline in Crema
- Anelli di Cipolle
- Pomodori Gratinati
- Verdure Miste alla Griglia
- Ceci al Rosmarino
- Crocchette di Patate Tradizionale
- Patate al Forno alla Parmigiana
- Patate Arrosto alla Fiamma
- Patate al Forno per le Feste
- Patate Casalinghe
- Puré di Patate
- Insalata Russa da Noi
- Frittelle di Patate
- Patate al Forno Semplice
- Patate al Forno Ripiene
- Insalata di Patate Aglio e Olio
- Patate Gratinate
- Insalata di Patate e Fagiolini
- Souffle di Patate
- Patate Dolci al Forno
- Patate Dolci Arrosto
- Puré di Patate Dolce

ZUCCHINI TRIFOLATI

Zucchini Sautéed with Garlic and Parsley

Here is a side dish that Franca introduced to Fr. Matt and he enjoyed from the onset. It is packed with flavor, and goes well with almost anything.

Ingredients:

3 Tbs. olive oil
4 medium Zucchini
2 garlic cloves
4 basil leaves
4 sprigs flat-leaf parsley
2 Tbs. grated Parmigiana-Reggiano cheese
Salt and pepper to taste

1. Wash and dry zucchini. Cut off and discard the ends. Slice zucchini crosswise in ¼-inch thick rounds.
2. Chop the garlic parsley and basil together.
3. Heat oil in a heavy skillet over moderate to high heat. Add zucchini and sauté over lively fire, stirring constantly so that they do not burn. Zucchini should cook in 5-6 minutes.
4. Lower heat, add the chopped garlic, parsley and basil and stir for an additional minutes. Add the salt and pepper to taste.
5. Place in a serving dish and sprinkle with cheese. Serve hot.

Serves 6-8

ZUCCHINI AL POMODORO FRESCO

Zucchini with Fresh Tomatoes

Here we have the added dimension of the flavor of the tomato that richly accompanies the zucchini.

Using preceding recipe for Zucchini Trifolati, add one onion, peeled and sliced, and sauté with zucchini at step 3.

1. Add two fresh tomatoes, seeded, peeled and chopped, and add at step 4 with the garlic, parsley and basil.

ZUCCHINI AL'ACETO

Zucchini with Vinegar

This is a true summer treat that goes well with grilled meat or fish. Fr. Matt recalls this from his childhood and at times that the fresh parsley can be replaced with fresh mint. In Italian cuisine, this preparation is called "Scapece," named after the cook, Marcus Apicius. The Ancient Romans would use vinegar to preserve and pickle their food.

Ingredients:

4 medium Zucchini
4 Tbs. olive oil
4 Tbs. red wine vinegar
2 basil leaves, chopped
2 sprigs flat-leaf parsley, chopped
Salt and freshly ground pepper to taste

1. Wash and dry zucchini, cutting off and discarding the ends. Slice crosswise in ¼-inch thick rounds.
2. Heat oil in a heavy skillet, add zucchini slices and fry over a lively fire until golden in color. Remove with a slotted spoon and place in a bowl.
3. When all the zucchini are fried, sprinkle with the vinegar and season with salt and pepper.
4. Sprinkle the chopped basil and parsley on top of the zucchini and serve warm or at room temperature.

Serves 6-8

Zucchini Fritti Impannati

Breaded Fried Zucchini

These are tasty and some will not even make it to the serving platter, but be eaten practically right from the frying pan since they are that good!

Ingredients:

4 medium Zucchini
1 Tbs. milk
Flour for dredging
3 eggs, lightly beaten, more if needed
2 cups flavored breadcrumbs
Oil for frying

1. Wash and dry zucchini, cutting off and discarding the ends. Slice lengthwise about ¼-inch thick.
2. In a deep bowl, beat the egg and milk lightly. Put the flour in a deep dish and the breadcrumbs in another.
3. Dredge each zucchini slice in the flour, then dip in the beaten egg mixture and lastly in the breadcrumbs. Continue until all zucchini are done.
4. Pour the oil about ½-inch deep in a heavy skillet and heat over moderate to high flame. Sprinkle a few breadcrumbs in the oil to test whether it is hot enough. When they crumbs begin to sizzle, start frying the zucchini to a golden color on each side.
5. Lay the fried zucchini on a paper towel to absorb the extra oil. Continue until all the zucchini are done.
6. Arrange on a serving dish and serve.

Serves 6-8

Zucchini in Pastella

Batter-fried Zucchini

Fr. Matt learned this recipe when visiting and dining near Lake Bolsena, close to Orvieto, but they are enjoyed throughout Italy.

Ingredients:

4 medium Zucchini
2 eggs, beaten
1 Tbs. olive oil
Pinch of salt

1 cup milk or water
½ tsp. baking powder
1 and ¼ cups flour
Oil for frying

1. Wash and dry the zucchini and remove and discard the ends. Cut lengthwise about ¼-inch thick.
2. Combine the milk and egg and mix well. Add the dry ingredients and blend into a smooth batter.
3. Pour the oil about ½-inch deep in a heavy skillet and heat over moderate to high flame and add a drop of the batter. When it sizzles, the oil is ready.
4. Dip each zucchini slice into the batter and place immediately into the frying pan. Fry until a golden color on each side.
5. Lay the fried zucchini on paper towels to absorb excess oil. Serve hot.

Serves 6-8

FIORI DI ZUCCHINI FRITTI

Batter-fried Zucchini Flowers

A summer treat that everyone looks forward to enjoying and the delicate taste is unique.

Ingredients:

12 Zucchini flowers
1 cup milk or water
1 egg, beaten
½ tsp. baking powder
1 Tbs. olive oil
1 and ¼ cups flour
Pinch of salt
Oil for frying

1. To prepare zucchini flowers, wash carefully to remove any dirt, then remove the green stem and the yellow seeds inside the flower. Rinse and pat dry with paper towels.
2. Prepare the pastella batter according to the preceding recipe and set aside.
3. Heat the oil in a heavy skillet over moderate heat.
4. Dip each flower in the batter and immediately place in hot oil. Fry until golden, about 2-3 minutes on each side. Drain on paper towels to absorb excess grease and serve hot.

Serves 3-4

FRITTELLE DI ZUCCHINI

Zucchini Pancakes

This pancake, made with shredded zucchini and a variety of savory flavors, can easily be served instead of pasta, risotto or polenta to accompany a main course.

Ingredients:

3 medium Zucchini
2 eggs, beaten
½ cup grated Parmigiana-Reggiano cheese
1 onion, grated
¾ cup flour
Salt and pepper to taste
Oil for frying

1. Wash and dry the zucchini, cut off and discard the ends. Shred zucchini, place in a bowl, add the onion and egg and mix well. Add the flour and seasoning.
2. Heat a thin coating of the oil in a heavy skillet over moderate heat. Test the temperature by adding a drop of the batter. When it sizzles, the oil is hot enough.
3. Place heaping tablespoonfuls in of the mixture in the pan and cook until golden on each side, about 2-3 minutes. Turn and continue to cook.
4. Place on paper towels to absorb grease. Serve hot.

Serves 6-8

ZUCCHINI RIPIENI

Stuffed Zucchini

Fr. Matt enjoyed this great dish during his very first visit to Rome and he has duplicated it here with the able help of the master, Franca.

Ingredients:

3 medium Zucchini

2 cloves garlic, chopped

2 basil leaves

3 Tbs. olive oil

2 Tbs. milk, if needed

1 onion, chopped

1 sprig parsley, chopped

1 cup breadcrumbs

¼ cup grated Parmigiana-Reggiano cheese

Salt and pepper to taste

1. Preheat oven to 350 degrees.
2. Wash zucchini. Cut ends off and discard them. Cut zucchini in half crosswise and also in half lengthwise. Scoop out the center pulp in the shell, leaving a border of ½ in around the sizes and ends.
3. Sauté the onion in a skillet with oil until softened. Add garlic and stir. Chop the zucchini pulp and sauté in the pan until soft.
4. Add parsley and basil to the skillet, stir and remove from heat.
5. Add breadcrumbs and grated cheese to skillet and mix well. If filling is too hard, add milk if needed.
6. Put a little water on the bottom of a baking dish. Stuff each zucchini with filling. Place in the baking dish and cover with foil. Bake 10 minutes, covered, to steam then uncover and bake an additional 20 minutes or until zucchini is tender when pierced with a fork.
7. Serve hot.

Serves 6

MELANZANE RIPIENE

Stuffed Eggplant

See Stuffed Zucchini recipe above and substitute accordingly.

ZUCCHINI ALL'OLIO E PARMIGIANA

Zucchini with Oil and Parmesan Cheese

This is very easy and healthy and has great taste to accompany the main course. Make sure that the oil is very fruity so that it can add a great flavor dimension.

Ingredients:

4 medium Zucchini
2 cloves garlic, finely chopped
3 Tbs. extra-virgin olive oil
¼ cup grated Parmigiana-Reggiano cheese

1. Wash and dry the zucchini and cut off and discard the ends. Cut in half lengthwise and crosswise. Steam the pieces by placing steamer in a pan with a cup of lightly salted water.
2. Bring water to a boil and cook 10 minutes.
3. Meanwhile, warm olive oil with garlic cloves, but do not allow the garlic to burn. Discard garlic.
4. Place zucchini in a platter, drizzle with garlic infused oil and sprinkle with grated cheese.
5. Serve warm or at room temperature.

Serves 6

MELANZANE FRITTE

Fried Eggplant

This side dish is well enjoyed whether served warm or even at room temperature. The eggplant rounds can even be cut into strips like French Fries before frying.

Refer to the preceding Fried Zucchini recipe, substituting one large eggplant for the zucchini.

1. Wash and dry the eggplant, cutting off and discarding the ends. Slice crosswise ¼-inch thick.
2. Proceed, using either breadcrumbs or batter as desired.

Serves 4-6

FRITTELLE DI MELANZANE

Eggplant Fritters

These are typical of Calabria on the southern tip of Italy, near to Sicily. They are almost like a vegetarian meatball. They are fragrant and superb, especially when eaten piping hot.

Ingredients:

2 lbs. Eggplant	2 garlic cloves, chopped
2 sprigs flat-leaf parsley, chopped	½ onion, chopped
3 basil leaves, chopped	½ tsp. salt
1 and ¼ cups breadcrumbs	½ cup grated Parmigiana-Reggiano cheese
3 Tbs. oil	Oil for frying

1. Peel and cube eggplant, cook in boiling water for 15-20 minutes. Drain and let cool.
2. Meanwhile, sauté onion in olive oil until softened, add garlic and stir. Do not allow to burn. Add parsley and basil, turn off flame and set aside.
3. Mix eggplant in a bowl with sautéed ingredients, breadcrumbs and grated cheese.
4. Form into patties and fry until golden. Place on paper towels to absorb excess grease.
   Serves 6

MELANZANE AL FUNGHETTO

Eggplant Mushroom-style

This goes well with either meat or fish and is moistened and enhanced by the tomato.

Ingredients:

2 medium Eggplant	1 onion, chopped
4 Tbs. olive oil	3 tomatoes, fresh or canned
1 Tbs. capers	salt and pepper to taste

1. Wash and dry the eggplant. Remove and discard the ends. Cut the unpeeled eggplant into ½-inch dice.
2. Place oil in a heavy skillet over moderate heat. Add the onion and soften for 3-4 minutes. Add the eggplant, capers and tomatoes and sauté for 15 minutes, stirring occasionally.
3. Test for tenderness and cook an additional few minutes if needed.
4. Season with salt and pepper and serve warm or at room temperature. **Serves 6**

RATATOUILLE

Vegetable Medley

The word ratatouille is based on the French word "touiller" which means, "to toss." It originated in the area near to Nice, France which is not far from the northwest Italian border. It is a lovely medley of vegetables, here further enhanced with herbs. It is a versatile side dish and can also be used on crostini as an antipasto.

Ingredients:

2 Eggplants, cut in ½-inch dice	2/3 cup olive oil
1 red bell Pepper	2 Onions, peeled and sliced thinly
1 green bell Pepper	2 garlic cloves, finely chopped
2 small Zucchini, cut in ½-inch dice	3 sprigs flat-leaf parsley, coarsely chopped
5 tomatoes, fresh or canned	3 basil leaves, chopped coarsely
	Salt and freshly ground pepper to taste

1. Sprinkle the diced eggplant with salt and set aside for 20 minutes.
2. Meanwhile, remove seeds from peppers and slice in strips. Remove seeds and skin from tomatoes and cut in chunks. Prepare all other vegetables.
3. Rinse the eggplant and pat dry with absorbent paper.
4. Heat the oil in a heavy skillet over moderate heat. Add the onion and soften for 5-10 minutes, but do not allow to brown. Add the garlic and stir well.
5. Add the rest of the vegetables and herbs and stir. Add salt and pepper to taste. Cover and bring to a boil. Remove cover and continue to cook for an additional 15-20 minutes, stirring frequently until the vegetables are soft, but not mushy.
6. Serve hot or at room temperature

Note: This recipe can also be cooked in the oven:

1. Preheat oven to 350 degrees. Soften onion and garlic in oil as in step 4.
2. Place all prepared vegetables and herbs in a baking dish. Pour onion and garlic mixture over the vegetables and stir well. Cover with foil and bake for 20 to 25 minutes or until vegetables are tender.

Serves 6-8

PEPERONATA

Sautéed Peppers

This side dish is well-known in both the north and south of Italy and many times can be added to sandwiches or on hamburgers as well.

Ingredients:

6 red bell Peppers

2 large Onions, peeled and sliced

3 basil leaves, coarsely chopped

½ tsp sugar

1 garlic clove, finely chopped (optional)

1/3 cup olive oil

5 fresh Tomatoes, seeded, peeled & diced

3 sprigs flat-leaf parsley, finely chopped

salt to taste

1. Wash peppers, remove seeds and cut lengthwise into ½-inch strips. Place oil in a heavy skillet. Add the peppers and onions and sauté over a lively fire, stirring constantly for 10 minutes.
2. Add the garlic, tomatoes, herbs and salt to taste and continue to cook, stirring until the peppers are tender. Serve hot or cold. **Serves 6-8**

GIARDINIERA DI PEPERONI

Bell pepper medley

This originated from the area of Puglia on the Adriatic coast and is very popular all year round.

Ingredients:

5 large bell Peppers in assorted colors

3 cloves garlic, chopped

Oil for frying

1 cup pitted Gaeta olives

½ cup capers

2 Tomatoes, chopped

1 sprig flat-leaf parsley, chopped

3 basil leaves, chopped

salt and pepper to taste

1. Wash and core the peppers and cut into slices. Fry garlic in oil until softened, but not brown. Add pepper slices and cook, stirring occasionally until tender.
2. Add olives, capers and tomatoes, stirring well to heat through.
3. Add parsley and basil, salt and pepper, stir and serve hot or at room temperature. **Serves 6-8**

PEPERONATA ALLA MAMMA

My mother's peppers

This is a very tasty side dish that has the surprising addition of the vinegar and breadcrumbs. Fr. Matt's mother learned from a dear friend some years ago.

Ingredients:

6 red bell Peppers
¼ cup balsamic vinegar
Salt and pepper to taste

1 cup extra virgin olive oil
½ cup unflavored breadcrumbs
2 cloves garlic, finely chopped

1. Wash and dry peppers, removing core and seeds and cutting each pepper into eight pieces.
2. Heat oil in skillet over moderate heat, add peppers and sauté until softened and light golden in color. Add garlic and cook until softened. Remove from heat.
3. Add the vinegar to the pan to deglaze. Add the breadcrumbs and mix thoroughly.
4. Place in a deep serving platter, season with salt and pepper to taste. Serve at room temperature.   **Serves 6-8**

PEPERONATA IN PADELLA

Fried peppers

This is one of the Mauriello family's favorite summer side dishes for many years now, and is best when served with a broiled steak.

Ingredients:

18 Cubanel Peppers
½ cup olive oil

½ cup grated Pecorino cheese
Salt and pepper to taste

1. Trim stems off peppers, wash with cold water and dry thoroughly with paper towels.
2. Heat oil in large frying pan over moderate heat. Fry peppers a few at a time, covered, until light golden in color – about 3-5 minutes on each side. Place on a deep serving platter and sprinkle with a layer of grated Pecorino cheese. Continue this process until all peppers are done.
3. Pour cooking oil over the peppers, add salt and pepper and sprinkle the remaining cheese on top. Serve warm or at room temperature.
4. Remove remaining seed core before eating.   **Serves 6-8**

FAGIOLINI AL BURRO E FORMAGGIO

String Beans with butter and cheese

Although a very simple recipe, it is nonetheless rich and tasty with the rich flavors of the butter and the grated cheese. It goes well with many main courses.

Ingredients:

1 and ½ lbs. fresh String beans
¼ cup grated Parmigiana-Reggiano cheese

½ stick sweet butter
salt and freshly ground pepper to taste

1. Snap ends off string beans and wash. Fill a large saucepan ¾ full with lightly salted water and bring to a boil. Add the string beans and cook approximately 10 minutes until tender, but firm.
2. Drain and set aside. Put butter in the pan, melt and return string beans, stirring to coat well. Place in a serving dish and sprinkle with freshly ground pepper and grated cheese. Serve hot.

Serves 6

FAGIOLINI ALLE MANDORLE

String Beans with almonds

This has always been considered a very elegant side dish over the years and the crunchy taste of the almonds adds a special texture to the string beans.

Using preceding recipe, omit the grated Parmesan cheese and substitute ¼ cup slivered almonds.

Fagiolini all' Estate

Summertime String Beans

This is a warm weather side dish, since the word "l'estate" means "the summer." The fragrant herbs and garden tomatoes add to the freshness of the recipe.

Ingredients:

1 and ½ lbs. fresh String beans
1 onion, peeled and chopped
2 sprigs flat-leaf parsley, coarsely chopped
Salt and freshly ground pepper to taste
2 ripe fresh tomatoes
2 basil leaves, coarsely chopped
2 Tbs. olive oil
2 Tbs. grated Parmigiana-Reggiano cheese

1. Prepare and cook string beans as in prior recipe. Drain and set aside.
2. Heat olive oil in saucepan, add the onion and cook until softened but not browned.
3. Meanwhile, wash, peel and seed the tomatoes and cut in large chunks. When onion is softened, add the tomato, basil and parsley and stir well. Cook an additional two minutes.
4. Return string beans to the saucepan. Stir to reheat. Add salt and pepper to taste.
5. Place in a serving dish, sprinkle with grated cheese and serve hot.

Serves 6

FAGIOLINI ALL' ARCOBALENO

Rainbow String Beans

The word "arcobaleno" refers to the rainbow, since there are various colors represented. Not only does it look festive with the various colors, but is very enjoyable in taste as well.

Ingredients:

1 and ½ lbs. green and white String beans

1 red bell pepper

1 small garlic clove

Juice of one lemon

1 yellow bell pepper

2 Tbs. olive oil

2 Tbs. capers

Salt and pepper to taste

1. Follow recipe for pepperoni trifolati alla fiamma steps 1 and 2 to prepare roasted peppers. Set aside.
2. Follow instructions for cooking string beans in prior recipes.
3. Peel garlic clove and squeeze through a garlic presser into a saucepan. Add the oil, lemon juice, capers, salt and pepper and mix with a whisk over low heat for one minute.
4. Add the string beans and pepper strips. Stir to coat ingredients.
5. Place in a serving dish and serve hot or cold. **Serves 6**

FAGIOLINI AL PREZZEMOLO

String Beans with Parsley

Here parsley serves as the main flavor feature and it helps to enhance the string beans and compliments them very well.

Ingredients:

1 and ½ lbs. fresh String beans

1 onion, finely chopped

3 sprigs flat-leaf parsley, finely chopped

2 garlic cloves, finely chopped

½ cup olive oil

Salt and pepper to taste

1. Cook string beans according to prior recipes.
2. In a large skillet, soften onion in oil but do not allow to brown. Add garlic, stir and cook 1-2 minutes.
3. Add drained string beans, salt and pepper to taste, stirring to coat. Place beans in a serving bowl, add chopped parsley and stir well. Garnish with additional chopped parsley and some sprigs of fresh parsley. **Serves 6**

INSALATA DI FAGIOLINI

String Bean Salad

This is a tangy and refreshing summer dish that is very well received and enjoyed, and it is just perfect for the summer months.

Ingredients:

1 and ½ lbs. fresh String beans
2 sprigs flat-leaf parsley, chopped
1/3 cup olive oil
1 clove garlic
4 basil leaves, chopped
2 Tbs. white wine vinegar (optional)
Salt and pepper to taste

1. Snap off ends of string beans and wash.
2. Fill saucepan ¾ full with lightly salted water and bring to a boil
3. Boil string beans until tender but firm, about 7-10 minutes. Drain and set aside.
4. Chop basil, parsley and garlic together until very fine.
5. Place beans in a bowl, add garlic mixture, oil and vinegar to bowl and toss well. Add salt and pepper to taste. Serve warm.

Serves 6

FAGIOLINI AL PROSCIUTTO

String Beans with Ham

The distinct and rich flavor of the prosciutto adds a depth to the otherwise plain flavor of the string beans.

1. Follow recipe for Insalata di Fagiolini.
2. Add ¼ lb. prosciutto ham, cut ¼-inches thick, then cut in chunks.
3. Sauté the ham in the oil, add to the string beans and toss well. Season with salt and pepper.

Serves 6

ASPARAGI BURRO E FORMAGGIO

Asparagus with Butter and Cheese

Here the asparagus are enhanced by the creamy and rich flavors of the butter and cheese.

Ingredients:

2 lbs. Asparagus
½ stick sweet butter, melted
¼ cup grated Parmigiana-Reggiano cheese
Salt to taste

1. Trim and discard tough asparagus ends. Place in a large frying pan, cover with lightly salted water, bring to a boil and cook until tender but not soft. Test for tenderness at the flower and tip. The stalk can be somewhat firm.
2. Drain, place in a serving dish, cover with heated melted butter and sprinkle with grated cheese. Serve hot.

Serves 6-8

ASPARAGI AL VOLTI IN PROSCIUTTO

Asparagus Wrapped in Prosciutto

The savory flavor of the prosciutto adds a special taste to the asparagus and the presentation on the table is somewhat different and definitely elegant.

Ingredients:

2 lbs. Asparagus
½ stick butter, melted
½ lb. prosciutto ham

1. Cook asparagus according to the Asparagi Burro e Formaggio recipe.
2. Cut prosciutto slices in half, lengthwise. Take three asparagus at a time, wrap with ham and place in a baking dish. Cover with melted butter and bake in a 350-degree oven for 10 minutes.

Serves 6-8

CARCIOFI RIPIENI MEDITERRANEO

Mediterranean Stuffed Artichoke

Artichokes are well enjoyed and both Franca and Fr. Matt collaborated in developing this delicious stuffing to help give a special and unique flavor to this side dish.

Ingredients:

6 fresh Artichokes
2 garlic cloves, finely chopped
1/3 cup grated Parmigiana-Reggiano cheese
Pinch of hot red pepper flakes
2 cups flavored breadcrumbs
3 basil leaves, finely chopped
¼ lb. prosciutto ham, finely chopped
1/3 plus 3 Tbs. olive oil
2 Tbs. water
Juice of one lemon
Salt to taste

1. Cut off artichoke stem, slice and reserve. Remove the small hard outer leaves toward the base and discard.

2. With a scissor, trim off about ½-inch off the tips of the remaining leaves. With a knife, slice off ½-inch from the top end of the artichoke. Open artichoke with your finger and remove the fuzzy choke in the middle.

3. Wash artichoke under cold running water and sprinkle the top with a little lemon juice. Place artichoke upside down to drain.

4. In a bowl, mix all the ingredients for the stuffing, using only 1/3 cup of the oil. Moisten with water and mix well, stuff artichokes between leaves and in the center.

5. Prepare a large saucepan by adding water about 1-inch deep. Add 3 Tbs. of the oil and place artichokes standing in the pan. Add the cut stems, bring the pan to a boil, cover and reduce heat. Cook for 45 minutes to an hour. Add more water if necessary to keep bottom of pan moist. The remaining liquid is used as a sauce. Serve hot.

Serves 6

CARCIOFI IN INTIGOLO AL LIMONE

Artichokes with Lemon Dip

This is a spring and summer dish that is a true classic and would be served on Lake Como in the north of Italy.

Ingredients:

6 fresh Artichokes
1 cup olive oil
1 garlic clove, peeled and crushed
Juice of one lemon
3 sprigs flat-leaf parsley, finely chopped
Salt and freshly ground pepper to taste

1. For cleaning and cooking the artichokes, follow same procedure as the stuffed artichoke recipe.

2. For sauce, mix all ingredients, let sit for 30 minutes to amalgamate flavors. Pour into 6 individual serving cups.

3. Cooked artichokes can be served hot or cold with the dipping liquid.

Serves 6

SPINACI AGLIO E OLIO

Spinach with Oil and Garlic

A very simple side dish where the garlic highlights the subtle flavor of the spinach.

Ingredients:

Three 10-oz bags of Spinach or 3 packages frozen
2 garlic cloves, peeled and crushed

1/3 cup olive oil
Salt and freshly ground pepper to taste

1. Remove thick stems and thoroughly wash spinach. Set aside with water that clings to leaves.
2. Place oil and garlic into a large saucepan over moderate heat. Sauté garlic lightly until it becomes fragrant and a light golden color. Do not allow to burn. Place wet spinach into pan, add ½ cup water and cover. Let cook for 2-3 minutes or until spinach is just wilted.
3. Add salt and pepper to taste, mix well to incorporate all flavors and serve immediately.

Serves 6

Variation: Fry 4 strips of bacon until crisp, drain on paper towels, crumble and sprinkle on top of spinach.

SPINACI ALLA PARMIGIANA

Spinach Parma-style

Here the typical elements of the creamy butter and cheese have a crunchy addition of the pine nuts for a special flavor.

Ingredients:

Three 10-oz packages of fresh Spinach or 3 packages frozen
3 Tbs. butter, melted
½ cup grated Parmigiana-Reggiano cheese

Salt and pepper to taste
2 Tbs. pignoli (pine nuts)

1. Thoroughly wash spinach, discard tough stems and set aside with the water that clings to the leaves.
2. Pour ¼ cup water in the bottom of a large, heavy pot. Add salt and pepper to taste. Bring water to boil. Add the spinach, cook 2 minutes until wilted, turn top leaves to the bottom. Continue to cook an additional 2-3 minutes.
3. Place in a serving dish, pour melted butter over spinach and mix well. Sprinkle with grated cheese and serve garnished with the pine nuts sprinkled on top.   **Serves 6-8**

SFORMATA DI SPINACI

Spinach Soufflé

This is a very delicate side dish and makes a positive impression when served at the table. It is good for an intimate dinner gathering of friends. Franca has added her own northern Italian dimension with the usage of the nutmeg.

Ingredients:

One 10-oz. package of fresh Spinach
4 Tbs. butter
6 large eggs, separated
2 Tbs. flour
Dash of ground nutmeg
¾ cup milk
½ cup grated Parmigiana-Reggiano cheese
Salt and pepper to taste

1. Trim tough stems from spinach leaves, wash thoroughly and cook in a pot of lightly salted water for one minute. Drain, cook, squeeze spinach dry and finely chop. Set aside.

2. Preheat oven to 350 degrees and place rack in the center position.

3. Use 2 Tbs. butter to grease a 12-cup soufflé dish.

4. Beat egg yolks, flour and nutmeg in a large bowl until thick – about 5 minutes. Bring milk to a boil in a saucepan and gradually beat the milk into the bowl with the egg mixture.

5. Return egg mixture to the same saucepan, heat until the mixture boils and thickens, about 2 minutes, stirring constantly

6. Remove from heat, stir in remaining 2 Tbs. butter and cool for 10 minutes.

7. Mix in the spinach and Parmesan cheese, season with salt and pepper. Blend with egg mixture. In a separate bowl, beat egg whites until stiff but not dry.

8. Fold egg whites into spinach and egg mixture, pour into a buttered baking dish and place in oven. Bake until puffed and golden – about 35 minutes. Serve immediately.

Serves 6

SPINACI AL BURRO E PROSCIUTTO

Spinach with Butter and Ham

The rather plain spinach is made more interesting by incorporating the treasures of Parma, considered by some as the culinary capital of Italy. Here we feature its two most famous products, Parmigiano-Reggiano Cheese and Prosciutto di Parma.

Ingredients:

2 lbs. fresh Spinach
½ cup chopped Prosciutto ham
¼ cup grated Parmigiana-Reggiano cheese
1/3 cup melted butter
Salt and pepper to taste

1. Remove any tough stems and thoroughly wash spinach.

2. Bring 2 cups lightly salted water to a boil in a large saucepan. Add spinach, cover and cook for 5 minutes.

3. Drain and squeeze spinach to remove most of the moisture.

4. Melt butter in a skillet, add ham, stir to coat then add the spinach, mix and add salt and pepper to taste. Place in a serving bowl, sprinkle with grated cheese and serve hot.

Serves 6

Variation: Substitute Parmesan cheese for crumbled gorgonzola and add to skillet to melt before placing in a serving bowl.

Broccoli alla Romana

Broccoli Roman-style

This style of broccoli is enjoyed in the beautiful of Rome, where they enjoy mixing a variety of flavors to give the dish extra taste and interest.

Ingredients:

2 bunches (approximately 3 lbs.) Broccoli
Salt and freshly ground pepper to taste
2 anchovy filets (optional)

3 garlic cloves, thinly sliced
½ cup olive oil
1 sprig flat-leaf parsley, chopped

1. Prepare the broccoli by cutting off the tough stem. Divide in florets and wash thoroughly under cold running water.
2. Fill a large saucepan 2/3 full with lightly salted water and bring to a boil. Add the broccoli and cook for 5-6 minutes. Drain and set aside.
3. Heat oil in a large skillet over moderate flame, add garlic and if desired, mash the anchovies and add them to the skillet.
4. When garlic browns, add the broccoli, season with salt and pepper and mix well. Place in a serving bowl, pour sauce from the pan over them and garnish with parsley. **Serves 6-8**

Broccoli al Limone

Broccoli with Lemon

Whether it is served cold or at room temperature, this is a refreshing summer side dish that goes very well with broiled or fried fish.

Ingredients:

2 bunches (approximately 3 lbs) Broccoli
¼ cup olive oil
1 lemon sliced crosswise for garnish

Juice of one lemon
Salt and freshly ground pepper to taste

1. Cook and drain broccoli according to steps 1 and 2 of prior recipe.
2. Mix oil and lemon juice with a whisk in a bowl. Add salt and pepper and pour over broccoli
3. Garnish with lemon slices. Serve hot or cold.
   Serves 6-8

BROCCOLI ALL' ABRUZZESE

Broccoli Abruzzi-style

The area of Abruzzo is well-known for their excellent cooks and there the use of Pecorino Romano cheese is more typically in the cuisine of this area that surrounds Rome. The Abruzzese people are called "forte e gentile" which means, "strong and kind."

Ingredients:

Two bunches (approximately 3 lbs.) Broccoli

¼ cup prosciutto ham, chopped

Salt and freshly ground pepper to taste

1 cup grated Pecorino cheese

1/3 cup olive oil

1. Cook and drain broccoli according to steps 1 and 2 of Broccoli alla Romana.
2. Heat oil in a large skillet. Add prosciutto and warm for a few minutes. Toss cooked broccoli in oil to coat. Place in a baking dish, sprinkle with grated cheese and bake for 5-10 minutes in a preheated 350-degree oven until the cheese is melted. Serve immediately.

Serves 6-8

BROCCOLI GRATINEE

Broccoli Swiss-style

Here is a very enjoyable and rich side dish that Franca has made over the years for her family and friends. Many years before Fr. Matt even met her, he enjoyed tasting it in the beautiful city of Lugano, Switzerland.

Ingredients:

Two bunches (approximately 3 lbs.) Broccoli

½ cup shredded Gruyere cheese

Salt and pepper to taste

½ cup grated Parmesan cheese

1 recipe basic Béchamel sauce

1. Prepare the béchamel sauce and set aside.
2. Cook and drain the broccoli according to steps 1 and 2 of Broccoli Romana
3. Put broccoli in a lightly buttered baking dish. Pour béchamel sauce over them, sprinkle with the shredded Gruyere and Parmesan cheese.
4. Place in a preheated 350-degree oven for 20 minutes or until a golden color. Serve hot.

Serves 6

CAVOLIFIORI FRITTI

Fried Cauliflower

This side dish is seen throughout all of Italy and is served with either fish or poultry. There are two options found below, that are equally enjoyed.

Ingredients:

1 head Cauliflower
1 garlic clove, unpeeled and crushed
1 and ½ to 2 cups flavored breadcrumbs
Oil for frying

1 Tbs. milk
2 eggs, beaten
Lemon wedges (optional)

1. Cut cauliflower into florets, rinse under cold water and dry. Fill a saucepan 2/3 full with lightly salted water and bring to a boil. Add florets and cook for 5-6 minutes. Drain and cool.
2. Mix eggs and milk in a bowl and beat lightly. Put breadcrumbs in a separate bowl. Dip each floret in the egg mixture and then coat with the breadcrumbs. Repeat the process until all florets are done.
3. Heat oil with unpeeled garlic in the skillet over moderate flame.
4. When garlic begins to sizzle, fry the breaded florets until golden on each side.
5. Serve hot garnished with lemon wedges.

Serves 6

Variation: Cauliflower in Batter

For the pastella or batter:

1 cup milk or water
1 egg, beaten
1 tsp. baking powder
Salt and pepper to taste

1 Tbs. olive oil
1 and ½ cups flour
pinch of salt
dash of ground nutmeg (optional)

1. Parboil cauliflower as in step 1 in the previous recipe. Combine all dry ingredients. Beat egg and milk together and add slowly to dry ingredients, mixing constantly to form a smooth batter.
2. To fry cauliflower, heat oil, dip cooked florets into batter, place directly into the hot oil and fry until golden. Repeat until all florets are done. Serve hot.

Note: Cauliflower can also be substituted for the preceding four broccoli recipes.

Broccoli Rape Aglio e Olio

Broccoli Rape with Garlic and Oil

Although this vegetable has a little bitter taste, it has a distinct flavor and is a very healthy vegetable that is rich in iron. It is more typical of the southern regions of Italy.

Ingredients:

Two bunches (approximately 3 lbs.) Broccoli Rape   4 cloves garlic, thinly sliced
½ cup olive oil   Salt and pepper to taste

1. Bring a large pot of lightly salted water to a boil.
2. Meanwhile, remove hard stems from broccoli rape, wash thoroughly and set aside. When water is ready, add broccoli rape, making sure all is submerged. Cover and bring to a boil, then reduce heat and cook for about 10 minutes or until stem is tender when pierced by a fork.
3. While broccoli is cooking, sauté the garlic lightly in the oil until light golden in color. Do not allow to burn.
4. Drain the broccoli rape when cooked, place in a large serving bowl, add the oil and garlic mixture and the salt and pepper. Mix well and serve hot.

Serves 6-8

Cavolini di Bruxelles alla Mamma

Mother's Brussels Sprouts

Fr. Matt learned this recipe from his mother many years back. It adds flavor and interest.

Ingredients:

Two boxes (approximately 3 lbs.) Brussels Sprouts   2 Tbs. grated Parmesan cheese
1 large onion, thinly sliced   Salt and pepper to taste
¼ cup olive oil   Parsley sprigs for garnish

1. Bring a large pot of lightly salted water to a boil. Rinse Brussels sprouts under cold running water. Boil for 10 minutes until tender but not overcooked.
2. While sprouts are cooking, sauté onion in a skillet until softened and light golden in color.
3. Drain cooked sprouts and return to pan. Add the onion and oil mixture and stir well. Add salt and pepper to taste. Place on a serving platter, sprinkle with grated cheese and garnish with fresh parsley sprigs.   **Serves 6-8**

SCAROLA VERDE E ROSSA

Red and Green Escarole

With the addition of the fresh tomatoes, this side dish is colorful and complements well a variety of main courses such as roasted or grilled meat.

Ingredients:

2 heads fresh Escarole

½ cup olive oil

Salt and pepper to taste

3 fresh tomatoes

2 cloves garlic, chopped

1. Thoroughly clean and wash escarole and cook in a pot of lightly salted water for about 10 minutes or until tender. Drain when done.

2. Meanwhile, blanch the 3 tomatoes by submerging them in hot water for one minute. Cool until able to handle, remove the skin, cut in half, remove the seeds and chop into cubes.

3. Put the oil and garlic in the same pot, heat until garlic is light golden in color. Return escarole to pot and stir to coat. Place on serving dish, add the chopped tomatoes, salt and pepper, mix well and garnish with fresh basil leaves.

Serves 6-8

ERBETTE CASALINGHE

Home-style Swiss Chard

This is that typical way that Franca learned to cook Swiss Chard from her mother, who picked it fresh from her garden. Over the years, her family and friends have enjoyed its subtle taste.

Ingredients:

2 lbs. Swiss Chard
2 cloves garlic, chopped
3 Tbs. butter
1 onion, chopped
¼ cup olive oil
Salt and pepper to taste

1. Thoroughly wash Swiss chard, set aside with water that clings to the leaves.

2. Heat oil and butter in a large pot. Add onion, cook until softened but not browned, add garlic and stir.

3. Add Swiss chard, stir and cover. Cook for 2-3 minutes, toss and cook an additional 2-3 minutes until tender. Add salt and pepper to taste. Serve hot.

Serves 6-8

Note: Swiss chard can also be substituted in recipes for spinach and escarole in these recipes: Spinach Aglio e Olio, Spinach alla Parmigiana and Scarola Verde e Rossa.

SEDANO COL PROFUMO DI ACCIUGA

Celery in Anchovy Sauce

The salty taste of the anchovies here adds a different and enhanced taste to the celery which could otherwise be somewhat bland. The olive oil helps to add an extra depth of richness as well.

Ingredients:

2 heads Celery
3 Tbs. extra virgin olive oil
6 anchovy filets
Juice of one lemon
2 garlic cloves, chopped
1 sprig flat-leaf parsley, chopped

1. Prepare celery by cutting off the hard base, tough outer stalks and leaves. Cut into 6-inch lengths. Place in salted boiling water and simmer for 15-20 minutes until tender.
2. Drain and dry on paper towels.
3. Heat oil and garlic over medium heat in a large skillet. Add the anchovies and mash with a fork. Add the lemon juice and the celery and mix until well-coated.
4. Cover and cook gently for 3-4 minutes. Add parsley and place in a serving bowl.

Serves 6-8

FINOCCHIO COL PROFUMO DI ACCIUGA

Fennel in Anchovy Sauce

This is very similar to the prior recipe, where the salty taste of the anchovies compliments the boiled fennel. Here the sweetness of the fennel adds a different taste dimension.

1. Following the preceding recipe, substitute 3 Fennel bulbs for the Celery.

FINOCCHIO IN PADELLA ALLA SUSANNA

Suzanne's Fennel

Fr. Matt watched his sister cook this while visiting her in Milan, and very much enjoyed it and wants to share it with others.

Ingredients:

3 Fennel bulbs
Salt and pepper to taste
½ stick (2 oz.) butter
¼ cup grated Parmigiana-Reggiano cheese

1. Prepare fennel by cutting off the base of the bulb, the hard outer stalks and leaves. Wash and cut in quarters lengthwise.
2. Melt butter in a large skillet over moderate heat. Add fennel, cover and reduce heat to low. Cook for 35-40 minutes. Check for tenderness with a fork. Cook an additional 5 minutes of necessary.
3. Place fennel on a platter, pour butter and juices over it, season with salt and pepper and sprinkle with grated cheese. Serve hot. **Serves 6-8**

INSALATA DI FINOCCHIO

Fennel Salad

Fr. Matt first tasted this in Israel and duplicated it upon his return. It is very refreshing.

Ingredients:

3 Fennel bulbs
½ cup Gaeta olives
½ cup olive oil
Salt and pepper to taste

Juice of 2 lemons
1 sprig flat-leaf parsley, chopped
1 red bell pepper
1 clove garlic, peeled & crushed (optional)

1. Cut off hard base from bulb of fennel, hard outer stalks and leaves. Wash and slice thinly and place in a bowl.
2. Core and cut the bell pepper, wash and dry and finely chop. Add to bowl with fennel.
3. In a smaller bowl, combine the oil, lemon, and garlic clove, and whisk together. Add the salt, pepper, parsley and olives and let rest a few minutes. Remove the garlic clove, pour over the fennel and pepper mixture and mix well. Serve chilled or at room temperature. **Serves 6-8**

CIPOLLINE AGRODOLCE

Sweet and Sour Onions

There is a legend that sweet and sour recipes come from the Arab tradition. Many times it is also associated with the Chinese flavors that developed in the Hunan province and the taste is now enjoyed worldwide. This is our own version.

Ingredients:

2 and ½ lbs. of pearl Onions or large Onions peeled and cut in quarters
¼ cup brown sugar
¼ cup oil
¼ cup white vinegar
Salt and pepper to taste

1. In a saucepan, bring salted water to a boil, add onions and blanch approximately 5 minutes. Drain.
2. In a skillet, add onions, oil, vinegar, sugar and salt and pepper.
3. Cover pan, cook slowly over very low heat for about 30 minutes, stirring frequently until tender. Serve warm or cold.

Serves 6

CIPOLLINE IN CREMA

Creamed Onions

This is from the north of Italy where dairy products are more prevalent. The cream and wine help to compliment the flavor of the onions.

Ingredients:

2 and ½ cups of pearl Onions
4 oz. dry white wine
2 Tbs. butter
8 oz. half and half

1 bay leaf
Salt and pepper to taste
1 clove
2 sprigs flat-leaf parsley, chopped

1. Boil onions for 5 minutes in lightly salted water. Drain.
2. In a large saucepan, melt butter, add onions and sauté for 5 minutes, stirring occasionally. Add wine and let evaporate by half
3. Add the cream, bay leaf and clove. Add salt and pepper to taste.
4. Cook slowly over low heat for 30 minutes until tender.
5. Discard bay leaf and clove.
6. Serve in a deep platter, garnished with chopped parsley.   **Serves 6-8**

ANELLI DI CIPOLLE

Onion Rings

These fried onion rings go well with the summer barbeque and are actually enjoyed with beef and lamb dishes as well as fried fish.

Ingredients:

3 large Onions
1 egg, beaten
½ cup flour
¼ cup grated Parmigiana-Reggiano cheese

1 Tbs. oil
Oil for frying
½ cup warm water
Salt and pepper to taste

1. Mix flour, oil, water, egg and cheese together with a whisk. Let batter rest for ½ an hour. Season with salt and pepper.
2. Peel onions and slice crosswise. Separate rings from slices.
3. Dip rings in batter and fry in oil until golden. Drain on paper towels and serve hot.

Serves 6

POMODORI GRATINATI

Parmesan Baked Tomatoes

These are just great for the summer months when everyone enjoys the abundant harvest of garden tomatoes. The stuffing adds a savory interest to the flavor.

Ingredients:

6 medium ripe Tomatoes
6 Tbs. breadcrumbs
2 Tbs. parsley, chopped
3 Tbs. olive oil

6 Tbs. grated Parmigiana-Reggiano cheese
Salt and pepper to taste
1 egg, beaten

1. Wash and dry tomatoes, remove stems and cut in half crosswise. Remove seeds but leave pulp.
2. Prepare stuffing by combining cheese, breadcrumbs, parsley, eggs and oil in a bowl. Season with salt and pepper. Mix well.
3. Fill tomatoes with stuffing. Arrange on a baking sheet and bake at 350 degrees uncovered for 30 minutes. Serve hot or warm.

Serves 6

VERDURE MISTE ALLA GRIGLIA

Mixed Grilled Vegetables

This side dish is just great for an outdoor summer gathering of family or friends. It is a perfect complement to any grilled meat, poultry or fish.

Ingredients:

3 medium Zucchini
3 bell Peppers, red green and yellow
2 Fennel bulbs
¾ cup oil
2 Eggplants
3 Onions
2 Leeks
Salt and pepper to taste

1. Wash and dry vegetables. Cut zucchini and eggplant into slices about ¼-inch thick.

2. Core and remove seeds from peppers and cut in slices ¼-inch thick. Cut bulb end off leeks and cut in half lengthwise. Be sure all sand in leaves is washed out and slice leeks lengthwise. Do the same with the fennel bulbs.

3. Mix oil, salt and pepper together in a small bowl.

4. Heat a large cast-iron grill pan over medium heat.

5. Brush vegetables with oil mixture and place them on the grill, cooking for 3-5 minutes on each side until soft and light brown. Some vegetables may need less cooking. Continue until all vegetables are grilled.

6. Arrange on a platter and serve. Sprinkle with salt and pepper and drizzle with additional oil if desired.

Serves 6-8

CECI AL ROSMARINO

Chickpeas with Rosemary

This is a sweet tasting bean and it is enhanced by the aromatic taste of the scallion and rosemary. It is a delightful salad for both summer and winter, and is a recipe more typical of the north of Italy.

Ingredients:

2 and ½ cups dry Chickpeas
1 small bunch scallions, chopped
5 Tbs. olive oil
2 Tbs. balsamic vinegar
Large sprig of rosemary, finely chopped
Salt and pepper to taste

1. Wash then soak chickpeas in water for 12 hours.

2. Bring a saucepan of lightly salted water to a boil. Add chickpeas and simmer gently for one hour. Test for tenderness. Cook an additional 15 minutes if necessary.

3. Drain chickpeas and place in bowl.

4. Meanwhile, sauté scallions in the oil in a frying pan to soften. Add vinegar, remove from heat, and pour over chickpeas.

5. Add rosemary to chickpeas. Add salt and pepper to taste.

6. Garnish with sprig of parsley.

Serves 6-8

CROCCHETTE DI PATATE TRADIZIONALE

Traditional Potato Croquettes

This comes from the French word, "croquettes" and this recipe arrived through Naples and there were called crocchè. They can also be enjoyed as afternoon snacks, but in most cases they accompany the main course.

Ingredients:

1 lb. Potatoes (4-5 medium)
½ cup grated Parmigiana-Reggiano or Pecorino cheese
2 Tbs. milk
Salt and pepper to taste
4 eggs, beaten
1 sprig flat-leaf parsley, finely chopped
¼ lb. Mozzarella, cut in small cubes
1 cup breadcrumbs
Oil for frying

1. Boil the potatoes in their skins. Cool slightly, mash while still warm.

2. Stir in one egg, grated cheese, parsley, salt and pepper to taste. Let cool to room temperature.

3. Form into small logs about the size and shape of an egg. Make a hole with your finger in the center of each and insert a mozzarella cube, then close, shaping into egg form. Set aside.

4. In a bowl, add milk to the remaining eggs. Beat well. Dip each croquette into the egg mixture and then into breadcrumbs.

5. Heat oil ½-inch deep in a skillet and fry the croquettes on each side until crisp and golden in color. Place on a paper towel to absorb the grease. Serve warm or at room temperature.

Serves 6

Variation: Place small cubes of cooked meat or diced prosciutto, salami or cooked ham into the center of the croquette in place of mozzarella.

PATATE AL FORNO ALLA PARMIGIANA

Parmesan Oven-roasted Potatoes

This features the Parmigiano-Reggiano cheese as the principle ingredient to enhance the potatoes and the other herbs accompany them with their distinct flavors.

Ingredients:

4 large baking Potatoes, scrubbed
2 Tbs. olive oil
¼ cup grated Parmigiana-Reggiano cheese
½ tsp. dried sage, crumbled, or 2-3 fresh sage leaves, chopped
One sprig flat-leaf parsley, finely chopped
¼ tsp. ground black pepper
Salt to taste

1. Preheat oven to 450 degrees.

2. Cut potatoes into 1-inch thick wedges. In a large bowl, combine potatoes and oil to coat well.

3. In a small bowl, combine grated cheese, spices, salt and pepper and mix well. Add this mixture to the potatoes and toss to coat evenly.

4. Arrange potatoes on a baking sheet in a single layer. Bake about 35-40 minutes, until potatoes are evenly browned.

Serves 4-6

Variations:

1. Substitute fresh rosemary sprig, chopped (about 1 Tbs. dried) and 3 finely chopped garlic cloves for the Parmesan cheese and spices.

2. Add one tsp. cayenne pepper to the mixture at step 3 for a more spicy taste.

PATATINE ARROSTO ALLA FIAMMA

Pan-roasted Potatoes

This is the perfect accompaniment to any kind of roast. They are the Italian version of French fries, but here we cut the potatoes in chunks and add the herbs for additional flavor.

Ingredients:

4-6 medium Potatoes, peeled
3 garlic cloves, unpeeled

½ cup olive oil
2 medium sprigs rosemary or 2 Tbs. dried

1. Peel and wash potatoes and cut into chunks about 1-inch thick.
2. Heat oil in a large skillet, add potatoes and rosemary and cook over moderate heat.
3. Crush garlic cloves with the palm of your hand and add to skillet.
4. Cook 3-4 minutes, turn potatoes and cook additional 3-4 minutes on the other side. Cover and cook an additional 10 minutes, turning potatoes once during that time.
5. Uncover and let cook to a golden color, stirring occasionally, about 10 minutes, or until tender when pierced with a fork.
6. Place on paper towels, discard garlic and add salt to taste. Serve with fresh rosemary sprig to garnish.

Serves 4-6

PATATINE AL FORNO PER LE FESTE

Holiday Oven-roasted Potatoes

This is the traditional accompaniment that Fr. Matt's Mom would make for the holidays. It is an adaptation to the United States, since sweet potatoes are not generally used in Italy.

Ingredients:

1 large Onion
Salt and pepper to taste
1 Tbs. oregano, fresh, or 1 tsp. dried and crushed

4 medium sweet Potatoes
6 medium white Potatoes
1 tsp. paprika

1. Preheat oven to 375 degrees.
2. Peel and thinly slice the onion. Peel and slice the potatoes.
3. Place onions and potatoes in baking dish, toss with oil, oregano and paprika, salt and pepper to taste, cover with foil and bake for 20 minutes.
4. Uncover and bake an additional 20 minutes. Test with a fork for tenderness. Serve hot.

Serves 6-8

PATATE CASALINGHE

Home-style Potatoes

This is a rustic style side dish that is typical of the mountain region.

Ingredients:

4 large medium Potatoes, peeled

Salt and pepper to taste

Small bunch of fresh scallions (approximately 1 cup), sliced

1/2 cup oil

1 large onion, peeled and sliced

1. Slice potatoes ¼-inch thick
2. Heat oil in a large skillet over medium flame. Add potatoes, cook 3 minutes on each side. Cover and cook an additional 10 minutes. Uncover, add onions and cook 10 minutes more until light golden in color.
3. Place on a serving dish, sprinkle with chopped scallions, season with salt and pepper and serve.

Serves 4-6

PURE' DI PATATE

Mashed Potatoes

A true classic that is international, but this version includes our own style and flavor with the addition of the grated cheese.

Ingredients:

6 Potatoes

1 stick butter

2 cups milk

½ cup Parmigiana-Reggiano cheese

Salt and pepper to taste

1. Wash potatoes, place in a large pot and cover with lightly salted water. Bring to a boil and cook until tender.
2. Remove from heat, remove potatoes from the pot and discard water. Peel the potatoes, place them back in the empty pot, and puree with a mill. Add butter, milk, Parmesan cheese, salt and pepper to taste. Mix well, adding some more milk if potato mixture is too thick.
3. Return to low heat, keeping warm until ready to serve. **Serves 6-8**

INSALATA RUSSA DA NOI

Our own Russian Salad

This is the European take on American potato salad and has added a greater variety of vegetables. It is said to have originated in Russia, hence the name. We have incorporated our own ideas in this version.

Ingredients:

4-6 medium Potatoes
½ lb. String beans
½ lb. frozen or fresh Peas
1 tomato, peeled and deseeded
2-3 scallions, finely chopped
2-3 cups mayonnaise
2 red bell Peppers, roasted (page36)
2 Tbs. capers
½ lb. Carrots
2 sprigs flat-leaf parsley
1 jar mixed vegetables in vinegar

1. Prepare roasted peppers and set aside.
2. Boil potatoes in skin until tender. Cool slightly and peel while still warm. Cut into small dice, and place in a large mixing bowl.
3. Wash string beans and cut into ½-inch pieces. Peel and wash carrots and cut in quarters lengthwise, then cut into small sticks ½ inch long.
4. Add peas, carrots and string beans into boiling water and cook until just tender – about five minutes. Be careful not to overcook. Strain and add to the potatoes.
5. Ad 1 Tbs. parsley, all the basil, and one of the roasted peppers, cut into small pieces ½-inch square. Add the scallions, one Tbs. of the capers and the mayonnaise, and mix well with the potatoes. Add salt and pepper to taste.
6. Place on a large oval serving dish and make into a football shape.
7. Cut the remaining roasted peppers into strips one inch wide and decorate the top of the salad with a starburst design. Continue to decorate with pickled vegetables, remaining capers and chopped parsley.
8. Chill if desired. Serve cold or at room temperature.

Serves 6-8

FRITELLE DI PATATE

Potato Pancakes

This has its origin in Germany and is well-known worldwide. It is generally served with sour cream or apples sauce as the accompaniment.

Ingredients:

3-4 medium Potatoes
1 onion, peeled and grated
¼ cup Parmigiana-Reggiano cheese
1 Tbs. chopped chives
oil for frying

2 eggs, beaten
½ cup flour
1 Sprig parsley, finely chopped
salt and pepper to taste

1. Peel and wash potatoes. Shred and place in a bowl, add eggs and mix well. Then add flour, cheese, parsley and chives.
2. Pour a thin coat of oil on a skillet, place over moderate heat. Test if the oil is hot enough by adding small drop of water. If it sizzles, the oil is ready.
3. Place heaping tablespoons of the potato mixture in the pan. Cook until golden on each side, about 3-4 minutes. Place on paper towels to drain. Serve hot.

Serves 6-8

PATATE AL FORNO SEMPLICE

Simple baked Potatoes

This is an American classic and Idaho potatoes are typically used.

Ingredients:

6 baking Potatoes
Salt and pepper to taste

6 tsp. butter

1. Preheat oven to 400 degrees.
2. Wash potatoes, pierce with tines of a fork in several places and place in oven on a baking rack.
3. Bake 45 minutes until tender when pierced with a fork.
4. Remove potato, slit with a knife, making a cross lengthwise across the top. Push with finger to the center and the potato will open like a flower.
5. Add a teaspoon of butter on the top of each, add salt and pepper to taste. **Serves 6**

PATATE AL FORNO RIPIENE

Stuffed Baked Potatoes

This is also an American tradition and here we offer five variations to help you decide which one might fit the right main course according to your taste and preference.

Five variations:

Variation I:

½ cup crumbled Gorgonzola
2 Tbs. butter, softened

1. Bake potatoes as in preceding recipe, slice off the top and reserve. Scoop out the pulp of the potatoes, place in a bowl, add the butter and cheese, salt and pepper to taste.
2. Refill the potato shells with the mixture. Cover with the reserved tops and bake an additional 10-15 minutes. Serve hot.

Variation II:

1 cup shredded Cheddar cheese
2 Tbs. butter
2-3 scallions
Salt and pepper to taste

1. Bake potatoes as in preceding recipe, slice off the top, scoop out the pulp, add to bowl with half of the cheese, butter and scallions.
2. Refill the pulp mixture into shells, discard the tops and cover with remaining cheese. Bake 10-15 minutes until melted.

Variation III:

¾ cups grated Parmigiana-Reggiano cheese
2 Tbs. butter
½ cup chopped Prosciutto
Salt and pepper to taste

1. Add cheese, prosciutto, butter, salt and pepper to scooped out potato pulp as in other variations. Cover with tops and reheat in the oven as above.

Variation IV:

1 cup blanched spinach, drained and chopped
½ cup Romano cheese
2 Tbs. butter

    1.   Mix spinach, cheese and butter with potato pulp. Refill shells and bake as per preceding recipe.

Variation V:

2 roasted red bell peppers, diced
¼ cup grated Parmesan cheese
6 slices bacon, cooked and crumbled
2 Tbs. butter

    1.   Mix peppers, bacon and butter with potato pulp. Refill shells and bake as per recipes above.

INSALATA DI PATATE AGLIO E OLIO

Garlic and Oil Potato Salad

Fr. Matt's grandmother put this together for his father who never cared for mayonnaise. It is a big hit in his family and we hope that you will try it.

Ingredients:

6 Potatoes
3 cloves garlic, peeled
Salt and ground pepper to taste

¼ cup olive oil
Sprig of flat-leaf parsley, chopped
splash of cider vinegar (optional)

1. Boil potatoes in skins, cool slightly, peel and cut in 1-inch cubes.
2. Crush garlic with the palm of your hand. Sauté in 2 Tbs. of the oil until golden. Discard garlic. Toss oil with potatoes, add chopped parsley and remaining oil, salt and pepper to taste and mix well.
3. Serve warm or at room temperature.   **Serves 6**

PATATE GRATINATE

Scalloped Potatoes

A well-known and much enjoyed side dish that originated in France, here we use the Italian version with the béchamel sauce, which makes it so much richer. It can be served for any festive occasion or even as a special treat for a week night dinner.

Ingredients:

6 potatoes, peeled
1 recipe Béchamel sauce (pg. 10)
Salt and ground pepper to taste

1 cup grated Parmigiana-Reggiano cheese
1 Tbs. butter

1. Preheat oven to 350 degrees.
2. Slice potatoes ¼ inch thick. Parboil for 5-6 minutes. Drain and cool slightly.
3. Grease a baking dish with butter. Make a single layer with potatoes, sprinkle with salt and pepper to taste, and spread on 1/3 of the béchamel sauce. Continue adding layers of potatoes and béchamel sauce until finished.
4. Sprinkle with Parmesan cheese and cover with foil.
5. Bake 15 minutes, uncover and bake an additional 10-15 minutes until golden. Serve hot. **Serves 6-8**

INSALATA DI PATATE E FAGIOLINI

Potato and String Bean Salad

A fun and bright enjoyable summer salad and it is perfect for packing and bringing to a picnic.

Ingredients:

1 clove garlic, peeled
3 basil leaves, chopped
½ cup olive oil
¼ cup white wine vinegar
6 potatoes
1 lb. String beans
1 sprig flat-leaf parsley, chopped
Salt and pepper to taste

1. Crush the garlic with the palm of your hand, add to the oil in a saucepan, brown, then remove and discard the garlic.

2. Mix the dressing by combining the oil, vinegar, chopped basil, parsley, salt and pepper and let sit.

3. Boil potatoes in skins until tender when tested with a fork. Let cool.

4. Cut string beans in half, boil until tender, drain and cool.

5. Peel the potatoes, cut into 1 and ½ inch dice. Mix with the string beans and dressing. Serve warm or at room temperature.

Serves 6-8

SOUFFLÉ DI PATATE

Potato Soufflé

This is well-known throughout the north and south of Italy. It originated in France and came in the northern regions through the border. In the Naples area, it has been called Gatò di Patate, from the French word, gateau. It is light and fluffy and is a wonderful feast day or special occasion treat.

Ingredients:

6-8 medium Potatoes
1 cup diced Prosciutto ham
½ lb. Mozzarella, cut in chunks
2 sprigs flat-leaf parsley, chopped
2-3 eggs, beaten
2 Tbs. butter
½ stick butter
½ cup grated Pecorino cheese
4 Tbs. breadcrumbs

1. Wash and boil potatoes in skins, until tender when tested with a fork. Peel, mash in a large bowl.

2. Add prosciutto, grated cheese, parsley and eggs and mix well.

3. Grease a round baking dish, sprinkle with 2 Tbs. bread crumbs. Place ½ of the potato mixture in the dish, cover with all of the mozzarella and remaining potato mixture.

4. Top with remaining bread crumbs and dot with additional butter.

5. Bake in a preheated 375-degree oven for 35 to 40 minutes until lightly raised and browned.

Serves 6-8

PATATE DOLCI AL FORNO

Oven-roasted Sweet Potatoes

Here sweet potatoes are used and they very welcome when they accompany a Roast Ham or Turkey for the holidays. We have incorporated sweetness by adding the brown sugar and orange juice rather than the traditional maple syrup.

Ingredients:

4 Sweet Potatoes
4 Tbs. butter
3 Tbs. brown sugar
½ cup orange juice
Dash of cinnamon (optional)
Dash of salt

1. Preheat oven to 400 degrees.
2. Wash potatoes, pierce with a fork and bake on rack for 45 minutes.
3. Test with a fork for tenderness. Remove, peel and slice ¼-inch thick.
4. Melt butter, add sugar, juice and cinnamon and salt. Place sliced potatoes in a baking pan, pour juice mixture over them and bake an additional 15 minutes at 350 degrees. Serve immediately.

Serves 4

PATATE DOLCI ARROSTO

Roasted Sweet Potatoes

The addition of the rosemary adds a special flavorful and aromatic touch to these oven-roasted sweet potatoes.

Ingredients:

4 Sweet Potatoes
1 Sprig fresh rosemary, finely chopped
Salt and pepper to taste

2 cloves garlic, finely chopped
1 Tbs. olive oil

1. Preheat oven to 375 degrees.
2. Wash, peel and cut the sweet potatoes lengthwise and place in a baking dish. Toss with oil, salt and pepper, to coat.
3. Sprinkle with garlic and rosemary and bake for 35-40 minutes. Test with a fork for tenderness. Serve hot.   **Serves 4**

PURE' DI PATATE DOLCE

Mashed Sweet Potatoes

This is a more recent American side dish that that is considered somewhat healthier that the typical mashed white potato. We have added our own flavor with the sautéed onion.

Ingredients:

6 Sweet Potatoes
1 Tbs. olive oil
1 large onion, peeled
2 Tbs. butter
Salt and pepper to taste
1 sprig of flat-leaf parsley, chopped

1. Bake potatoes in a preheated 400-degree oven for 45 minutes.

2. Meanwhile, chop onion and sauté in olive oil and butter.

3. Peel potatoes and mash. Mix with onion mixture and season with salt and pepper to taste.

4. Sprinkle with chopped parsley.

Serves 6

Chapter VI: Dolci/Desserts

The ending of the meal with the right dessert makes it complete and special. This is a selection of those we have enjoyed through the years and hope you will enjoy them too.

- Tiramisú
- Zeppole
- Basic Sponge Cake
- Dolce alla Crema Pasticcera
- Zuppa Inglese
- Crostata di Marmellata
- Crostata di Frutta
- Biscotti Zia Giuseppina
- Cantucci di Prato
- Biscotti di Pinioli
- Biscottini al Sesamo
- Amaretti
- Mezzelune di Noce
- Biscotti con Marmellata
- Chiacchere di Carnevale
- Dolcetti Emiliana
- Mousse di Cioccolata
- Latte in Piedi
- Flan a la Portuguesa
- Zabaglione
- Pizza Dolci di Pasqua
- Croccante di Natale
- Cream Puffs
- Cannoli alla Siciliana
- Struffoli
- Fragole Cento Volte
- Macedonia di Howard
- Pesche Ripiene di Pasta Frolla
- Torta di Limone alla Meringa
- Torta di Pesche Fresche
- Torta di Mele
- Torta di Mirtilli
- Dolce di Zucca
- Dolce Torino
- Torta di Rhum
- Torta di Cioccolata alla Franca
- Torta di Carote
- Torta di Ananas
- Biscotti di Vino
- Limoncello

TIRAMISÚ

"Pick-me-up"

We have never met a person who did not enjoy Tira-mi-su. This is our own version, where the yolks are cooked as a zabaglione before being incorporated into the other ingredients. It adds more volume and is lighter as well.

Ingredients:

3 eggs, separated
3 Tbs. fine sugar
8 oz. Mascarpone cheese
1 cup espresso coffee
1/3 cup milk
¾ cup Marsala or Amaretto
24 Ladyfingers
4 Tbs. unsweetened cocoa powder
Fresh raspberries and mint sprigs for garnish

1. Make the zabaglione by beating the egg yolks and sugar in the top of a double boiler until pale in color. Add 1/3 cup of liqueur and continue to whisk over double boiler until the mixture becomes creamy. Remove and cool.
2. Beat the egg whites until stiff and set aside. Mix the mascarpone until a creamy consistency. Fold in the zabaglione mixture and incorporate well. Fold in the stiff egg whites and incorporate.
3. Combine the coffee, milk and liqueur. Dip half the ladyfingers, one by one, in the coffee mixture and arrange on the bottom of a serving dish. Cover with half of the mascarpone mixture. Repeat with the remaining lady fingers, forming a second layer, and cover with the other half of the mascarpone.
4. Sprinkle with unsweetened cocoa powder. Let set in refrigerator for 2-3 hours before serving.
5. Garnish with raspberries and mint.

Serves 6-8

ZEPPOLE

Fried Pastry Puffs

These are a tradition during Italian street fairs, usually part of the festivities when honoring the patron saint. Of course, they are a special treat any time of the year. Some people prefer it sprinkled with granulated sugar rather than the confectioner's.

Ingredients:

1 package (1/4 oz. active dry yeast)
5 cups flour
½ tsp. salt
Oil for frying
4 cups warm water
Confectioner's sugar (optional)

1. Dissolve yeast in warm water. Mix flour and salt in bowl, add yeast mixture and mix well. Cover and let rise until double in size.

2. Meanwhile, heat oil in a medium pot over medium to high heat.

3. Using a small ladle, pull a heaping tablespoon of dough and drop into hot oil, frying until golden brown.

4. Drain on paper towels and sprinkle with sugar if desired.

Serves 10-12

BASIC SPONGE CAKE

This is the base for a variety of desserts. You can also simply frost it with whipped cream and top with fresh strawberries for a truly delightful strawberry shortcake.

Ingredients:

6 egg whites

4 egg yolks

½ cup vegetable oil

1 and ½ cups flour

3 tsp. baking powder

1½ cups sugar

½ cup water

1 tsp. vanilla extract

Dash of salt

1. Preheat oven to 350 degrees. Generously butter two 10-inch round cake pans, that is 2" high or one rectangular pan that is 9" by 12".

2. In a large bowl, beat egg whites until soft peaks form, gradually adding ½ cup sugar while beating until very stiff. Set aside.

3. In a small bowl, mix egg yolks, oil, water and vanilla.

4. Sift together the dry ingredients in a large bowl. Add egg yolk mixture to the dry ingredients and mix well with an electric beater. Fold in the stiffly beaten egg whites and gently incorporate them.

5. Pour into the prepared pan and bake for 25 minutes or until side shrinks and top springs back in the center. Turn into a rack immediately and let cool.

Serves 6-8

DOLCE ALLA CREAM PASTICCERA

Pastry Cream Cake

This was developed by Franca when there were special occasions to celebrate in the Rectory, especially when the bishop was invited to dine there.

1 Recipe Basic Sponge Cake (above)

1 pint heavy cream, whipped

1 cup water

1/3 cup Dark Rum or Gran Marnier liqueur

1 Recipe Crema Pasticciera (pg. 11)

2 pints mixed berries, cleaned and washed

½ cup. granulated sugar

fresh mint leaves for garnish

1. Make the pastry cream; cool in the refrigerator until ready to use. Bake the sponge cake in 9" by 12" baking pan. Cool.

2. Boil the water and sugar over moderate heat until the sugar is dissolved and some of the water evaporates and it becomes like a slightly thickened syrup. Cool and add the liqueur and set aside.

3. To assemble, cut the cake into two layers. Wet both halves with the sugar syrup. Place one half on a serving platter and cover with the cooled pastry cream. Place other half over it and cover with the whipped cream. Cut in 3" to 4" inch squares and place on individual dishes and spoon with the mixed berries over each piece. Garnish with fresh mint leaves, if desired.

Serves 12

ZUPPA INGLESE

English Trifle Dessert

This is the traditional trifle that is known and enjoyed throughout England. The Italians who visited there brought back the concept and adapted it, so by using the word "Inglese" it gives due credit to the English people.

Ingredients:

1 recipe Sponge Cake (page 295)
1 recipe Crema Pasticcera (page 11)
1 cup shipping cream
4 Tbs. Marsala
½ cup candied fruit peel
Grated semisweet chocolate for garnish

1. Bake one recipe sponge cake and one recipe pastry cream and allow them to cool. Whip cream and keep chilled.

2. When ready to assemble, cut the cake into fingers, approximately 1-inch thick.

3. Place half of the sliced cake on a deep serving platter or in a bowl. Sprinkle with half of the Marsala and half of the candied fruit. Spread the chilled cream over the cake.

4. Repeat the cake, Marsala, fruit and cream for the second layer. Finish with the whipped cream and chocolate shavings.

5. Chill for at least one hour before serving.

Serves 6

CROSTATA DI MARMELLATA

Jam-filled Tart

This is a very popular and tasty flaky tart that can sometimes be enjoyed at breakfast with an inviting cup of cappuccino.

Ingredients:

1 recipe Crostata crust (page 13)
1 1/2 cups Apricot jam

1. Prepare the Crostata crust, cover and refrigerate.

2. Preheat oven to 350 degrees.

3. Reserve ¼ of the dough for the top. You can roll out the remaining dough between wax paper or it can be pressed with your fingers into a 9-inch tart pan.

4. Overlap the edge a little to form an outer crust.

5. Spoon on the jam and spread evenly.

6. Roll out the remaining dough and cut into six strips. Place on the tart crisscrossing to make a lattice pattern.

7. Bake for 25-30 minutes until the dough is a golden color.

Serves 8-10

CROSTATA DI FRUTTA

Fresh Fruit Tart

This is a very refreshing tart with delightful and healthy fruit to help you not feel quite so guilty about enjoying that piece or two.

Ingredients:

1 recipe Crostata crust (page 13)
1 recipe Pasticcera cream (page 11)
1 pint blueberries
1 and ½ pints raspberries
½ cup apricot preserves
2-3 fresh nectarines, pitted

1. Prepare the Crostata crust, cover and refrigerate.

2. Prepare the Pasticcera cream and refrigerate.

3. Preheat oven to 350 degrees.

4. Roll out crust and place into a 9-inch tart pan. Overlap the edge to form a crust.

5. Pour in the cream and spread evenly. Place in oven and bake for 30 minutes until the crust is golden. Remove from oven and cool.

6. Wash berries and dry with paper towels. Slice the nectarines thinly.

7. Heat the apricot jam in a small saucepan until liquefied.

8. Place raspberries around the edge of the pie, on top of the pasticcera cream. Next, lay the slices of nectarine on the top of the pie in a ring and place the blueberries in the center.

9. Brush over the fruit with the warm apricot jam, as a glaze. Let set and chill at least one hour before serving.

Serves 8-10

Please Note: You may substitute any fruit you wish for the Crostata topping, such as bananas, strawberries, kiwi, blackberries, etc. If using bananas, dip in lemon juice to prevent discoloring.

BISCOTTI ZIA GIUSEPPINA

Aunt Josephine's Cookies

These were the specialty of Fr. Matt's much beloved paternal aunt. No matter whose biscotti he tried, when he was asked how he liked them, he would always say, "Yes, they are tasty, but not as good as my Aunt Josephine's." Here, her secret recipe, which she had given to him, is finally revealed for all to enjoy.

Ingredients:

1 cup vegetable shortening
1 and ¼ cups sugar
6 eggs
2 Tbs. vanilla extract
3 cups flour
2 Tbs. baking powder

1. Mix shortening and sugar until creamy. Add eggs and extract and mix in well.

2. In a separate bowl, mix flour and baking powder together. Gradually add to the egg mixture, incorporating well.

3. Place on two lightly greased cookie sheets with a spoon, forming a total of four logs.

4. Bake in a preheated, 350-degree oven for 20 minutes. Cool for 5 minutes, slice diagonally, place on cookie sheets and return to oven until both sides are lightly toasted.

5. You can also cool the baked logs completely, then and spread the lemon icing, found below on them and slice. Do not return them to the oven to toast.

Note: For individual cookies, this batter can also be placed by the tablespoon on the cookie sheets before baking. Then, after they are baked and cooled, they can be iced with the following:

Lemon Icing:

Using 1 ½ cups of Confectionary sugar: for each ½ cup of confectionary sugar, mix in 2 teaspoons of fresh lemon juice. You can also substitute Anisette in place of the lemon juice. Mix to a smooth but not runny consistence. Add more sugar or juice a bit at a time if needed to get a spreadable consistency. You can decorate with colored sugar or rainbow sprinkles.

Serves 12 or more

CANTUCCI DI PRATO

Prato Almond Cookies

These are a specialty of the city of Prato in Tuscany, not far from the beautiful city of Florence. They are perfect for dunking in a glass of Vin Santo at the end of a meal.

Ingredients:

2 cups flour

1 cup white sugar

1 cup brown sugar

2 eggs

2 Tbs. cinnamon

12 oz. almonds

¼ cup oil

2 Tbs. water

2 Tbs. baking powder

1. Mix eggs, sugar, oil and water together in a large bowl.
2. Add additional dry ingredients. Combine well.
3. Use a small amount of oil on your hands and form the mixture into four logs. Place them on 2 lightly greased cookie sheets. Brush tops with beaten egg.
4. Bake in a 350-degree, preheated oven for about 25 minutes or until golden brown.
5. Slice logs diagonally while still hot.   **Serves 8-10**

BISCOTTI DI PINOLI

Pine Nut Cookies

A very festive cookie that is often enjoyed at weddings and other happy occasions.

Ingredients:

2 and ½ lbs. Almond paste

1 and ½ lbs. confectioner's sugar

2 lbs. Pinoli (pine nuts)

1 and ½ tsp. baking powder

6 egg whites

1. Beat egg whites until stiff and set aside
2. Break up almond paste with a wooden spoon or by hand until it resembles crumbs.
3. Add sugar and baking powder and mix well. Add egg whites and mix with a fork.
4. Drop a teaspoon of dough in the nuts, roll and place on a lightly greased baking sheet.
5. Bake in a preheated, 325-degree oven for 15 to 20 minutes until golden brown.

Serves 8-10

BISCOTTINI AL SESAMO

Sesame Cookies

These traditional cookies are also called "Biscotti della Regina" meaning "of the Queen." They originated in Torino, in the region of Piedmont, where the royal family of Italy resided.

Ingredients:

½ cup butter	3 eggs
1 cup sugar	2 tsp. vanilla extract
3 tsp. baking powder	1 cup milk
3 cups flour	Sesame seeds

1. Cream butter and sugar together, add eggs and vanilla and mix well.
2. Sift flour and baking powder and add gradually to wet ingredients.
3. Use a tablespoon full of dough and roll into a small logs. Dip each one into the milk then the sesame seeds, and place on a greased cookie sheet.
4. Bake in a preheated, 350-degree oven for 12-15 minutes or until lightly brown.

Serves 8-10

AMARETTI

Almond Treats

These are more of a northern Italian area, from the area where the liqueur Amaretto di Saronno was developed in Lombardy, not far from Milan, but they are enjoyed worldwide.

Ingredients:

½ cup sugar	3 egg whites
1 lb. Almond paste	Flour

1. Beat sugar and egg whites together with an electric mixer until well combined.
2. Crumble the almond paste, add and mix an additional two minutes.
3. Knead the dough with your hands until smooth. Add a small amount of flour if necessary to form a thicker dough.
4. Using teaspoon fulls, form into small balls with your hand.
5. Bake in a preheated, 350-degree oven for 15 minutes.

Serves 6-8

MEZZELUNE DI NOCE

Walnut Crescent Cookies

These are a special holiday treats that melt in your mouth. There is very little flour since the walnuts are the main ingredient. They are very popular in the north of Italy where there are many walnut trees.

Ingredients:

2 and ½ cups Walnuts
¼ cup sugar
1 tsp. vanilla
1 and ½ cups flour
1 and ¾ sticks butter, room temperature
Powdered sugar

1. Preheat oven to 350 degrees.

2. Grind the walnuts until very fine. Combine walnuts in a bowl with the flour and sugar and mix together.

3. Add the butter and vanilla and mix well. Form into a ball and chill, covered, for an hour.

4. Using a tablespoon-full of dough, roll it in your hands about 2-3 inches long and shape into a crescent.

5. Repeat with the rest of the dough. Place crescents on an ungreased cookie sheet for 12-15 minutes or until lightly browned. Cool in the pan for 10 minutes, but while still warm, you can roll in the powdered sugar.

Makes 20-15 crescents

BISCOTTI CON MARMELLATA

Raspberry Tart Cookies

These delicate butter cookies, filled with jam are perfect for an afternoon tea with friends or any special gathering. They are similar to the German Linzer Torte cookie.

Ingredients:

1 and ½ cups flour
½ cup sugar
Grated rind of ½ lemon
3 egg yolks
¾ stick butter, softened, raspberry or apricot jam
Confectioner's sugar

1. Preheat oven to 350 degrees.

2. Sift sugar and flour together. Mix in the lemon rind. Make a well in the center and add the yolks and butter.

3. Mix with a fork to incorporate well. Knead with your hands until of a smooth consistency.

4. Roll out dough about 1/8-inch thick. Use a 2-inch round cookie cutter to make the cookie shape. Place on an ungreased baking sheet and bake for 10-12 minutes or until light golden.

5. Cool in the pan. Spread the raspberry jam on half the cookies, and cover with the other half. Dust with confectioner's sugar.

Serves 8-10

CHIACCHIERE DI CARNEVALE

Mardi Gras Cookies

These are enjoyed each year as part of the Carnival that precedes Lent. This recipe is known throughout the north and south of Italy and enjoyed even throughout the year.

Ingredients:

5cups flour
Confectioner's sugar
½ cup sugar
3 eggs
6 Tbs. butter
2 Tbs. Cognac
1 tsp vanilla extract
Oil for frying

1. Mix all dry ingredients together. Make a well, add the eggs, butter, cognac and extract.
2. Mix well with a spoon, then continue to knead with your hands for about 15 minutes until very smooth in texture.
3. Let dough rest, covered, at room temperature for 10-15 minutes.
4. Cut into eight pieces and roll out one piece at a time on lightly floured board as thinly as possible.
5. With a fluted cutter, cut into rectangles 4-inches long by 2-inches wide. Make a slit lengthwise in the center of each rectangle about 2-inches long. Take one end and pass it through the slit.
6. Heat oil until very hot in a deep pot. Deep fry the cookies a few at a time until a golden brown color.
7. Place on paper towels to absorb excess grease. Let cool and dust with powdered sugar

Serves 8-10

DOLCETTI EMILIANI

Emilia-style Filled Cookies

This cookie is typical of the region of Emilia–Romagna, where Donald, Franca's husband has his roots. This recipe was shared with them while they were on vacation there.

Ingredients:

3 cups flour
2 tsp. baking powder
Confectioner's sugar
1 cup regular sugar
Grated peel of one lemon
3 eggs
Apricot preserves

1. Sift together dry ingredients and lemon rind. Make a well and add the eggs and butter. Combine with a spoon and then kneed until dough becomes smooth.

2. Roll out about ¼ inch thick. Cut into 3-inch circles. Spoon one tsp. full of preserves and fold over to seal. Cookies should look like a half moon.

3. Place on an ungreased cookie sheet, and pierce the tops with a fork to allow steam to escape.

4. Bake for 10-15 minutes or until golden in color. Cool 10 minutes in a pan, then with a spatula, transfer to a rack to cool completely.

Serves 8-10

MOUSSE DI CIOCCOLATA

Chocolate Mousse

This is Father Matt's special occasion treat dessert, and always well received. Franca's version is very similar.

Ingredients:

8 oz. semisweet Chocolate

1 cup heavy cream

4 eggs, separated

¼ cup Grand Marnier liqueur

1. Melt chocolate over a double boiler. Beat the egg yolks until a light color, then add to the melted chocolate and incorporate well.
2. Transfer to a bowl, add the liqueur and let cool.
3. Beat the egg whites until stiff and refrigerate. Whip the cream until stiff and refrigerate.
4. Fold the whipped cream into the chocolate mixture, then fold in the egg whites until no streaks of white appear.
5. Spoon into footed serving glasses and refrigerate. Serve well chilled.

Serves 6-8

LATTE IN PIEDI

Crème Caramel

This recipe is typical of the hometown where Franca's husband Donald was raised. It was handed down from his dear grandmother, Terenzia.

For the caramel:

½ cup sugar

1/3 cup water

For the cream:

4 and ½ cups milk

3 egg yolks

2 tsp. vanilla

1 cup sugar

5 whole eggs

1. Preheat oven to 325 degrees

2. Put sugar and water in an ovenproof mold. Place on low flame and mix until the sugar dissolves. Increase the heat moderately high and bring to a boil, cooking for 3-4 minutes without stirring, until the caramel becomes light brown. Remove from stove and coat the mold entirely.
3. Scald the milk, add the sugar, mix until dissolved and set aside.
4. Beat the eggs and yolks together in a large bowl until they thicken and become pale yellow. Add the milk and vanilla and stir well.
5. Pour the liquid into the baking mold and put the mold into a larger pan filled halfway with boiling water.
6. Bake for 40-45 minutes until the center is firm.
7. Let cool completely at room temperature. Loosen the edges with a small knife and turn into a deep serving dish.

Serves 8-10

FLAN A LA PORTUGESA

Portuguese-style Custard

Fr. Matt learned this recipe from dear friend who was born and raised in Portugal, when he was stationed as a priest in Danbury. It is light and delicate.

Ingredients:

2 ½ cups sugar	*2 Tbs. water*
1 quart whole milk	*7 eggs*
1 tsp. vanilla	*Dash of salt*

1. Preheat oven to 350 degrees
2. Combine 1 and ½ cups sugar and 2 Tbs. water in a saucepan and cook over high heat until caramelized. Do not allow to burn. Pour immediately into an ovenproof mold.
3. Whisk the milk, remaining sugar, eggs, vanilla and salt until smooth. Pour into mold.
4. Place mold into a hot water bath (a larger container with hot water) and place in oven uncovered for one hour.
5. Insert a knife into the center of the flan to see if the knife comes out clean.
6. If knife is clean, remove flan from oven, remove from hot water bath and chill completely before serving. Dip outside of mold in hot water to loosen. Turn onto a deep serving dish.

Serves 8-10

ZABAGLIONE

Egg Custard

This recipe originated in 16th century Florence and in France it is called Sabayon. It is well-known throughout Italy and the world. The Marsala wine comes from Sicily, however Vin Santo from Toscana or any sweet white wine can also be used.

Ingredients:

6 Egg yolks
½ cup Marsala wine
½ cup granulated sugar

1. Fill a double boiler halfway with water and place a pot on top, making sure the bottom of the pot does not touch the water.

2. Add the yolks and sugar and beat constantly with a whisk until they are a light color and begin to thicken.

3. Add the Marsala wine and continue beating until the mixture has thickened and increased in volume.

4. Place in serving glasses and serve warm or cold.

Serves 6

PIZZA DOLCE DI PASQUA

Easter Sweet Pie

This is the Easter traditional dessert that Fr. Matt has enjoyed ever since the days of his childhood. It is typical of the region of Campania, near to Naples. He learned this recipe from his grandmother and mother. The orange extract is reminiscent of the smell of orange blossom flowers and sometimes, orange flower blossom water is used instead of the extract.

For the crust:

1 egg

1/8 cup sugar

1/8 tsp. salt

½ tsp. baking powder

1/8 lb. (1/2 stick) butter

1 and ¼ cups flour

¼ tsp. vanilla

For the filling:

1 and ½ lbs. Ricotta cheese

¾ cup sugar

½ tsp. vanilla extract

5 eggs, separated

1/3 tsp. salt

½ tsp. orange extract

1. Preheat oven to 350.

2. In a bowl, combine the ingredients for the crust in the order listed, knead slightly, form into a ball, wrap in plastic and place in refrigerator to keep cool.

3. For the filling combine ricotta, egg yolks, sugar, salt and extracts and mix until very smooth with an electric mixer.

4. Beat whites until stiff and gently fold into the ricotta mixture.

5. Roll out dough for crust and place in a deep dish 9-inch pie plate. Flute the edges and roll out the leftover scraps into 2 strips, ½-inch wide by 10-inches long.

6. Pour filling into crust, place dough strips crosswise on top and bake for one hour. Insert a toothpick into the center and if it comes out dry, the pie is done. Let cool completely before serving.

Serves 8

CROCCANTE DI NATALE

Christmas Almond Candy

Fr. Matt would enjoy watching his grandmother Serafina make this candy at Christmas time.

Ingredients:

1 and ½ cups sugar

8 oz. whole Almonds

½ cup water

Candy sprinkles

1. Combine sugar and water in a saucepan. Bring to a boil, stirring frequently with a wooden spoon. Reduce heat and simmer on a low flame, stirring constantly until water evaporates.
2. Add almonds and continue cooking until sugar mixture turns brown. Do not allow to burn. Remove from heat.
3. Lightly oil an aluminum pan. Pour almond mixture into pan, spread out rapidly with a wooden spoon, sprinkle with candy sprinkles and allow to cool completely.
4. When mixture becomes hard, place on paper towels to absorb oil. To serve, break off pieces and arrange on the serving plate. **Serves 6-8**

CREAM PUFFS

A favorite of many, they can be sprinkled with confectionary sugar or frosting before serving.

Ingredients:

1 recipe Pasticcera cream (page 11)

1 cup water

4 eggs

1 stick (1/4 lb.) butter

1 cup flour

pinch salt

1. Prepare pasticcera cream and cool.
2. Combine butter and water in a saucepan and bring to a full boil.
3. Add sifted flour and salt all at once, beat mixture until it is thick and leaves the sides of the pan.
4. Remove from heat and add eggs, one at a time, beating vigorously after each addition. Mixture should be smooth and satiny.
5. Drop heaping tablespoons of the mixture, 2 inches apart, on a greased baking sheet
6. Bake in a preheated 425-degree oven for 25 minutes. Cool, slit and fill with cream filling.

Makes 12

Cannoli alla Siciliana

Ricotta-filled Pastry Shells

These originate in Sicily. When the Arabs went there, they brought the crops of sugar cane and almonds that were incorporated into the many well-known desserts that originated there. The ingredients in this particular recipe make for a very fulfilling delight.

For the shells:

2 cups flour
1 tsp. sugar
¾ cup Marsala wine
2 Tbs. shortening
¼ tsp. salt
1 egg white
Vegetable oil for frying

For the filling:

1 and ½ lbs. Ricotta cheese
½ square of unsweetened chocolate, grated
3 Tbs. candied orange peel, chopped
½ cups Confectioner's sugar
1 egg white

Please Note: To make shells, metal tubes, approximately 7-inches long and 1 and ½-inch in diameter, are needed.

1. Combine the flour, shortening, sugar and salt. Wet gradually with Marsala. Form the dough into a ball with your hands, cover and refrigerate one hour.
2. Cut dough in half and roll out until ¼-inch thick. Cut into 4-inch squares. Place tubes diagonally across the square, overlap and seal with egg white.
3. Pour oil about 3 inches in pan and heat. Fry tubes in hot oil until a golden brown color. Cool slightly and remove shell from the tube. Repeat until all shells are made.

To make filling:

1. Mix ricotta with other ingredients. Chill mixture before filling shells. Sprinkle with confectioner's sugar.

Serves 6-8

STRUFFOLI

Honey Clusters

A wonderful Neapolitan delight that originated in 1600's and is well-known in the south of Italy. The recipe was brought to the new world by the immigrants and is part of the tradition in many Italian-American households at Christmas.

Ingredients:

6 eggs
½ tsp. salt
¼ cup candied citron, chopped
Candy sprinkles

3 cups flour
1 and ½ cup honey
Oil for frying

1. Beat eggs, ½ cup flour and salt until smooth. Add additional cup flour and incorporate well.
2. Place mixture on a board and knead the remaining flour until a smooth texture.
3. Place dough in a lightly greased bowl and let rest, covered for 2 hours.
4. Roll dough into ropes ½-inch in diameter and cut into ½-inch lengths. Let rest, covered, before frying in moderately hot oil, turning until golden.
5. Drain on paper towels.
6. Heat the honey until liquefied for 15 minutes, stir in the citron and struffoli.
7. Pour onto serving dish and pat into a ring. Scatter the colored sprinkles. Let set before serving. **Serves 10-12**

FRAGOLE CENTO VOLTE

Strawberries 100 Times

This recipe was learned by Fr. Matt's from his cousin Vittoria when visiting her in Rome over 30 years ago and one of his favorites ever since. It is very refreshing.

Ingredients:
2 pints fresh Strawberries
¼ cup orange juice

3 Tbs. sugar
Juice of one lemon

1. Rinse strawberries, cut off green stems and cut on quarters.
2. Drain berries, put in a bowl, add the sugar and juices and stir one hundred times. Chill at least ½ hour before serving. Note: It may be served with whipped cream or over ice cream.

Variation: Substitute Grand Marnier or your favorite liqueur for one or both of the juices. **Serves 6-8**

MACEDONIA DI HOWARD

Howard's Fruit Salad

This is a specialty that Franca used to make for one of the dear friends of her family and she wanted to name it in his honor. We hope that you will enjoy this variety of delicious fruit which is enhanced by the combination their juices that give us a special taste.

Ingredients:

¼ cup fresh lemon juice
1 apple
1 pear
2 peaches
2 oranges
2 kiwi
2 bananas
1 pint strawberries
2 cups seedless grapes
2 cups fresh orange juice
½ cup sugar
2 plums
1 pint raspberries

1. Pour lemon juice into a large bowl.

2. Wash and peel apple, pear, peaches and plums, remove core and seeds and cut into small chunks. Place in a bowl and toss with lemon juice.

3. Peel and cut oranges into sections, remove seeds, peel kiwi and banana, and place in the bowl.

4. Wash and drain berries, removing green stems from the strawberries, quarter them and add to the bowl as well.

5. Wash grapes, drain and cut each in half and add to bowl. Add the orange juice and sugar, mix well, and chill before serving.

Serves 6-8

PESCHE RIPIENE DI PASTA FROLLA

Custard-filled Pastry Peaches

This is an example of art imitating life, where a ripe fresh peach is depicted in a pastry. It is a specialty of the family of Franca and she brought it back to us after one of her visits to her family there.

Ingredients:

3 cups all-purpose flour
3 tsp. baking powder
1 cup sugar
1 and ¾ stick butter, softened
1 tsp. vanilla extract or grated rind of one lemon
3 eggs
1 recipe Zabaglione, room temperature
½ cup liquid from Maraschino cherries
1 oz. light rum
granulated sugar for dredging

1. Preheat oven to 350 degrees.

2. Sift dry ingredients, place in a bowl or on a board, make a well in the center and add the butter, eggs and vanilla or rind. Mix well.

3. Take two Tbs. dough, roll into a round ball the size of a golf ball, and place on a lightly greased baking sheet. Repeat process with all of the dough, and bake for 15 minutes or until golden.

4. Let cool slightly. With a knife or spoon, hollow out the center from the flat side of each cake. Fill with the zabaglione and unite the two halves to resemble a peach.

5. Mix the rum and maraschino liquid in a bowl. Lightly roll the assembled pastry in the juice, then in the sugar. Refrigerate until ready to serve. Serve chilled.

Serves 6-8

TORTA DI LIMONE ALLA MERINGA

Lemon Meringue Pie

A refreshing American favorite that has become one of our favorites as well!

Ingredients:

½ recipe Sweet pie crust (page 13)
6 eggs
1 and ¾ cups sugar
1/3 cup corn starch or flour
1 and ½ cups water
1/3 cup fresh lemon juice (2-3 lemons)
3 Tbs. butter
2 tsp. grated lemon rind
1/8 tsp. cream of tartar
Pinch of salt

1. Preheat oven to 350 degrees. Roll out crust and place in a 9-inch pie pan. Bake until light golden – about 6-7 minutes. Remove and cool.

2. Separate eggs, placing 4 yolks in a small bowl and six whites in a large bowl. Remaining yolks may be reserved in a small cup, covering them with cold water. They should last a few days.

3. In a medium saucepan, mix 1 cup sugar and the corn starch. Add the water, stir until smooth. Stir in the egg yolks and place pan over medium heat. Bring to a slow boil, stirring constantly, for one minutes.

4. Remove from heat, stir in lemon juice, butter and lemon peel. Set aside to cool.

5. Add cream of tartar and salt to the egg whites and beat with an electric mixer until foamy. Gradually add in the remaining ¾ cup sugar and continue to beat on high speed until stiff peaks form when the beaters are lifted.

6. Spoon the cooled filling into a prebaked pie shell, smoothing with the back of a spoon. With a large clean spoon, spread the ¼ of the meringue mixture over the filling, sealing the edges to prevent shrinking. Pile the remaining meringue into high peaks and shape with the back of a spoon.

7. Bake for 6-8 minutes in a preheated, 400-degree oven. Cool on a wire rack. Serve or refrigerate.

Serves 6-8

TORTA DI PESCHE FRESCHE

Fresh Peach Pie

There is nothing like the flavor of luscious ripe peaches in the summer months. When served warm, it is usually accompanied by vanilla ice cream for an extra special treat.

Ingredients:

For the crust:

2 cups sifted, unbleached all-purpose flour
½ cup (one stick) chilled unsalted butter
1 tsp. grated orange peel
¼ cup peach nectar, well chilled
¾ tsp. salt
¼ cup solid vegetable shortening
1-2 Tbs. fresh orange juice

For the glaze:

1 and ¼ cups peach nectar
½ cup plus 2 Tbs. peach jam
2 Tbs. amaretto liqueur

For the filling:

¾ cup granulated sugar
3 and ½ Tbs. corn starch
2 Tbs. fresh orange juice
Pinch of nutmeg
1 egg beaten with 2 Tbs. water
¼ cup firmly packed brown sugar
8 medium Peaches (2 and ¼ lbs.)
¼ tsp. cinnamon
Pinch of salt

For the crust:

1. In a food processor, combine flour, salt, butter cut in pieces and shortening and blend lightly. Add the orange peel, peach nectar and fresh orange juice. Blend until mixture forms a ball.

2. Remove and flatten into a circle, Cover with plastic wrap and refrigerate for at least 30 minutes.

315

For the glaze:

1. Combine all ingredients in a small saucepan and stir to blend. Cook over medium heat until reduced to about ¾ cup. This will take approximately 40-45 minutes. Strain and cool slightly.

For the filling:

2. Combine the sugars and corn starch in a small bowl and mix well. Transfer ½ cup of this mixture to a large bowl.

3. Peel peaches and cut into ½-inch slices and arrange on the sugar mixture, covering with the remaining mixture. Toss gently to blend.

4. Add remaining ingredients and blend thoroughly.

To assemble:

1. Preheat oven to 425 degrees and position rack in the lower third of the oven.

2. Roll dough out on a lightly floured surface to a circle ¼ inch thick. Put over the 9-inch pie pan and press dough into it. Trim the edges, leaving a ½-inch overhang. Brush the bottom and sides of the pastry with the glaze. Layer the peaches neatly in the pastry.

3. Gather the dough trimming and roll out Cut in strips ½-inch wide. Form a lattice pattern over the peaches, folding the pastry overhand over the lattice.

4. Brush the lattice and edge with the egg mixture. Cover the edge of the crust with foil.

5. Bake for 20 minutes, remove foil and continue to bake until golden, an additional 20-30 minutes. Serve warm.

Serves 6-8

TORTA DI MELE

Apple Pie

This is a well-known traditional American specialty, with a variety of spices that help to enhance the flavor of the apples. Some of the first recipes go back to the 1700's from the New England colonies.

Ingredients:

½ recipe Sweet pie crust (page 13)
5-6 Granny Smith apples
½ cup white granulated sugar
½ tsp. cinnamon
1 Tbs. fresh lemon juice
¼ cup brown sugar
2 Tbs. corn starch
¼ tsp. nutmeg

1. Prepare crust and refrigerate. Preheat oven to 400 degrees.

2. Prepare apples by peeling, coring and slicing into ½-inch slices. Place in a large bowl and add the remaining ingredients. Mix well and set aside.

3. Cut the crust dough in half equally. Roll out dough approximately ¼-inch thick. Roll out a large circle to fit the 9-inch pie pan. Place crust in the pan, and trim the ½-inch overhang.

4. Pour the apples into the crust. Roll out the top crust and cover the pie. Trim to meet the overhang and crimp with your thumb and finger.

5. Pierce the top crust with a small knife in several places.

6. Bake for 10 minutes at 400 degrees. Reduce heat to 325 degrees and bake an additional 40-45 minutes or until golden brown. Serve warm or at room temperature.

Serves 6-8

Variation: Add ½ cup raisins, ¼ cup chopped pecans or ¼ cup chopped walnuts in with the apples.

TORTA DI MIRTILLI

Blueberry Pie

This is a true American specialty. Blueberries are known and cultivated particularly in the northeastern part of the country, but this pie is enjoyed throughout the U.S.A.

Ingredients:

1 recipe Sweet pie crust (page 13)
2 pints fresh Blueberries
2 Tbs. corn starch
¾ cup sugar
1/3 cup water

1. Prepare crust and refrigerate. Preheat oven to 400 degrees.

2. Wash blueberries and drain on a paper towel. Place the cornstarch, sugar and water in a medium saucepan and mix well. Add the blueberries and stir.

3. Bring to a boil over moderate heat and cook for 2 minutes. Remove from heat and let the mixture cool.

4. Cut the crust dough in half equally. Roll out dough approximately ¼-inch thick. Roll out a large circle to fit the 9-inch pie pan. Place crust in the pan, and trim the ½-inch overhang.

5. Fill with blueberry mixture, cover with top dough and make a vent in the center with a small knife.

6. Bake for 10 minutes at 400 degrees. Reduce heat to 325 degrees and bake an additional 40-45 minutes or until golden brown. Serve warm or at room temperature.

Serves 6-8

DOLCE DI ZUCCA

Pumpkin Pie

This, as well, is an American tradition, usually served for Thanksgiving dinner, but welcome as a comfort food, usually in autumn and in the cold weather months.

Ingredients:

1 recipe Sweet pie crust (page 13)
¾ cup granulated sugar
2 eggs, slightly beaten
½ tsp. salt
½ tsp. ground ginger
1 tsp. ground cinnamon
¼ tsp. ground nutmeg
¼ tsp. ground cloves
2 cups cooked or canned Pumpkin
1 tsp. sugar
1 can (12 oz.) evaporated milk or half and half

For garnish:

1 cup heavy whipping cream, whipped

1. Preheat oven to 400 degrees.

2. Prepare pie crust according to recipe and refrigerate.

3. Combine sugar, salt, cinnamon, ginger and cloves in a medium bowl. Beat eggs slightly in a large bowl. Stir in pumpkin and sugar-spice mixture. Gradually stir in evaporated milk.

4. Roll out dough to approximately 1/8-inch thick and fit bottom and sides of a 9-inch pie pan. Pour filling into crust and bake for 15 minutes at 400 degrees, then reduce heat to 350 and bake an additional 40 to 50 minutes. Pie is done when a knife inserted in the center comes out clean.

5. Serve with whipped cream, if desired.

Serves 6-8

DOLCE TORINO

Dessert from Torino

Franca learned this recipe from her sister Maria Grazia when she went to visit her in Italy a few years ago. It is rich and full of flavor. You can also substitute an Amaro, such as Averna, for the Frangelico liqueur.

Ingredients:

3 eggs, separated
½ cup granulated sugar
½ cup sweet butter, softened
4 squares semisweet baking Chocolate
½ cup milk
1 cup espresso coffee
4 Tbs. Frangelico liqueur
24 ladyfingers
¼ cup toasted, slivered almonds

1. Beat the egg yolks with the sugar until pale yellow. Add the softened butter a little at a time until well incorporated and set aside.

2. Melt the chocolate with two Tbs. of milk over very low heat. Set aside.

3. Beat the egg whites until stiff. Refrigerate.

4. Add the melted chocolate to the egg yolk mixture and blend well. Fold in the egg whites and set aside.

5. Mix the coffee, Frangelico and milk together

6. Prepare a serving dish. Use half the ladyfingers, dip each into the coffee mixture and place on the serving dish. Cover with half of the chocolate cream. Repeat with ladyfingers and chocolate cream.

7. Sprinkle with sliced almonds. Let set in refrigerator two hours before serving. May be served with berries on top and/or sprinkled with cocoa powder.

Serves 6-8

TORTA DI RHUM

Rum Cake

This is typically a specialty of the south of Italy and has been a favorite at birthday parties and other special celebrations over the generations in many Italian-American households.

Ingredients:

1 recipe basic Sponge cake (page 294)
1 recipe Pasticcera cream (page 11)
½ cup water
¼ cup sugar
¼ cup light Rum
2 cups whipping cream
12 maraschino cherries
1 cup toasted, slivered almonds

1. Prepare the sponge cake recipe and let cool completely.

2. Prepare the crema pasticcera recipe and refrigerate.

3. Make the rum syrup by combining water and sugar in a small saucepan. Dissolve the sugar completely and bring to a boil. Remove from heat, stir in the rum and cool completely.

4. Whip heavy cream until stiff peaks form and then refrigerate.

To assemble:

1. Use a serrated knife and cut each cake into two layers, making a total of four layers.

2. Place the first layer on a serving platter, brush with rum syrup and 1/3 of the cream filling. Repeat with the second and third layers. Place the fourth layer on top and brush with the rum syrup only. Frost the cake with the whipped cream, press the almonds around the side and place the 12 cherries on top.

Serves 8-10

Torta di Cioccolata alla Franca

Franca's Chocolate Cake

This is her true dessert masterpiece... a bit of extra work, but well worth it!

For the cake batter:

½ cup sifted flour
½ cup unsweetened cocoa powder
6 eggs, room temperature
1 cup superfine sugar
1 tsp. vanilla
½ cup melted butter, cooled to lukewarm

For the syrup:

½ cup water
¼ cup brandy
¼ cup sugar

For the butter cream:

3 sticks unsalted butter, cut in pieces and at room temperature
8 oz. bittersweet Chocolate, coarsely cut in chunks
3 Tbs. brandy
1 Tbs. instant espresso powder
3 egg yolks
¼ tsp. cream of tartar
¾ cup water
1 and ½ cup sugar

For garnish:

½ lb. semi-sweet or white chocolate, shaved

For the cake:

1. Position rack in center of oven and preheat to 350 degrees.

2. Butter a 10.5 by 15.5-inch jellyroll pan. Line with lightly buttered and floured parchment paper.

3. Sift together the flour and cocoa powder and set aside. In a large bowl, mix the eggs and sugar. Place over a pan of simmering water, stir until mixture is warm to the touch, about 3-4 minutes.

4. Remove bowl from water, beat with an electric mixer at high speed until it is cool and tripled in quantity. Fold the flour mixture into the egg in three batches.

322

5. Blend vanilla in to the butter and fold into batter.

6. Pour into a prepared pan and bake 25-30 minutes, until the cake feels springy to the touch. Carefully remove cake from the pan and allow to cool completely on a rack.

For the syrup:

1. Cook water and sugar in a small heavy saucepan until sugar dissolves. Increase heat and bring to a boil. Cool syrup completely and stir in the brandy.

For the butter cream:

2. In a bowl, beat butter with electric mixer until it is light and fluffy. Set aside.

3. Stir chocolate, ¼ cup of water, brandy, and espresso powder in a small pan over very low heat until the chocolate melts.

4. Beat the egg yolks in a large bowl with an electric mixer until slightly thickened.

5. Cook sugar, ½ cup water and cream of tartar in a heavy small saucepan over low heat until sugar dissolves. Increase heat and bring to a boil. Let boil until a candy thermometer registers 225 degrees.

6. Add syrup to yolks in a slow stream, beating constantly at low speed. Continue beating until mixture is thick and cool.

7. Beat in butter, a little at a time, incorporating completely.

8. Add the chocolate mixture to the egg, beating until incorporated, and refrigerate until spreadable.

To assemble:

1. Cut cooled cake crosswise into three equal pieces, that wioll becomethree layers. Place first layer on a serving dish and brush it generously with the syrup. Spread with ¼ of the butter cream.

2. Continue in the same manner with the second and third layers.

3. Spread the remaining butter cream on the sides of the cake. Garnish with the shaved chocolate on the side and on top.

Serves 12

TORTA DI CAROTE

Carrot Cake

A lovely specialty of Franca, as well as Fr. Matt's sister... but Fr. Matt's feels that the best part in the preparation is helping to "clean up" the leftover frosting.

Ingredients:

3 cups sifted flour
2 tsp. baking powder
2 tsp. baking soda
½ tsp. salt
2 tsp. ground cinnamon
2 cups sugar
1 and ½ cups vegetable oil
3 cups grated raw Carrots
4 eggs
½ cup white raisins
½ cup chopped walnuts

For the frosting:

8 oz. package of cream cheese
3 and ½ cups Confectioner's sugar
1 Tbs. fresh lemon juice
6 Tbs. (3/4 stick) butter, softened

1. Preheat oven to 350 degrees.

2. Sift the flour, baking powder, baking soda, salt, and cinnamon together.

3. In another bowl, combine the sugar and oil and mix thoroughly. Add the carrots and blend well. Add the eggs, one at a time to the carrot mixture, beating well after each addition.

4. Fold in the nuts and raisins and gradually add the flour mixture, blending well.

5. Butter and flour two round pans, 10-inches by 2-inches each. Pour half the batter evenly into each.

6. Bake at 350 degrees for one hour. Turn cake out onto a wire rack to cool. Cut the cake in half.

7. Blend together the frosting ingredients. Frost the center of the cake, place the other half on top, then frost the top and outside of the cake.

Serves 8-10

TORTA DI ANANAS

Pineapple Upside-down Cake

Fr. Matt's mom and sister would make this each year on the Fourth of July and the entire family looked forward to it. We hope that you will make it a holiday tradition as well.

Ingredients:

1 cup (2 sticks) butter, softened
1 and ½ cups sugar
2 eggs
2 tsp. vanilla extract
3 cups flour
2 and ½ Tbs. baking powder
Pinch of salt
1 and 1/3 cups milk
1 and ½ cups brown sugar
1 can Pineapple slices, drained
Maraschino cherries

1. Preheat oven to 350 degrees.

2. Cream 1 and ½ sticks butter with the sugar in a bowl. Add the eggs and vanilla and mix well.

3. Sift together the flour, baking powder and salt. Add alternately with milk to the egg mixture and beat until smooth.

4. Melt the remaining butter and coat the bottom of an 11-inch by 14-inch or similar rectangular pan or a large round baking pan.

5. Sprinkle the brown sugar on the bottom, arrange the pineapple slices and place a cherry in the center of each pineapple ring.

6. Pour the batter over all and place in the oven. Bake for 45 minutes. The cake is ready when a toothpick placed in the center comes out clean.

Serves 8-10

BISCOTTI DI VINO

Wine Cookies

Fr. Matt learned this recipe from dear parishioners from his priest assignment in Danbury in the 1990's and they are a big hit wherever he brings them. They can also be made with red wine, but the white gives them a lighter color.

Ingredients:

4 cups flour
1 cup sugar
1 cup white Wine
2 Tbs. Baking powder
¾ cup vegetable oil
2 Tbs. Anise seeds, lightly crushed, optional
Granulated sugar

1. Preheat oven to 350 degrees.

2. In a large bowl, combine the sugar, flour and baking powder together. Make a well in the center and add wine and anise seeds.

3. Mix with a wooden spoon to incorporate well. Knead with your hands until a ball forms. It should be of a smooth and wet consistency.

4. With a tablespoon, scoop out a rounded tablespoon of the dough at a time. Roll the dough into a 5-6 inch rope, and form the rope into rings. Make sure to pinch the ends together firmly. Dip one side of each ring in granulated sugar and place on a lightly oiled baking sheet, with the sugared side up.

5. Bake for 25-30 minutes, until golden brown. Cool in the pan.

Makes about 40 cookies

LIMONCELLO

Lemon-flavored Liqueur

This treat, originally from Amalfi, is so easy to make and a truly delightful way to end a meal. But do be careful and drink just a bit, otherwise the delicious lemony flavor might make you forget that there is a pretty hefty alcohol content!

Ingredients:

10 organic Lemons
1 liter of grain alcohol
2 liters water
4 cups granulated white sugar

1. Wash the lemons well and dry them. Peel the lemons, trying to avoid the white pith. Try to choose thick skinned lemons, as they are easier to peel.

2. Put the lemon peel and the alcohol in a large wide mouthed jar. Seal tight and put in a cool, dry and dark place, like a closet, for 7 days. Shake the jar once each day to reposition the peel.

3. On the seventh day, boil the water and add the granulated sugar. Stir until the sugar is completely dissolved. Turn off the heat and let rest.

4. Strain the alcohol mixture over cheesecloth into a bowl. Discard the lemon peel.

5. Combine the lemon-infused alcohol into the sugar and water mixture and mix well. Chill and serve. This mixture can be put into various bottles and stored in the freezer, so as to be served very cold. Serve in chilled cordial glasses.

INDEX

Basic Pasta:

Sauces and Custards:

Pastry Crust & Cake:

Bread and Pizza dough:

Antipasti:

Pasta:

Lasagne, Stuffed and Filled Pasta:

Gnocchi:

Risotti:

Polenta:

Soups:

Meat:

Beef and Veal:

Pork:

Lamb:

Chicken:

Fish:

Dolce: